THE EUROPEAN UNION AND THE REGIONS

The European Union and the Regions

Edited by
BARRY JONES
and
MICHAEL KEATING

CLARENDON PRESS · OXFORD

Oxford University Press, Walton Street, Oxford OX2 6DP

Oxford New York
Athens Auckland Bangkok Bogota Bombay
Buenos Aires Calcutta Cape Town Dar es Salaam
Delhi Florence Hong Kong Istanbul Karachi
Kuala Lumpur Madras Madrid Melbourne
Mexico City Nairobi Paris Singapore
Taipei Tokyo Toronto
and associated companies in
Berlin Ibadan

Oxford is a trade mark of Oxford University Press

Published in the United States by
Oxford University Press Inc., New York

. *British Library Cataloguing in Publication Data*
Data available

Library of Congress Cataloging in Publication Data
The European Union and the Regions / edited by Barry Jones and Michael
Keating.
Includes index.
1. Regionalism—Europe. 2. European federation. 3. Nationalism—
European. 4. Europe—Politics and government—1989– . 5. Europe—
Civilization—1945– . I. Jones, J. Barry (James Barry), 1938– .
II. Keating, Michael, 1950– .
JN94.A38R4382 1995 320.5'4'09409049—dc20 94–43462
ISBN 0–19–827999–X

3 5 7 9 10 8 6 4 2

Printed in Great Britain
on acid-free paper by
Ipswich Book Co., Suffolk

Preface

In 1985 we published a collected volume, *Regions in the European Community*, which examined the impact of European integration on regions and stateless nations and the developing relationships between these and the decision-making apparatus of the Community. At that time, the subject was regarded as interesting but of limited importance. Indeed, the partial coverage of the then member states reflected the patchy academic interest in this area. By the early 1990s, the subject had moved to centre stage. The southern enlargement of the Community had accentuated regional disparities. Several member states had introduced or reformed their systems of regional government. The impact of the Single European Act and later the Maastricht Treaty had further developed the decision-making capacity of the Community. Spending by the Community on regional policy had increased to around a quarter of its budget. The nation-state, while it showed no sign of fading away in favour of a Europe of the Regions, was increasingly penetrated by supranational and subnational influences. The turbulence in eastern Europe had led observers to question the permanence of states and boundaries more generally.

It seemed time for another examination of the question. On this occasion, we sought to cover all member states of what is now the European Union—though we must confess to failure in our search for a specialist on Luxembourg regionalism. Each contributor addresses a common set of concerns, including the impact of the Community on regional policies and politics, the channels of influence from the regions to the Community, and the new forms of triangular politics in which regions, states, and the Community interact to make and implement policy. We do not find a uniform pattern. Rather, issues and channels of influence vary considerably from one case to another. Even the term region varies in meaning, from the historic nationalities of Scotland, Wales, and Catalonia, through the German federal *Länder*, to the Dutch provinces. Policy issues too are often peculiar to individual states, or their regions and national minorities. Yet there is a common dynamic towards increasing regional assertion and a challenging of the decisional monopoly of the nation-state.

At the time the book went to press, the Maastricht Treaty had just been ratified and the term European Union was begining to displace that of European Community. The book's title reflects the new terminology, but individual chapters continue to refer mainly to the Community.

The draft papers were discussed at a conference at the University of Wales, Cardiff and subsequently revised and updated. Funding was provided by the Commission of the European Communities, the Nuffield Foundation, the Welsh Development Agency, the Assembly of Welsh Counties, the Council of Welsh Districts, and the University of Wales. We are particularly grateful to Bruce Millan, European Commissioner for Regional Policy, and to Elizabeth Haywood, European Affairs manager at the Welsh Development Agency, for help with this. Knut Diekman, Adriaan Deerx, David Hanley, Mark O'Donovan, Adam Price, and Jean Williams acted as discussants, and helped us organize our thoughts more clearly. We are also grateful to Jeffrey Anderson (Brown University), John Bachtler (Strathclyde University), Paul Hainsworth (University of Ulster), and Roland Sturm (University of Tübingen) for advice.

In 1992, our group suffered a severe loss with the death of George Yannopoulos. His draft chapter was completed by Kevin Featherstone and we present it as a tribute to George's scholarship.

M.K.

B.J.

Contents

List of Maps

List of Tables

Contributors

Barry Jones — University of Wales, UK

Michael Keating — University of Western Ontario, Canada

Harvey W. Armstrong — University of Lancaster, UK

Richard Balme — University of Bordeaux, France

Carlo Desideri — Istituto di Studi Sulle Regioni, Rome, Italy

Kevin Featherstone — University of Bradford, UK

Hans-Georg Gerstenlauer — European Commission

Frank Hendriks — University of Leiden, Netherlands

Michael Holmes — University College, Dublin, Ireland

Liesbet Hooghe — University of Toronto, Canada

Francesc Morata — Autonomous University of Barcelona, Spain

Armando Pereira — Commissao de Coordinaçao Regio Norte, Porto, Portugal

Jos C. N. Raadschelders — University of Leiden, Netherlands

Nicholas Reese — University of Limerick, Ireland

Alastair H. Thomas — University of Central Lancashire, UK

Theo A. J. Toonen — University of Leiden, Netherlands

Abbreviations

ARE	Assembly of European Regions
AWC	Assembly of Welsh Counties
BON	*Bestuur Op Niveau*
CAP	Common Agricultural Policy
CBI	Confederation of British Industry
CCRs	Commissions of Regional Co-ordination
CDU	Christian Democratic Union
CIPE	Interministerial Committee for Economic Planning
CIS	Commission for International Collaboration
CODER	*Commission de Développement Economique Régional*
COR	Committee of the Regions
CSFs	Community Support Frameworks
CSU	Christian Social Union
DATAR	*Délégation à l'Aménagement du Territoire et à l'Action Régionale*
EAGGF	European Agricultural Guidance and Guarantee Fund
EAGGF(Gu.)	European Agricultural Guidance and Guarantee Fund (Guidance Section)
EC	European Community
ECSC	European Coal and Steel Community
ECU	European Currency Unit (single currency)
EEC	European Economic Community
EFTA	European Free Trade Area
EIB	European Investment Bank
EMU	European Monetary Union
ERDF	European Regional Development Fund
ESF	European Social Fund
FDP	German Free Democratic Party
FEOGA	Agricultural Guidance Fund
FNLC	*Front National de Libération de la Corse*
GATT	General Agreement on Tarrifs and Trade
GDP	Gross Domestic Product

GDR	German Democratic Republic
GRP	Gross Regional Product
IDA	Industrial Development Authority
IMCs	Interministerial Conferences
IMPs	Integrated Mediterranean Programmes
IRA	Irish Republican Army
MP	Member of Parliament
MEP	Member of European Parliament
ND	New Democracy
NICE	Northern Ireland Centre in Europe
NPCI	National Programmes of Community Interest
NUTS	Nomenclature of units for territorial statistics
P11	Directorate for European Politics
PU	Political Union
RPR	*Rassemblement pour la République*
SDP	Social Democratic Party
SEA	Single European Act
SEM	Single European Market
SGCI	Secretariat of the International Committee for European Affairs
SLP	Scottish Labour Party
SMEs	Small and medium-sized enterprises (SMEs)
SNP	Scottish National Party
SPD	German Social Democratic Party
STUC	Scottish Trades Union Congress
TUC	Trades Union Congress
UDF	*Union pour la Democratie Française*
UK	United Kingdom

1

Europeanism and Regionalism

MICHAEL KEATING

European Integration and Regionalism

European integration and regionalism have posed twin challenges to the nation-state in western Europe. Developing simultaneously in the post-war era, both have had a political and an economic dimension. There is at first glance a contradiction between the two trends, since European integration takes matters to a supranational level, while regionalism is concerned with strengthening the subnational level. Yet there are also elements of consistency and mutual reinforcement in the two movements.

The creation of the European Community can be traced back to political and economic arguments in the context of post-war reconstruction. Politically, European unity provided a framework for containing Germany and insurance against a new war, as well as bolstering western solidarity in the cold war. Economically, it corresponded to the logic of large-scale industrial development. Free-trade theory predicted that the removal of tariff barriers would increase allocative efficiency, while the creation of a large home market would allow European firms to compete with their American and later Japanese rivals. Political and economic logic came together in the functionalist argument that spillovers from one area would lead to integration in others. So economic integration would lead ineluctably to political co-operation and ultimately European unity. For the more idealistic, the dream was of a United States of Europe, a political and economic union to take its place beside the superpowers. In practice, integration was largely subordinated to the needs of national governments and proceeded only in those areas where it suited their interests. Later, the political emphasis on

I am grateful to Gary Marks for comments on this chapter.

strengthening of European institutions and an expansion of their competence was subordinated to the *laissez-faire* deregulating fashion of the l980s which underlay the initiative for the creation of the internal market in 1992. Proposals for monetary union and an independent central bank, together with the continued 'democratic deficit', confirmed fears that Europe was less a new form of the democratic State than a scheme to remove important issues from political control altogether. Hence, on the one hand, a series of oppositions to the project, many of which took a territorial form; and on the other, a series of proposals for strengthening the Community's institutions and their accountability.

Regionalism is a more complex phenomenon but is also inspired by both economic and political impulses. It has taken two forms, 'top-down regionalism' in the form of national regional policies, and 'bottom-up regionalism' in the form of regional political and economic mobilization. In the 1960s, many European states adopted regional development policies as an extension of schemes of national and sectoral planning. Economically, these were justified in terms of the need to tap under-utilized resources in peripheral and declining regions and increase national output. Politically, they served to enhance national solidarity and secure support from peripheral regions for the State regime or the party in power. Such diversionary policies could be presented as a non-zero-sum game in which all could win, the depressed regions through growth, the advanced regions through the relief of congestion, and the national economy through additional output and an easing of inflationary pressures. They also helped governments to integrate their peripheral territories and served to strengthen national unity and legitimate the expanding State.[1]

Gradually, as governments saw a need to institutionalize regional policies and involve regional political and economic leaders in their elaboration and implementation, regional development became more politicized. Tensions arose between the central top-down perspective and pressures arising from within regions. For regions themselves were becoming more assertive in a variety of ways. In some cases, this was a matter of resistance to change in traditional societies. In others, new social forces emerged, commit-

[1] M. Keating, *State and Regional Nationalism: Territorial Politics and the European State* (Brighton: Harvester-Wheatsheaf, 1988). S. Biarez, *Le Pouvoir local* (Paris: Economica, 1989).

ted to modernization on a regional basis, altering the image of regionalism from archaic defence of the old to a dynamic force for change. Historical claims for regional and national distinctiveness were reasserted. The tension between this indigenous regionalism and regionalism as State policy became more acute in the 1970s as central governments, giving increased priority to national competitiveness in the global market, found it more difficult to plan their spatial economies and began to reduce regional policy expenditure. By the 1980s the efficacy of the old models of territorial management by national states was placed seriously in question.

Yet, while economic restructuring followed an increasingly global logic, this did not entail the end of territorial politics. The impact of global change varies across territories. The fact that it is at the regional and local levels that the impact of change is felt has helped create new coalitions of territorial defence and increased the political salience of regions. At the same time, it is increasingly recognized that combinations of factors of production in specific places are a vital element in economic growth and change, even within a globalized market. The region has thus become a key level of political dialogue and action, where national, continental, and global forces meet local demands and social systems, forcing mutual adaptations and concessions.

The political character of territories themselves is a key element here. Some areas have a strong sense of identity, rooted in historical experience, language, culture, or political traditions. Some have distinctive civil societies, with a locally based business class, associative life, and sense of spatial solidarity. Some have autonomist or secessionist movements. Others lack these features or have been reduced to political dependencies of national states or dominant political parties and client systems. In some territories, regional assertion is confined to culture; in others it is a matter of lobbying for economic favours; in others again there is a demand for regional autonomy. In some cases, all three elements are combined, not without tensions: for example, between the demand for autonomy and that for more aid from the State.

Regions have also become increasingly important as a level of government, though the experience varies greatly. In France and Italy, national governments established regions slowly over a period of years, proceeding from mere consultative organs, to indirectly elected, then elected regional councils, and then conceding powers and functions. Although regional government is stipulated in the 1948 Italian Constitution, it was not until the 1970s that the ordinary-status regions came into being. In France, the process, starting in 1972, was not completed until the elections of 1986. In Spain and Belgium, regions and autonomous communities are more of a response to demands from within the regions themselves and both countries are heading in a federalist direction. The German Basic Law of 1949 provided for a federal system in response both to German traditions and to the insistence on decentralization in the new democracy. In the United Kingdom, a revival of historical pressures from the periphery led the Labour Government of 1974–9 to propose elected assemblies in Scotland and Wales but opposition in Parliament combined with fears of separatism in the peripheral territories themselves to wreck the scheme. In England, gradual moves towards the institutionalization of regions in the 1960s and 1970s were later reversed and little remains even at the administrative level. Denmark, Ireland, the Netherlands, Greece, and Portugal likewise remain centralized, though pressures for decentralization exist, reinforced by the process of European integration.

Issues and Conflicts

The convergence of European integration and regionalism raises a further set of economic and political issues. Neo-classical economic theory generally holds that in a free-trade area with capital mobility, less developed and peripheral regions will be able to exploit their comparative advantages of low cost to attract investment, so producing a convergence in output and living standards. Even if disparities remain, the overall rise in prosperity generated by the open market will raise their incomes alongside everyone else's. This was the assumption underlying the Cecchini report on the 1992 initiative.[2] Critics have responded that in the absence of the perfect competition and factor mobility assumed by the neo-classical model, peripheral regions may suffer. In a free-trade area, there may be pressures to economic concentration, with peripheral regions disadvantaged by their distance from markets, the quality of

[2] P. Cecchini, *1992—The European Challenge: The Benefits of a Single Market* (Aldershot: Wildwood House, 1988).

their infrastructure, and technological backwardness. Central regions, by contrast, will enjoy agglomeration economies, building on their existing advantages. This simple core-periphery model probably represents a gross simplification of the complex processes of adjustment in the single market and proposed monetary union. New patterns of spatial inequality are emerging which often cut across the old geography of need and in some cases divisions within regions and urban areas may be as important as between them. Yet the general point remains valid that change will have uneven spatial impacts, exacerbating existing disparities and creating new ones. Community rules on tariffs and subsidies and the inability to manipulate exchange rates within the Exchange Rate Mechanism of the European Monetary System, inhibit states from responding to these problems. Given not only the move to continental economic integration but more specifically its free-market orientation, there is a danger of regions being reduced to mere elements in the continental or global division of labour, subordinated to the vicissitudes of international capital flows.

Enlargement of the Community has increased regional disparities very considerably, while changing their nature. British entry in 1973 posed the problem of reconversion of declining industrial regions. The accession of Greece, Spain, and Portugal added to the number of underdeveloped rural areas. The poorest regions in Greece and Portugal have a per capita gross regional product of around 40 per cent of the Community average while the poorest region of the nine members of 1973–81 (Calabria) comes in at 59 per cent of the average (1987 figures). National GDP per head ratios in 1989 were 2.1:1 between Denmark and Portugal, compared with a maximum of 1.5:1 among American states.[3] German unification poses a new set of development issues while change in eastern Europe creates further competition for investment.

Like the concerns about the social consequences of the internal market, this gives rise to two types of response. The first is a set of oppositions to the project and defence of the nation-state as the body best able to reconcile social and market considerations, as well as manage the relation of territories to the market. The second is an attempt to use the institutions of the Community itself to introduce a more socially and spatially sensitive model of growth,

[3] C. Andre, J-F. Drevet, and E. Landaburu, 'Regional Consequences of the Internal Market', *Contemporary European Affairs*, 1/1–2 (1989), 205–14.

so engaging in the politics of Community building. Both types of response are visible in the countries considered here, with a strong tendency to move from opposition to constructive dialogue. Successive enlargements have raised the salience of regional policies in the Community and spurred demands for equalization mechanisms of various sorts. Peripheral regions with low output and unfavourable economic structures can claim to be in need of substantial, long-term development assistance[4] and use this as the price of acquiescence in further integration. Spain has emerged as the leader of the poorer states pushing for a Community anti-disparity policy. While Spain and member states would generally prefer simple intergovernmental transfers, the Commission has insisted so far that this would not be *communautaire* (in the spirit of European unification) and that transfers must take the form of Community policy measures. The most important of such measures has been the structural funds.

Other Community policies also have an uneven regional impact. The Common Agricultural Policy (CAP) both pre-empts resources which could otherwise be used for other sorts of development policy, and itself has an uneven spatial impact. It is difficult to quantify this but it is estimated that generally the CAP serves to reinforce rather than combat existing regional disparities.[5] The neo-liberal bias of many Community policies may serve to exacerbate regional disparities.[6] The competition policy, strengthened in the approach to 1992, was inspired under the influence of the 'Thatcherite' commissioner Leon Brittan, by a purely market and competitive vision and frequently comes into conflict with the needs of regional development. The competition directorate has become vigilant in rooting out national and local aids to economic development as distortions of the market, and has proved hostile to the development of a Community regional policy. Requirements under Economic and Monetary Union to cut budget deficits will have a severe impact on southern European countries depending on government borrowing to finance the infrastructure needed to

[4] D. Keeble, J. Offord, and S. Walker, *Peripheral Regions in a Community of Twelve Member States* (Luxembourg: Commission of the European Communities, 1988).

[5] J. D. Strijker and J. de Veer, 'Agriculture', in W. Molle and R. Cappelin (eds.), *Regional Impact of Community Policies in Europe* (Aldershot: Gower, 1988).

[6] T. Cutler, C. Haslam, J. Williams, and K. Williams, *1992—The Struggle for Europe: A Critical Evaluation of the European Community* (Oxford: Berg, 1989).

allow them to compete effectively. Even Germany, faced with the need to invest in the eastern *Länder*, finds this a difficult restriction.[7] Rules on public procurement have also hit certain regions that are traditionally highly dependent on government orders for their economic survival. Deregulation in telecommunications and transport, with the outlawing of various types of cross-subsidy, has caused difficulties in regions such as the Italian Mezzogiorno.[8] Environmental regulations have posed severe burdens on the less developed regions in Spain, undercutting their cost advantage. Sectoral policies in agriculture, fisheries, steel, coal, and textiles have all had an uneven regional impact.

European integration has also had political effects in regions, bringing into being new social and political movements and alliances. Some of these are linked to economic restructuring, such as the movements to defend declining industries or inter-class movements to promote development. Unable to rely on national diversionary policies, regional governments and movements have started to consider possibilities for indigenous development as well as ways to influence Community policies. Community structural fund interventions have stimulated political mobilization around programmes and spending projects and have encouraged people to articulate their demands in regional terms, just as did the national regional policies of the 1960s and 1970s.

Europe also provides a new context for older political demands. Autonomist and separatist movements, which in the past often saw the Community as one step more remote, and therefore more objectionable, than national governments, have increasingly come to frame their demands in European terms. Free trade potentially lowers the economic costs of separation considerably, a factor which, in Catalonia, as in Quebec and Scotland, has led nationalist movements to abandon protectionism in favour of autonomy within the free-trade regime.[9] In some cases, this takes the form of a policy of independence in Europe, the Community providing an

[7] U. Bullman and D. Eisel, 'Europa der Regionen: Entwicklung und Perspectiven', *Aus Politik und Zeitgeschichte*, 21/93 (1993).

[8] B. Fullarton and A. Gillespie, 'Transport and Telecommunications', in Molle and Cappelin, *Regional Impact of Community Policies*.

[9] J. Clavera, 'El debat sobre el lluire canvi: El cas de Catalunya davant la integració en la Comunitat Europea', in M. Parés i Maicas and G. Tremblay (eds.), *Catalunya, Quebec: Autonomía i Mundialitazió* (Barcelona: Generalitat de Catalunya, 1990).

external support system for a move which otherwise appears fraught with danger, uncertainty, and cost. Elsewhere, Europe is evoked more vaguely, as providing an arena in which the regional personality can be projected and as an alternative frame of reference to the State. In some instances, it merely provides an opportunity for local politicians to engage in diplomatic posturing, trying to create the impression of having their own foreign policy or bypassing the nation-state. Yet even the politics of empty gestures may serve in the longer run to consolidate regional sentiment. Spain's three historic nationalities illustrate all three styles. The governing Basque Nationalist Party has demanded the right to be represented directly in the Council of Ministers on matters of regional competence.[10] Jordi Pujol, nationalist president of Catalonia, limited himself to speculating that the autonomous communities might in future be allowed on occasion to represent the Spanish State in Europe.[11] Manuel Fraga, conservative president of Galicia and formerly a Spanish centralist, has for his part merely used Europe to project his own region (and his own personality) without making constitutional demands in relation to the Community.

While Europe may provide an external support system for national minorities seeking to escape from the embrace of the State, it may, however, threaten their cultures and languages.[12] Hooghe (Ch. 6) draws attention to some Flemish groups which see Europe as an 'Americanizing' influence.

Regionalism, Europeanism, and the State

Assessing the long-term significance of European integration and regionalism is more difficult. European integration has sometimes been presented as a form of internationalism, a transcendence of the nation-state. This perspective can be disputed on two counts, firstly because the Community is the work of states, and secondly because the project is for the construction of a continental order precisely to enable Europeans to compete in world markets with Americans, Japanese, and newly industrializing countries while

[10] *El País*, 14 Dec. 1993.   [11] Ibid., 15 Dec. 1993.
[12] S. Cardus, 'Identidad cultural, legitimidad política e interés económic', in *Construir Europea: Catalunya* (Madrid: Encuentro, 1991).

helping to set the terms of trading for the rest of the world. This has nothing to do with internationalism in the broad sense. Others have argued that the Community represents the culmination of those very functional, integrative, and diffusionist trends which were responsible for creating the existing states of western Europe from their original components. In this vision, the Community is a state in the making. This perspective too is misleading. The European nation-state was a product of its place and time (the seventeenth to nineteenth centuries) and it would be anachronistic to project these processes into the late twentieth century. Besides, the Community consists precisely of nation-states which have shown great reluctance to efface themselves in favour of a fully fledged European government. So the Community must be seen as a new type of political order or regime, within which new types of politics are possible.

Regionalism similarly has been seen in various ways. Some see it as an atavistic reaction, a rejection of modernization and progress. Others see it precisely as an element in modernization and democratic assertion. Some see it as a threat to the State, carrying dangers of incohesion, fragmentation, and/or separatism; others as a mechanism for rationalizing State authority and administration, so consolidating its authority. Regionalisms in fact differ in their character as well as their strength, depending on the conditions in particular local societies and the impact on them of national and international forces.[13] It is not possible to construct a single model or theory explaining all cases, though comparative analysis can help in the elaboration of partial theories and explore the dynamics and processes of territorial mobilization. The chapters in this book show how the phenomenon varies from one Community state to another.

The combined effects of regionalism and European integration on the nation-state create a further set of dynamics. To analyse these, we might pose two contradictory hypotheses. The first is that regionalism and European integration serve to strengthen the State by off-loading the less gratifying functions and externalizing difficult tasks like agricultural and industrial restructuring, coping with the social and political fall-out of economic change or, more recently, maintaining monetary and fiscal rectitude and exchange-

[13] Keating, *State and Regional Nationalism*.

rate stability. Europe may provide an external support system for small, weak, or threatened states, while regionalism may ward off separatist and other disintegrative threats. As long as national governments can maintain their control over the processes of European integration and regionalism, then they will use these to strengthen their own power, retaining the functions which they consider essential and ensuring that Community institutions will remain intergovernmental rather than supranational.

The counter hypothesis is that European integration and regionalism will weaken the State by eroding its authority and functional competence simultaneously from above and below. A new political regime is created, in which national governments are no longer masters of the game and, in extreme versions, states disappear altogether in favour of a Europe of the Regions.[14]

Such a scenario is advanced from two very different perspectives. On the one hand are technocratic and rationalist observers, who note that, with competences distributed in the most efficient manner between the Community and the regions, the nation-state will become functionally redundant. This is reminiscent of the early functionalist arguments, inspired by pre-war theories, which argued that functional linkages would increasingly bypass the nation-state.[15] On the other are romantics, utopians, ethnic activists, and a variety of movements inspired by post-industrial values, who wish to remove the 'artificial' and oppressive structures of the nation-state in favour of 'natural' ethnic or spatial communities, within a democratic and pluralist Europe. Both forms of the 'Europe of the Regions' scenario, however, ignore the very real power of nation-states, the resilience of their political and bureaucratic élites and the powerful private interests which have invested in them. Functionalist theories were soon found to be wanting and were replaced by more sophisticated approaches giving a greater role to states and political strategy.[16]

Yet in the longer run the two hypotheses might be reconciled. Although the processes of European integration and regionalism

[14] M. Keating, 'Regional Autonomy in the Changing State Order: A Framework of Analysis', *Regional Politics and Policy*, 2/3 (1992).

[15] E. Haas, *The Uniting of Europe* (Stanford, Calif.: Stanford University Press, 1958) and *Beyond the Nation-State: Functionalism and the Theory of Regional Integration* (Stanford, Calif.: Stanford University Press, 1964).

[16] P. Taylor, *The Limits of European Integration* (New York: Columbia University Press, 1983). Haas himself also retreated from the functionalist position.

have in general advanced only as far and as fast as national governments have wished, the latter do not have complete control over events. Territorial pressures have forced governments to concede more than they might have wished, while continental integration is also driven by economic and strategic interests which nations do not entirely control. The processes and institutions of European integration and regionalism have brought into being new actors and new networks which themselves become an element in the political game. It is also important to bear in mind the precise form which European integration has taken and the ideological climate of the late twentieth century. Both emphasize privatism, deregulation, and a general roll-back of the State, eroding the power of government horizontally just as it is challenged vertically from Europe and the regions. European integration, together with global market integration (through GATT, the rise of the multinational firm, and capital mobility) have dealt a severe blow to traditional models of territorial management in which national states were able to use protectionism, subsidies, and a variety of collective and individual clientelist methods to secure support in peripheral regions. It would be an exaggeration to say that the Community is simply characterized by deregulation, yet in Europe as elsewhere traditional modes of authority based on universal norms and law are giving way to more complex forms of regulation tailored to individuals or circumstances.[17] The market is not, *pace* the neo-classical school, a homogeneous and value-free entity. Rather, it is shaped by states and systems of regulation and heavily influenced by cultural factors, so that it takes different forms in different places.[18] In the new Europe, markets will be shaped crucially by internationally mobile capital, but also by European, national, and regional forms of regulation and cultural norms. What is certain is that the post-war model of the nation-state facing the nationally defined market is a thing of the past. The rise of the northern leagues discussed in Desideri's chapter is witness to the collapse of the Italian model of territorial management. Territorial explosions have similarly marked the end of the French model, while the British experience offers parallel examples. The nation-

---

[17] A. Bressand and K. Nicolaïdis, 'Regional Integration in a Networked World Economy', in W. Wallace (ed.), *The Dynamics of European Integration* (London: Pinter, 1991).

[18] M. Albert, *Capitalisme contre capitalisme* (Paris: Seuil, 1991).

state may not be about to disappear, but it is certainly being transformed, increasingly penetrated by supranational and subnational
influences.

Patterns of Influence

The new political linkages and channels of influence among the
Community, states, and regions, are the main subject of the following chapters. The principle of 'subsidiarity', that matters should be
decided at the lowest level possible, is often invoked in discussions
about the EC. It has obvious applicability in this context, where it
would require a substantial devolution to the regions both of national and Community power. This is, by and large, the position
taken by the Commission. Yet the chapters show that, the Community being an association of states, most links between regions and
the EC continue to pass through national governments. The quality
of national intergovernmental relations is thus the main influence
on that of EC–regional relations. In centralized states, without
regional institutions, it is extremely difficult for regional interests to
articulate their demands. At best, the central State may be penet-
rable by local interests through the activities of parties, territorial
notables, and clientelist practices. In the United Kingdom, the
absence of regional government is compensated for by the presence of territorial ministers of central government with a brief to
argue the case of their respective areas but, as Keating and Jones
show, this model has come under extreme strain and doubts can be
cast on its present efficacy. Where states have a system of regional
government, a capacity exists to articulate a regional interest but
making this effective is another matter. In some cases, national
states have insisted that Europe is an aspect of foreign affairs and
therefore the exclusive responsibility of central government. This
has led not merely to the exclusion of regions from European
matters but to the intrusion of national government in regional
matters where there is a European policy to be formulated or
directive to be implemented. So, in violation of the subsidiarity
principle, the Community has proved a force for centralization
within states. Spain and Italy present examples of the tensions
arising from such a centralist approach to Community matters. In
Belgium, on the other hand, Hooghe shows how the national

government has effaced itself in various policy matters, allowing the regions to deal with Brussels directly. In Germany, the consensual tradition of co-operative federalism has allowed the *Länder* a role in determining German positions in Europe, though not without some tensions, as Gerstenlauer notes. In France, the traditional model of territorial influence through the accumulation of mandates and collaboration among political and administrative élites has been extended to Community affairs. So, despite the limited competences of regional councils, they are not without influence over national policy.

The Maastricht Treaty for the first time explicitly allows regional ministers to represent their respective states in the Council of Ministers, a provision first used by the Belgians. Germany also now has provision for a *Land* minister to represent the State, part of the concessions made to secure ratification of the treaty by the *Bundesrat*. It is too early to see how these arrangements will operate in practice but it should be emphasized that regional representatives must represent the whole State, not merely the region, and that agreed positions must be reached domestically before the issue in question comes to the Council of Ministers.

In several countries, regional government has come to be rivalled by the rise of urban politicians as cities seek to project themselves on the national and international stage. French regional presidents have found themselves overshadowed by powerful mayors and, with the limitation of the accumulation of mandates, many, though not all, senior politicians have surrendered the regional mandate. In the UK (especially in England), the dismantling of regional institutions has been accompanied by a new assertiveness on the part of cities, with both major parties emphasizing urban needs over regionalism. In several countries, it is subregional agencies which are involved in spending structural fund moneys and which insist on involvement in the determination of the respective programmes. Yet the Community, with its emphasis on the regional dimension, has helped sustain a sense of regional identity and regional politicians have looked to it with more hope than to their national governments.

Many regional governments and other interests have attempted more direct links with the decision-making instances of the Community. The value of this strategy depends on the permeability of the institutions in question and their capacity to respond. The

Council of Ministers, representing member states, is responsive only to the extent that member governments are responsive. Most lobbying has therefore concentrated on the Commission, with a constant succession of delegations and the establishment of offices in Brussels by several regions. By 1989, representation in Brussels included all ten West German *Länder* and west Berlin (in ten offices); four Spanish regions (each with its own office); six French regions and two departments (in four offices); and four British local authorities (each with its own office).[19] Since then, other offices have been set up, as detailed in the chapters, and at one count there were fifty-four such offices in all.[20] Meetings are also convened by the Commission to discuss the implementation of structural-fund interventions. There is a great deal of noise created by this regional lobbying and politicians seek to extract the maximum political capital out of a strategy which allows them to project themselves internationally and appear to circumvent the national state. The concrete benefits are more questionable. While the Commission is always happy to talk to regions, thus extending its own information sources, it is rarely able to respond to specific demands, given the rules about funding and programmes. More important, perhaps, is the gradual creation of networks of influence around the Commission, exchanging information, planting ideas, and gradually developing policy. In this area, the quality of intelligence assembled by regions and their technical capacity are more important than offices in Brussels. The directorates-general responsible for regional and structural policies have to some extent become allies of the regions in promoting a more *communautaire* perspective and maintaining pressure on the Council. For the same reason, the Commission encourages the activities of European-wide organizations of local and regional authorities. It is not only national governments who fear the effects of this. National representative bodies may resent being bypassed, as in the case of the French Economic and Social Council, which complained about the establishment of the Consultative Council of Regional and Local Authorities which, it claimed, merely created expectations and encouraged demands among which the national government would have to choose.[21]

[19] M. Serignan, M 'L'Évolution des relations entre la CEE et les Collectivités territoriales', *Après-demain*, 314–15 (1989), 4–7.
[20] Information provided by Gary Marks.
[21] Conseil Economique et Social, report on meeting of 25 and 25 April 1989, *Journal officiel de la république française*, no. 12, 26 May 1989.

The International Union of Local Authorities and the Council of Communes and Regions of Europe are both wider in scope than the Community and have been closely associated with the Council of Europe which they persuaded to establish a Permanent Conference of Local and Regional Authorities in 1957. In 1986, they opened a joint office to deal with the EC.[22] In 1985, the Council (later Assembly) of European Regions was launched, with 107 members including eleven Swiss cantons and Austrian *Länder*. The establishment of formal rights of consultation with the Community owed a great deal to the pressure of the European Parliament which, in the course of the reforms of the Community regional fund, stressed the need for greater involvement of regions themselves. In 1988, the Commission finally established a Consultative Council of Regional and Local Authorities with consultative rights over the formulation and implementation of regional policies as well as the regional implications of other Community policies. Its forty-two members are appointed by the Commission on the joint nomination of the Assembly of European Regions, the International Union of Local Authorities, and the Council of Communes and Regions of Europe.[23] The Maastricht Treaty provides for a Committee of the Regions with the same status as the Social and Economic Committee, with rights to be consulted by the Commission and Council of Ministers. Arguments are taking place within member states as to how this will be nominated and whether national and municipal representatives will balance those of regional governments. The Council of the Regions represents a significant step forward in institutionalizing the presence of regions in Community decision-making, but it is a long way short of the ideals of some of the more ardent regionalists, who looked to a regionally based second chamber of the European Parliament.

Other regional organizations seeking to influence policy-making in Brussels are the Conference of Peripheral Maritime Regions, the Association of European Frontier Regions, the Working Group of Traditional Industrial Regions, and three Alpine groups. In addition, the development of the Community has encouraged the formation of a number of transnational frontier organizations.

Intergovernmental co-operation, in Europe as elsewhere, does tend to enhance the role of executives and exacerbate the demo-

---

[22] J.-P. Chauvet, 'Participation des collectivités territoriales aux décisions européenes: Le Rôle des lobbies locaux et régionaux', *Apres-demain*, 314–15 (1989), 9–12.   [23] Ibid.

cratic deficit. Procedures for involving regions in Community decision-making as part of a triangular system of intergovernmental
relations may further enhance the role of executives against legis-
latures. The evidence of the chapters certainly suggests so.

The European Parliament is usually seen as one remedy for the
democratic deficit but its capacity to remedy a deficit of territorial
representation is limited. Systems of election differ among member
states and not all have a territorial basis. Denmark, Greece,
Luxembourg, and the Netherlands have national list systems.
France also has a national list system of election but the parties
make sure that their lists have a balanced regional representation
to the extent of including the territorial designation of each
candidate in their publicity. Elsewhere, candidates are elected on
constituency and regional bases and have explicit territorial mandates. The Parliament, struggling to assert itself against the Commission and national governments and parliaments, has on
occasion shown itself sympathetic to the similar plight of regional
governments. This attitude may also owe something to the influence within the Parliament of regional and local notables and especially those French notables who continue to hold local office.
Several prominent French politicians, forced by the law on accumulation of mandates to surrender an elective office, have given
up their national parliamentary mandate, choosing to retain their
local and European ones. In 1988, having succeeded in persuading
the Commission to establish a Consultative Council of Regional
and Local Authorities, the Parliament pleaded for a charter of
regionalization for member states, providing for democratic election, adequate powers and finance, autonomy, and the participation of regions in defining the negotiating position of member
states in Community institutions. Of course, this remains a non-
binding recommendation adopted neither by the Commission nor
by the member governments.

Several of our chapters draw attention to the international
groupings of regions which have emerged within the Community or
Europe more widely. Again, the problem of distinguishing substance from gesture (and opportunities for foreign travel) is posed,
but there does seem to be a learning process at work. Regions learn
from each other about problems and policies, about how to organize for development and about the preparation of effective intelligence. After a period of rather naïve imitation, they may now be

learning how to adapt each others' experiences to their own cultures, institutions, traditions, and problems. Transfrontier co-operation initiatives are particularly important, enabling regions to take advantage of the dismantling of barriers across what, in the absence of states, would be regarded as single economic regions. This theme of co-operation, which is the subject of numerous research projects, must however be balanced against that of interregional competition for capital investment in the single market.

European Regional Policies

Many supporters of European integration have long recognized that a vigorous anti-disparity policy would be an essential concomitant of the project, though they have had to contend with a strong *laissez-faire* element within both the Commission and national governments. In the early years, it was believed that integration itself would largely solve regional problems through market processes. The only regional policy instrument included in the Treaty of Rome at Italy's insistence was the European Investment Bank. However, as early as the Treaty of Paris establishing the European Coal and Steel Community, it had been recognized that exceptions would have to be made to the provision banning subsidies and later regional subsidies were explicitly allowed. Since then, European regional policies have developed on three lines: the co-ordination of national regional policy measures to ensure their conformity to the treaties; the development of Community funds for regional development; and a slow series of moves towards a positive Community regional policy. Initially, the Commission was dependent on national databases, nationally defined regions, and national policy instruments. This has gradually changed. There is now a hierarchy of regional and local units used by the Community, the NUTS (nomenclature of units for territorial statistics), as shown in Table 1.1. The Commission also has its own database of regional conditions and a synthetic index of regional problems.

Policing of national regional subsidies is the responsibility of the competition directorate, which fixes ceilings for total permissible subsidies for each region. This is a matter of contention not only

TABLE 1.1. *Nomenclature of units for territorial statistics (NUTS)*

Country	NUTS 1	NUTS 2	NUTS 3
Belgium	Regions	Provinces	Arrondissements
Denmark	—	—	Ämter
Germany	Länder	Regierungs-be zirke	Kreise
Greece	NUTS 2 groupings	Development regions	Nomoi
Spain	NUTS 2 groupings	Comunidades autónomas	Provincias
France	ZEAT	Régions	Départements
Ireland	—	—	Planning regions
Italy	NUTS 2 groupings	Regioni	Provincie
Luxembourg	—	—	—
Netherlands	Landsdelen	Provinces	COROP-regios
Portugal	NUTS 2 groupings	NUTS 3 groupings	Groupings of concelhos
United Kingdom	Standard regions	NUTS 3 groupings	Counties, Scottish regions

Source: Commission of the European Communities, *The Regions of the European Community: Third Periodic Report on the social situation and development of the regions of the European Community* (Luxembourg, 1987).

with national and regional governments, but also with the directorate for regional policy within the Commission itself.

Moves towards a positive Community regional policy are inspired by the notion of 'cohesion'. This term, more often used than defined, encompasses economic, social, and political aspects of anti-disparity policies in the same way as did national regional policies in the past. Indeed, with the run-down of national regional policy, the Commission is left as the leading exponent of the regional approach. Economically, the idea is to permit all regions to compete in the internal market, by endowing them with the requisite infrastructure and skills. Politically, there is a need to demonstrate the value of Community membership in peripheral regions. In this respect cohesion bears comparison with regional development policies in the consolidation of the European State in the nineteenth century and, particularly, after the Second World War.

This has been at least partially successful. Survey data show a sharp rise in support for EC membership in Portugal and Greece in the 1980s, linked to a growing awareness and appreciation of the structural funds.[24] Ireland's large positive vote for the Maastricht Treaty had much to do with the feeling that Ireland stood to gain from the enlarged funds.

This interregional distributive logic is in practice inextricably linked with interstate distribution, the major priority of national governments. Unwilling to concede the principle of direct payments among states, the Commission and the more *communautaire* of the members have insisted that they should take the form of Community policy instruments. So the European Regional Development Fund (ERDF) was established in 1975 to accommodate the UK which was about to become a net contributor to the Community. Later the structural funds were doubled as the price for the southern members agreeing to the internal market programme. In the most recent reform, there has been an attempt to integrate the ERDF with the other, older structural funds, the European Social Fund (ESF) and the Guidance section of the European Agriculture Guidance and Guarantee Fund (EAGGF), together with Coal and Steel Community and European Investment Bank moneys. Armstrong traces the development and implementation of this policy. The various chapters on individual countries look at its implementation on the ground.

What emerges is that there has been a struggle for the control of the regional policy instrument among the Commission, member states, and regions. In the early years, the funds were largely handed over to states to distribute according to their own criteria to their chosen regions. Several states, such as Britain, France, and Spain, continue to manage the funds in a centralized manner, deciding themselves on how to distribute them internally. Indeed, the reform of the funds, the greater geographical concentration, and the need for co-ordinated programmes has in some respects strengthened national control in these states. Yet in other respects, the Commission has extended its control, moulding the structural funds into an instrument of Community policy rather than a series of compensations to national governments. Eligible regions are determined according to a single Community map, though the

[24] *Eurobarometer*, 36 (Dec. 1991) (Brussels: EC Directorate General for Communications).

eligibility criteria are still subject to some political manipulation
and bargaining. Governments are obliged to negotiate over programmes and, where they have failed to demonstrate additionality
and transparency, the Commission has held up money.[25] It has
further used the funds as an instrument of Community building,
strengthening solidarity and demonstrating the benefits of memberships to marginal regions. In this it has found allies in the
regions themselves, hence the insistence on partnership arrangements for Community programmes within states. Although the
quality of these varies, as the chapters show, they have taken on a
major political significance as a Community impact on the ground.
They have also brought into contact a range of actors at all three
levels, strengthening the sense of regional identity and establishing
new networks for the exchange of data, ideas, and influence. This
creates a potential for new types of policy-making in which the
states lose their traditional monopoly.[26] This effect is likely to be
subtle and long term but could prove very important in strengthening regional identity, modernizing it and linking it to the theme of
economic development, in much the same way that national regional policies in European states did in the 1960s and 1970s.[27] The
significance of the funds themselves varies, as the chapters again
show, from the purely symbolic to a real contribution to national
investment in the cases of Greece and Portugal.

Towards a Europe of the Regions?

Regions are becoming more important in the EC policy process.
Yet serious barriers remain to a Europe of the Regions. In the first
place, regions vary greatly in their economic capacity, their institutional structures, and the political, economic, and social demands
which they articulate.

Completion of the internal market, monetary union, and global
capital mobility are going to increase interregional competition.
Some regions are clearly better equipped in this respect than

[25] P. McAleavey, 'The Politics of European Regional Development Policy:
Additionality in the Scottish Coalfields', *Regional Politics and Policy*, 3/2 (1993).

[26] G. Marks, 'Structural Policy in the European Community', in A. Sbragia (ed.),
Euro-Politics (Washington, DC: Brookings, 1992).

[27] Keating, *State and Regional Nationalism*.

others. Southern countries are particularly vulnerable, caught between the technologically advanced states of northern Europe and the low labour-cost producers in the non-Community Mediterranean and eastern Europe. Just to bring the lower-performing regions up to Community average for basic infrastructure would require, according to a Commission study, a tripling of objective 1 expenditures between 1994 and 2010. With other pressures on the Community budget and a reluctance on the part of richer members to countenance further transfers, this is a stiff challenge. It is likely that further transfers to the south will be the price of continued progress to integration but it is less certain that these will take the form of regional as opposed to new forms of solidarity funds and there is still resistance from northern members to any new expenditure programmes.

There is equally a differentiation in the political capacity of regions in the strength of their business and social networks, their civic cultures, and their institutional structure.[28] It is notable that Germany and Belgium are the only European Union states with a level of government corresponding to the NUTS 1. Some states lack regional governments altogether, their regions often lacking internal cohesion or the capacity to mobilize politically or even to use Community financial instruments effectively.

In some regions and stateless nations, there are powerful autonomist movements or even separatist parties, which have come to see Europe as a way to circumvent the nation-state. In others, these pressures are absent and politics remains focused on the national capital.

So regions do not all have common interests in policy or institutional change. Needy regions may spend a lot of effort in trying to extract funds from Brussels, but they know that most of their resources come from the national level. Further market integration is likely to enhance the position of the better endowed regions. Similarly, strengthening of the regional dimension of Community decision-making at the expense of national governments could enhance the already privileged position of the stronger regions. It is

[28] J. Anderson, 'Skeptical Reflections on a "Europe of the Regions": Britain, Germany and the ERDF', *Journal of Public Policy*, 10/4 (1991), 417–47. R. Putnam, R. Leonardi, and R. Nanetti, *La pianta e le radici: Il radicamento dell'Istituto Regionale nel Sistema Politico Italiano* (Milan: Il Mulino, 1985). R. Putnam with R. Leonardi and R. Nanetti, *Making Democracy Work: Civic Traditions in Modern Italy* (Princeton, NJ: Princeton University Press, 1993).

for this reason that we are unlikely to see regions as a whole teaming up against national governments or the Commission to press a common policy or institutional agenda.

Developments within the new European Union may also militate against a Europe of the Regions. Popular resistance to the Maastricht Treaty has already produced a new emphasis on 'subsidiarity'. Much to the chagrin of regionalists, this is generally interpreted as indicating a need to pass powers back to national governments but not further. It may well be that responsibility for territorial management will revert to member states. It is significant that the new convergence funds agreed in the Maastricht Treaty were not tied to regional development, but were for transport networks firmly under the control of national governments.

Maastricht also effectively sanctioned the idea of a 'variable geometry Europe' by permitting Britain and Denmark to opt out of significant parts of it. This means that regions in different countries will face different patterns of opportunities and constraints in relation to Europe. Already, political controversy has arisen over Britain's opt-out of the social chapter and the advantage which this appears to give British regions in attracting industrial investment. The increased complexity of policy-making in the new Europe may create further opportunities for regions to intervene in the interstices of policy sectors and institutional competences. Within the Commission, and in the triangular negotiations among the Union, member states, and regions, the debate is likely to continue both on regional policies and the institutionalization of regions within the decision-making process. Some of the future implications are taken up by Jones in the conclusion.

2

The Role and Evolution of European Community Regional Policy

HARVEY W. ARMSTRONG

Introduction

Regional economic theory . . . suggests that in the absence of appropriate accompanying policies, market forces will not of themselves be sufficient to eliminate regional divergencies . . . but rather the reverse.[1]

This quotation sets out succinctly the great fear that underlies European Community (EC) regional policy. The forces unleashed by economic integration carry with them not only the hope for a more prosperous Europe, but also a threat to the already disadvantaged areas. The EC's regional policy is its response to this threat.

The 1986 Single European Act set out in general terms the objective of using EC regional policy for the purpose of 'strengthening . . . economic and social cohesion' (Article 130A). This is a laudable objective, but is unfortunately rather vague as it stands. In practice, emphasis tends to be placed on economic cohesion, with the narrowing of regional economic disparities being given great priority (e.g. unemployment rates and GDP per capita). Social cohesion is a more difficult concept to come to grips with, and is concerned with not only the social well-being of the Community and its citizens, but also with trying (via EC regional policy) to ensure a fairer spread of the benefits of economic integration.

[1] M. F. Doyle, 'Regional Policy and European Economic Integration', in Committee for the Study of Economic and Monetary Union, *Report on Economic and Monetary Union in the European Community*, Papers submitted to the Committee (Luxembourg, 1989), 70.

In this chapter the Community's regional policy is described and its strengths and weaknesses assessed. The next section examines the ways in which economic integration affects regional problems. Particular attention will be concentrated on the recent boost to integration arising from the Single European Market (SEM) process and the possible effects of Economic and Monetary Union. The third section turns to the EC regional policy. What were its origins? How has it evolved since its inception? What reform has it undergone? In the following section the currently constituted EC regional policy is subjected to close scrutiny. The existing EC regional policy owes many of its features to a major set of reforms introduced in 1989 as part of the single market process. The 1989 reforms mark the most significant set of changes to EC regional policy since its inception in 1975. More recent (1993) revisions essentially represent a fine-tuning of the 1989 policy in order to accommodate the effects of the anticipated implementation of the Maastricht Treaty on European Union. The fifth section reviews EC regional policy and assesses its strengths and weaknesses. In the final section conclusions are drawn and the possibilities for the future evolution of EC regional policy are considered.

Economic Integration and EC Regional Problems

It is important to realize that economic integration in Europe is a process which existed long before the Treaty of Rome establishing the EC in 1958, and would have occurred at a slow pace even had the EC not existed in the years since 1958. Improvements in transport infrastructure and transport technology, combined with more efficient methods of producing goods, have meant a steady decline in transport costs per unit of output. Moreover, world trade has been stimulated by the negotiation of simpler and easier trading arrangements and by the gradual integration of world financial and capital markets. The countries of the EC have all shared in this ongoing process of economic integration.

The distinctive role of the EC has been to give an additional fillip to integration among its member states. It has launched the member states on a process which began with tariff removal and which is likely to end with full Economic and Monetary Union. The latter, of course, is still some considerable way from being achieved.

In some ways the processes at work can be regarded as a continuum of ever-increasing integration. At the simplest level we have a free-trade area, a collection of countries which remove tariff barriers between themselves, but retain their own individual tariff policies for trade with non-members. The UK was a member of the European Free Trade Area (EFTA) prior to its admission to the EC in 1973. A customs union is essentially a free-trade area in which members go one step further and set up a common policy for trade and tariffs with non-member countries. Beyond customs unions lie common markets. In a common market member states ensure completely free trade in goods and services amongst themselves, together with full internal mobility for labour and capital from one member state to another. The EC as it is currently constituted is basically a common market on to which a number of special policies such as agriculture, social policy, or industry policy, have been grafted. The SEM process currently being phased in is essentially a series of tidying-up measures designed to remove as many as possible of the remaining non-tariff barriers to a full common market.

The closing months of 1991 witnessed two major further steps in the EC integration process. The first was the agreement at the Maastricht Summit in the Netherlands to move gradually over the 1990s towards Economic and Monetary Union. The stage-by-stage process for achieving this ultimate stage in the integration process[2] has been the subject of fierce controversy and intense negotiation. The monetary union part of EMU will almost certainly involve a single currency, the ECU. In monetary union all capital transactions between member states will be completely liberalized and banking and other financial markets will be fully integrated, under the aegis of a gradually developing EC central banking system. The economic union part of EMU will require the successful completion of SEM (i.e. free movement of goods, services, labour, and capital within the EC), the close co-ordination of member-state monetary and fiscal policies (including constraints on the size of budget deficits run by member states), and much stronger EC competition policy, regional policy, and other central policies designed to encourage industry to restructure and adapt to the new economic environment which is emerging.

---

[2] Under the Delors Plan, Committee for the Study of Economic and Monetary Union, *Report on Economic and Monetary Union in the European Community.*

The second major agreement in 1991 of major importance to the integration process was the decision to create a single EC/EFTA European Economic Area. This basically involves the majority of EFTA countries joining the EC's single market. Since most of the EFTA countries are prosperous by European standards, this agreement not only widens the SEM, it also goes some way towards balancing the mix of prosperous and depressed regions in the single market. Prior to the agreement, the entry of Greece, Spain, and Portugal had greatly increased the numbers of depressed regions relative to prosperous regions in the EC. Under the European Economic Area agreement EFTA countries will provide some funding for the depressed EC regions.

At the present time, the EC is in the rather paradoxical position of trying to complete its role as a common market (the SEM process), whilst simultaneously pushing onwards towards EMU. Before examining the implications for the disadvantaged regions of this ongoing process of economic integration, it is important to look more closely at what SEM and EMU involve, and what benefits will flow from their achievement.

The SEM process was launched in 1986 by the Single European Act.[3] By the end of 1992 some 300 separate pieces of EC legislation had been implemented, each designed slowly to edge the EC in the years after 1992 towards a genuinely free market in goods, services, and factors of production. The targets of the SEM process are not tariff and quota barriers to trade, most of which are now ended in the EC. Instead, it is non-tariff barriers which the legislation seeks to end. These are many and complex. Some will be unlikely ever to be overcome fully (e.g. language differences). Those being tackled by the SEM legislation can be classified into three categories.[4] The first are cost-increasing barriers, such as customs formalities or differing technical specifications for products. These raise costs for exporters. The second are market-entry restrictions, such as the preferential placing of government contracts with domestic firms ('public procurement'). The third are market-distorting practices such as collusion and other restrictive practices of firms, and differing member-state government price controls, taxes, and subsidies on goods.

[3] Commission of the European Communities, Single Europe Act, Dec. 1985.
[4] F. McDonald, 'The Single Market: The Likely Impact on the UK Economy', *British Economic Survey*, 18/2 (1989).

The successful eventual full implementation of SEM would significantly boost trade amongst the member states and should lead to more efficient production and lower priced goods for consumers in all regions of the EC, prosperous and depressed alike. The type of benefits flowing from SEM will be very similar to those which emerged when formal tariffs and quotas were removed earlier in the life of the EC. Economists distinguish between the static and dynamic effects of freer trade. Not all of these effects are necessarily beneficial. When the static effects are considered, the benefits of trade creation (the replacement of expensive local production by cheaper imports from a partner member state) must be set against the problems caused by trade diversion (the replacement of cheaper initial imports from a non-member by more expensive imports from a partner member state). Dynamic effects are also complex, and may be spread over a very long period of time. They include such things as the exploitation of economies of scale by bigger firms supplying the larger common market, the possibility of a whole range of external economies leading to reduced costs for firms, improved investment volumes, lower costs from greater competition, and a series of 'polarization' effects favouring locations for industry close to the central core of the EC.

Measuring the size of the benefits and costs of further integration, such as SEM, is an exercise fraught with difficulties. From the point of view of the EC as a whole a major study by the EC itself suggests that, if successful, SEM could eventually lead to gains of the order of 4.5 per cent of the combined GDP of the EC.[5] These would be in the form of extra output and hence consumption at lower prices by consumers in all EC regions. At the same time prices could be 6 per cent lower and perhaps 1.75 million more jobs would be created in the EC. Further benefits in the form of lower public-sector deficits and improved trade balances are also claimed. These benefits will not be achieved immediately. They will accrue gradually over a prolonged period after 1992. The EC has now

[5] M. Emerson, M. Aujean, M. Catinet, P. Goybet, and A. Jacquemin, *The Economics of 1992: The EC Commission's Assessment of the Economic Effects of Completing the Internal Market* (Oxford: Oxford University Press, 1988), 218. See also Commission of the European Communities (The Cecchini Report), *Research on the Cost of Non-Europe: Basic Findings*, 16 vols. (Brussels, 1988); P. Cecchini, *The European Challenge: 1992 The Benefits of a Single Market* (Aldershot: Wildwood House, 1988). For a more critical view see J. Pelkmans and A. Winters, *Europe's Domestic Market* (London: Routledge, 1988).

launched a post-1992 initiative designed to follow up the initial SEM legislation and maintain the pressure for full implementation.

It is important to keep in mind the overall benefits of economic integration when considering the effects on the different regions of the EC of changes such as tariff removal, SEM, or EMU. Any disadvantages faced by a given region must be weighed against greater prosperity for all from a more dynamic EC-wide economy.

The effect of economic integration on regional disparities in the EC is a very controversial issue. The pattern of existing regional disparities reflects previous rounds of integration, with tariff-removal and the entry of a series of new member states all having their own distinctive effects. Map 1 shows a widely used measure of regional disadvantage: GDP per capita. The picture which emerges is very much one of core and periphery. More prosperous regions tend to lie at the geographical centre of the EC. The more disadvantaged regions tend to be peripheral regions, particularly in the Mediterranean south (Greece, southern Italy, Spain, and Portugal), but also in Ireland and parts of the UK. More recent data than that shown in Map 1 would pick out eastern Germany as an additional peripheral disadvantaged region.

The pattern of regional disparities revealed by Map 1 is a very long-standing one. Prior to the mid-1970s regional disparities had shown some tendency to converge. Between the mid-1970s and mid-1980s this went into reverse, before stabilizing in more recent years.

Economic integration of the type which has helped to shape the pattern of disparities revealed in Map 1 has a profound effect on regional economies. All regions of the EC are affected by the structural changes which arise as the static and dynamic effects of integration work through the system. The more far-reaching the integration, the more are a region's firms faced with major restructuring decisions. In each region we would expect to see some industries being run down or even closed, while other industries expand and prosper. A major reallocation of capital and labour resources must occur if the benefits of integration are to be enjoyed.

That integration will affect every single part of the EC is beyond doubt. A more interesting question is why some regions are more affected than others, leading to a systematic pattern of regional disparities in the EC. In part this may be because of the initial mix

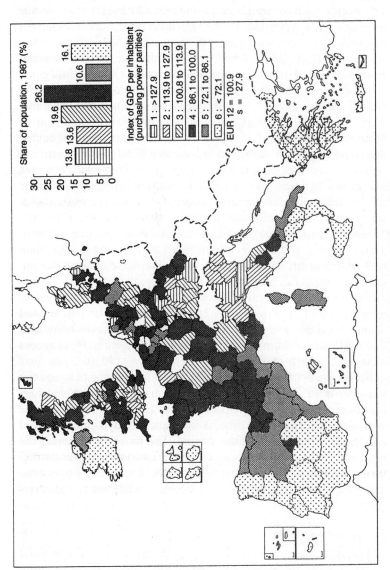

Share of population, 1987 (%)

Index of GDP per inhabitant
(purchasing power parities)

1 : >127.9
2 : 113.9 to 127.9
3 : 100.8 to 113.9
4 : 86.1 to 100.0
5 : 72.1 to 86.1
6 : <72.1

EUR 12 = 100.9
s = 27.9

MAP 1. Regional GDP per inhabitant, 1988.

of industries in the region prior to the integration occurring. If the region is particularly heavily dependent on industries most likely to be affected by freer trade, such as manufacturing rather than service industries during tariff-removal, or industries not enjoying the protection of high transport-cost inputs, then subsequent integration will cause painful restructuring effects. The EC has also long recognized the particular problems that integration poses for border regions. Regions lying along the internal frontiers of the EC, or along the external border with non-members, face particularly serious structural adjustment problems. Border regions frequently develop distinctive types of industries exploiting differences in tariffs, legal regulations, and break-of-bulk opportunities arising from the presence of a border. These industries are threatened by integration. External border regions face even more severe problems. Their trade is usually oriented towards non-member countries and must be slowly reoriented towards the EC.

Each 'round' of integration has its own distinctive regional pattern of effects, and it is dangerous to assume that the same regions will be adversely affected each time. The SEM process has attracted a good deal of research on the regional effects of further integration.[6] The selective nature of the barriers to trade being removed by SEM means that certain types of industry will be most heavily affected, and that regions initially heavily dependent upon them will suffer the greatest effects of restructuring. It is thought that perhaps forty manufacturing industries will eventually be most affected, particularly those heavily reliant on contracts from their member-state governments such as transport equipment, telecommunications, or where other barriers such as distinctive technical product standards have offered protection from free trade, for example electrical engineering or agri-food products. There is evidence that some of the already weak regions of the EC, notably in Ireland, Portugal, Spain, and Greece, are heavily dependent on the types of industries likely to face major restructuring after 1992.[7]

---

[6] Much of this is summarized in Commission of the European Communities, *The Regions in the 1990s: Fourth Periodic Report on the Social and Economic Situation and Development of the Regions of the Community* (Brussels, 1991), ch. 9.

[7] See Booz, Allen, and Hamilton, *Effects of the Internal Market on Greece, Ireland, Portugal and Spain*, Study for EC Commission, 1989; and Commission of the European Communities, 'The Impact of the Internal Market by Industrial Sector: The Challenge for the Member States', *European Economy*, special edition (1990).

The effects of SEM will by no means be confined to manufacturing. The SEM process envisages freer trade in a range of service industries, including major employers such as banking, finance,[8] transport, and communication services. Restructuring effects will therefore also be of great significance in regions heavily dependent on the service sector. Some of these regions have not yet experienced the painful process of restructuring. Earlier rounds of integration tended to affect manufacturing most since it was manufacturing which was formerly most protected by the tariffs and quotas being removed at that time.

It is clear then that integration affects all EC regions to some degree, but causes restructuring problems which are more severe in some regions than others. This in itself is serious, but suggests that the role of EC regional policy should be only a temporary one, designed to help regions to switch out of declining industries and into those which are expanding. Eventually, so the argument goes, resources will have had time to switch into those sectors where the region has a comparative advantage. The result will be a more prosperous EC as a whole. Unfortunately, there are processes at work which suggest that integration may be causing certain types of effects which are systematically biased against the already weaker peripheral regions of the EC. Neven, for example, has shown that trade between regions in the relatively prosperous core of the EC—France, Germany, Benelux, and parts of the UK—is mostly of the intra-industry type, that is in similar, slightly differentiated products. Trade between core and periphery regions in the EC by contrast is of the more traditional inter-industry type, that is trade in different commodities, with peripheral areas concentrating on labour-intensive, lower technology goods. The SEM process is likely to intensify the existing pattern of specialization, with the peripheral regions concentrating even more heavily on labour-intensive, low technology products. This could, paradoxically, be good for the peripheral regions in the short run, as the SEM stimulates demand for their products. It does nothing, however, to bring their incomes up to those of the more prosperous core, and leaves them vulnerable to competition in the longer run from countries in eastern Europe and the Third World which also specialize in labour-intensive, low technology goods.

[8] PA Cambridge Economic Consultants, *The Regional Consequences of the Completion of the Internal Market for Financial Services*, Study for EC Commission, 1989.

Perhaps most disturbing of all for the disadvantaged peripheral regions of the EC are the longer-term dynamic effects of further integration. The SEM process will enhance corporate restructuring, with mergers, take-overs, and plant restructuring occurring as firms adjust to the more competitive environment in which they must operate and as they seek to exploit economies of scale. This process is likely to favour the major metropolitan areas, and the financial and administrative centres of the EC, almost all of which lie in the already prosperous core of the EC. Regions at the centre of the EC already have the advantage of being best placed to serve the whole EC market, being located at the hub of the EC's integrating road, rail, and telecommunications systems. These advantages are reinforced by a whole series of agglomeration and localization external economies which arise when economic development becomes highly concentrated geographically. Indeed, it is possible that the central regions could benefit from polarized growth as capital and labour are drawn into these areas by job and investment opportunities not available in the periphery. The 1980s slow-down in internal migration is almost certainly only a short-run cyclical phenomenon caused by inadequate job opportunities in central Community regions.

The process of polarized growth is reinforced by the fact that labour migrants tend to be more economically active, better educated, and younger than those left behind. Their arrival simultaneously strengthens the attraction of the central regions for further industrial location, while weakening the attractiveness of the periphery.

To view the cumulative growth of the EC as potentially explosive is probably too extreme. Central regions will not experience massive, unlimited growth at the expense of their weaker peripheral counterparts. Language and culture differences, together with other costs and barriers, will slow the migration from peripheral to core regions. Countervailing forces are also at work. Growth at the centre triggers land-price rises and wage increases. These in turn make peripheral locations more attractive for business investors. So too does the increasing congestion and poorer quality of the environment in the big cities of the central regions. The overall result of integration is therefore likely to be an uneasy balance of forces. On the one hand the centre has formidable advantages for industry and services and acts as a magnet for migrants from peripheral regions. On the other hand lower costs for labour and land, together with excellent quality-of-life considerations, will favour at least some of the peripheral regions. The chances of an explosive growth of the centre at the expense of the periphery are remote. Indeed, it is possible that regional disparities could narrow in the very long term as market forces come into play. They may, however, widen somewhat in the immediate future.

It would be unwise to end this section without some discussion of the possible regional effects of EMU. In one sense EMU is simply a continuation of what has gone before—the customs union and SEM. A further boost to integration will occur and the familiar forces affecting the regions will be again set in motion. Trade, for example, will be easier if there is a single currency since transactions costs and exchange-risk premiums on interest rates will be eliminated. Very little research has yet been conducted on the regional effects of EMU. What little work has been done suggests, as already argued, that there will be a balance of countervailing forces at work, some of which help the peripheral areas, and some of which do not.[9] In one respect, however, EMU represents a distinctive new break from what has gone before. No longer will member states on the periphery of the EC be able to use exchange rate depreciation or massive public-sector deficit spending to help to protect or boost their flagging local economies. EMU will have removed two macro-policy instruments previously widely used to mitigate the consequences of depressed local economic conditions. Such member states will have lost some of the power they currently have to preserve local incomes.

Whether the existing structure of EC regional policy will be sufficient to meet the new challenges posed by EMU is an important question, though one beyond the scope of this chapter. Simply increasing again the size of budget appropriations set aside for EC regional policy may not be sufficient. The trends, already observed in EC regional policy, towards greater help for indigenous development, notably in smaller firms, and innovation may also not be sufficient in themselves. A whole range of other possibilities have also been discussed. These range from using regional policy funds to accelerate the creation of the single market or EMU in the hope

---

[9] See 'One Market, One Money: An Evaluation of the Potential Benefits and Costs of Forming an Economic and Monetary Union', *European Economy*, 44 (Oct. 1990).

that the free market itself will eventually eliminate disparities, to suggestions that the whole EC budgetary system may need to be reformed to generate intergovernment and interpersonal transfers in favour of more depressed parts of the Community.

The Evolution of EC Regional Policy

The EC regional policy which we observe today had its origins in 1975 when the European Regional Development Fund (ERDF) was established. Before this, EC regional policy was fragmentary and of very limited extent. What policy there was tended to be given via funds and programmes whose main purposes were those not concerned with regional policy. The European Coal and Steel Community (ECSC), for example, and the European Agricultural Guidance and Guarantee Fund (EAGGF) offered financial help in depressed regions by virtue of the industries they were designed to assist. The European Investment Bank (EIB) was also involved in making loans to projects in many depressed areas. In addition, the EC's competition policy had become involved in a fairly weak manner in attempting to regulate the way in which member states used their own regional policy subsidies to firms. The intention here was to prevent regional subsidies being used too aggressively to bid competitively for mobile investment projects, and to prevent subsidies from significantly distorting competitive forces within the EC. In practice, before 1975 the depressed areas of the EC looked almost entirely to their own member-state governments for regional policy assistance.

The EC Regulations which established the ERDF in 1975 created a threefold structure for EC regional policy which has persisted through to today:

1. A financial instrument for EC regional policy: the ERDF.
2. A series of measures designed to improve co-ordination between the EC, member states, regional and local authorities in their efforts to promote regional development.
3. Other EC funds and institutions which, as part of their more general objectives also operate with a deliberate regional bias.

The EC regional policy set up in 1975 underwent reforms in

1979, 1984, 1989, and 1993. The 1989 reforms were an integral part of the SEM process and will be considered at length in the next section. The 1993 reforms essentially retain the structure established in 1989 and introduce amendments necessary to accompany the anticipated ratification of the Maastricht Treaty and the expected step-by-step progress towards EMU. In this section the manner in which EC regional policy has evolved over the period 1975–93 is considered.

The European Regional Development Fund (ERDF)

The 1975 ERDF Regulation had its origins at the 1972 Paris Summit. With UK entry to the EC agreed, considerable pressure built up to strengthen the existing rudimentary EC regional policy. Much of this pressure was led by the UK, which was keen to see a more active EC regional policy, partly as a way of channelling EC funds to the UK and partly because the UK had a strong tradition of regional policy and was also bringing into the EC a number of problem regions in need of help. Indeed, on entry to the EC in 1973 one of the UK Commissioners (George Thomson) was appointed as the Commissioner with responsibility for EC regional policy. The result was a process which was to become all too familiar in the years which followed. The Commission pushed hard for a radical set of policy measures,[10] while the Council of Ministers responded by approving a watered-down version[11] which basically restricted the amount of regional policy powers transferred from member states to the EC. The member states themselves simultaneously preserved and continued with their own individual regional policies much as before. Table 2.1 compares the ERDF as proposed by the Commission and the regulations actually agreed by the Council of Ministers in 1975. The resulting ERDF was a rather peculiar creature in a number of respects. First, although it was ostensibly the EC's own regional policy financial instrument, it was effectively structured in such a way that individual member states exerted very strong influence over how the money was spent and who received

[10] Commission of the European Communities, 'Proposals for a Community Regional Policy', *Official Journal of the European Communities*, OJ C86 of 16 Oct. 1973 and OJ C106 of 6 Dec. 1973 (Brussels).
[11] Commission of the European Communities, 'Regulations Establishing a Community Regional Policy', *Official Journal* OJ L73 of 21 Mar. 1975 (Brussels).

the assistance. The whole of the budget, for example, was allocated on the basis of predetermined, negotiated, shares or quotas. The UK initial quota, for example, was 28 per cent of ERDF allocations. These quotas were determined by the Council of Ministers by negotiation, and not by the Commission on the basis of relative need and extent of problems faced (although the quotas did reflect 'need' to a certain degree). Similarly, there was to be no Commission-determined map of areas to be eligible for ERDF aid (as proposed by the Commission in 1973). Instead, the areas delimited by each member state for their own regional policies were used. Moreover, by controlling the flow of project applications for ERDF

TABLE 2.1. *The 1975 ERDF: actual and proposed*

1973 Proposals	1975 Regulations
(a) SIZE	
1500 million units of account (£940 m) over the three years 1974, 1975, 1976.	856 million units of account (£540 m) over the three years 1975, 1976, 1977. To be allocated on a 'quota' basis with member states obtaining a predetermined share:

UK	28.0%
Italy	40.0%
France	15.0%
Germany	6.4%
Belgium	1.5%
Denmark	1.3%
Luxembourg	0.1%
Eire	6.0%

(and 4 million u.a. (£2.5 m) from all others except Italy).

1973 Proposals	1975 Regulations
(b) ELIGIBLE PROJECTS	
(i) Investment in industrial and service activities. Must not be too small and must involve the maintenance or creation of jobs. Partial aid only and must also receive member-state regional aid.	(i) Investment in industrial, handicraft, and service projects. Conditions as in 1973 proposals but with some relaxation of percentage of fund contribution and more rigid limits on the cost per job created or maintained.

TABLE 2.1. *Continued*

1973 Proposals	1975 Regulations
(ii) Infrastructure projects—directly related to industrial or service development. Must also be aided by member-state public authorities. Up to 30% of member-state public authority expenditure can be met.	(ii) Infrastructure projects related to or a prerequisite for industrial, handicraft, or service development 30% of public (or similar) authority expenditure for small projects and 10–30% for larger projects. Otherwise conditions as 1973 proposals.
(iii) Priority Agricultural Areas. A parallel proposal to use EAGGF (Gu.) funds for industrial projects in designated areas.	(iii) Infrastructure projects in mountain and hill farming and certain less-favoured farming areas. Use of fund aid for eligible infrastructure projects in these areas (where conditions of aid are as in (ii) above).
(c) ELIGIBLE AREAS Detailed delimitation using multiple indicators. Areas must be also eligible for member-state regional aids, have GDP per head below the EEC average, be above a certain minimum size, and be either dependent on agriculture, have declining industries, or suffer structural underemployment.	Those areas also eligible for member state regional aids. Requirement to direct assistance to 'national priority areas'.

grants, member-state bureaucrats were left with the power to determine to a large extent which projects, firms, and local areas within their member state, had access to ERDF help, pre-empting the EC itself in taking these decisions.[12]

The second peculiar feature of the 1975 ERDF was the narrowness of the help given. Assistance was confined largely to grants for infrastructure investments and for investment in industrial and service-sector schemes. Member-state regional policies typically offer a much wider array of types of help in addition to investment

[12] H. W. Armstrong, 'Community Regional Policy: A Survey and Critique', *Regional Studies*, 12 (1978), 511–28.

grants. These include tax incentives, loans, advice, the provision of industrial premises, and so on. Another interesting feature of the original ERDF was its complete focus on project-by-project aid, with no attempt to package up the projects into coherent groups targeting particular regional problems (what is now known as programme assistance).

The third rather odd feature of the 1975 ERDF was the extraordinarily meagre financial resources devoted to it from the EC budget. Only 856 million units of account (£540 million) was set aside for a three-year period (1975–7), despite the Commission's original request, itself very modest, for 1,500 million units of account (£940 million). This amounted, in 1976, to a mere 0.04 per cent of the combined GDP of the then nine EC member states.

As noted earlier, the ERDF underwent major reform in 1979 and 1984.[13] By 1979 the size of the resources devoted to ERDF had been slowly increased and was being determined annually as part of the EC budget decision. The sums of money involved remained very small and were dwarfed both by other EC spending, notably on agricultural support, and by the spending of member states on their own individual regional policies. The 1979 reforms, however, were noteworthy not so much for a change in the scale of help given by ERDF, but for certain small changes at the margin in the manner in which help was to be given. These changes, in retrospect, proved to be the testing-ground for subsequent much larger reforms. In the 1979 reforms the vast bulk of ERDF spending (95 per cent of the total—subsequently known as the 'quota section') was left as project-by-project assistance, overwhelmingly in the form of investment grants, and allocated on the basis of predetermined national shares or quotas. The reforms made changes in the details of the regulation terms for these grants, but by and large little was to alter—manufacturing industries, services, and infrastructure projects continuing to be the main beneficiaries. The remaining 5

[13] For the 1979 reforms see: Commission of the European Communities, 'Principal Regulations and Decisions of the Council of the European Communities on Regional Policy', *Office for the Publications of the European Communities*, Luxembourg (1981). For the 1984 reforms see: *Official Journal*, OJ L169 of 28 June 1984 (Brussels). The reforms are examined in: H. W. Armstrong, 'The Reform of the European Community Regional Policy', *Journal of Common Market Studies*, 23/4 (1985), 319–43; and in H. W. Armstrong, 'Community Regional Policy', in J. Lodge (ed.), *The European Community and the Challenge of the Future* (London: Pinter, 1989), 167–85.

per cent of the ERDF (the non-quota section) did, however, involve radical change. This money was much less hedged around with detailed regulations and became a proving-ground for newer types of help. The non-quota section could be used more at the discretion of the EC and was less under the control of the member states. Special eligible areas, not necessarily those already designated as assisted areas by member states, could be given non-quota assistance. Most importantly of all, the non-quota assistance was to be given via programmes and not on the project-by-project basis of the quota section. Programmes are carefully co-ordinated packages of help (including other types of help as well as investment grants) targeted on a range of projects and policies designed to alleviate specific regional problems. They typically are designed to be rolling programmes lasting a number of years and in which ERDF help is closely tied in with assistance provided by member states and regional and local agencies. They are essentially a partnership between the EC and member states. Early programmes in which the UK participated were for areas affected by the run down of textile, steel, fishing, and shipbuilding industries, and along the Northern Ireland–Republic of Ireland border. The 1979 reforms also enabled the ERDF to begin to develop on a small scale newer types of flexible assistance designed to stimulate indigenous development in depressed areas, particularly for small firms, and to begin to help disadvantaged inner-city areas in Integrated Development Operations, as pioneered in Belfast and Naples.

The 1979 reforms were small, involving only 5 per cent of the ERDF, but were to lay the foundations for the much more significant 1984 reform package. In the 1984 reform, the distinction between the quota and non-quota sections was retained but they were renamed project assistance and programme assistance respectively. The reforms envisaged a rapid decline in project assistance (from 95 per cent to 80 per cent of all ERDF allocations within three years, and further falls thereafter). Programme assistance was earmarked for rapid expansion. Since programme assistance is more flexible and more at the discretion of the EC, this change involved a shift of power away from the member states towards the EC.

The 1984 reforms also tackled project assistance head on. Formal quotas for each member state were abolished and a set of 'indicative ranges' for each member state was introduced. The initial UK indicative range was 21.42 per cent–28.56 per cent. The 21.42

per cent represented the UK's guaranteed minimum share of all project assistance from ERDF. More (up to a maximum of 28.56 per cent) was available subject to suitable projects being put forward to the ERDF for approval. The 1984 reforms also relaxed a number of the detailed regulations governing project assistance.

Finally, the 1984 reforms broadened out programme assistance by defining two distinct types of programme. The first were Community Programmes, to be initiated by the EC and encompassing all of the member states. These are designed to tackle EC-wide problems. Early examples were Star (telecommunications) and Valoren (energy supply). The second type of programme envisaged by the 1984 reforms were National Programmes of Community Interest (NPCI) initiated by the member state and drawing in ERDF aid. These were to be confined to single member states. Community Programmes were given priority over NPCIs.

The radical changes of the 1984 reforms signalled not only a degree of extra EC control over its own fund, together with a boost for the programme approach to aid, but also a renewed emphasis on helping small firms and indigenous development (in preference to inward investment), and a commitment to a rapid expansion of the size of the ERDF. As we will see, the 1989 reforms were to take this process much further.

Co-ordination Initiatives and the Role of Other EC Instruments

Running alongside the ERDF throughout the period 1975–89 were the two other component parts of EC regional policy: co-ordination initiatives and other EC financial instruments operating with a deliberate regional bias.

The original 1975 EC regional policy began with a rather faltering attempt at encouraging co-ordination. Member states were required to supply the EC with annual information and statistical summaries of their own regional policies and of the use to which EC money was being put within the boundaries. The states were also required to prepare and submit periodic regional development programmes designed to analyse regional problems and set out the objectives and planning of the member states to tackle the problems. Periodic reports were published in 1980, 1984, 1987, and 1991. In its turn, the EC instituted a regional analysis system leading to two-yearly periodic reports on regional problems in the EC as a whole. These reports formed the basis of regular sets of priorities or guidelines for regional policy into which member-state plans were expected to dovetail. EC competition policy regulations controlling certain aspects of member states' own regional policies, which existed prior to 1975, were also continued in the period after 1975.

By 1979 the EC had also implemented a Regional Impact Assessment system to monitor the regional effects of all major EC decisions and to ensure a co-ordinated response by all EC directorates to any adverse effects which might arise.

The 1979 reforms themselves provided a major boost to co-ordination by introducing programme assistance, which by its very nature requires the parties involved, notably the EC and member-state governments, to act together in a carefully planned manner. The 1984 reforms, as we have seen continued to strengthen the programme approach.

Various other EC instruments have supplemented ERDF assistance during the period 1975–89. Most important of these have been structural funds other than the ERDF. These comprise the Guidance Section of the Agriculture Fund (EAGGF), giving a variety of types of help in depressed farming areas, and the European Social Fund, which offers help for retraining, training, and migration of workers. There is also the help given by the European Coal and Steel Community (ECSC) for retraining and for new industries in depressed coal and steel areas. The European Investment Bank (EIB) also continued to be active in providing loans on advantageous terms in depressed regions. These four EC instruments represent a considerable volume of help targeted on depressed regions.

The 1989 Reform of EC Regional Policy

The SEM process, triggered by the 1986 Single European Act, has led to the most thoroughgoing reform of the EC regional policy which has yet occurred. The reform was implemented via a series of new EC regulations.[14] The new EC regulations were published in 1988 and became effective on 1 January 1989.

[14] Commission of the European Communities, Regulation (EEC) No. 2052/88— Tasks of the Structural Funds ('The Framework Regulation'), *Official Journal* OJ

The 1989 reform of EC regional policy must be seen as an integral part of the SEM process. The process of abolishing as many as possible of the remaining barriers to free trade and factor movement within the EC is thought likely, as we have seen, to pose severe problems for the already depressed regions. It will also involve major restructuring in all parts of the EC. In order to avoid a new round of widening regional disparities as SEM is implemented, the EC decided upon a wide-ranging and fundamental reform of its regional policy. The main features of the 1989 reform are set out below. The recent 1993 upgrading of the 1989 reforms is also examined.

ERDF Reform as Part of a Comprehensive Reform of the Structural Funds

The challenge of the SEM for the disadvantaged regions is essentially one of structural change, and how to respond to it successfully. The 1989 reform of ERDF was therefore designed to be part of a comprehensive reform of all three EC structural funds (the ERDF, ESF, and the Guidance Section of EAGGF). The intention was to strengthen the degree to which all three funds simultaneously and in a co-ordinated manner were to be used to tackle EC regional problems. This involved strengthening the deliberate regional bias in the way in which the ESF or EAGGF Guidance Section were operated. It also involved the development of a common framework or set of objectives under which all three funds operate.

Concentration on Five Priority Objectives

The key Framework Regulation (EEC No. 2052/88) for the structural funds set out five major objectives for the reformed funds (see Table 2.2). By no means all of these objectives were of a 'regional' nature. Objective 3, the 'combating of long-term unemployment' was strictly speaking non-regional, although, of course, depressed regions tend to have more unemployed of this type. The regional

L185/9 of 15 July 1989. Commission of the European Communities, Regulations 4253/88, 4254/88, 4255/88, and 4256/88 ('The Implementing Regulations'), *Official Journal* OJ L374 of 31 Dec. 1988. See also Commission of the European Communities, *Guide to the Reform of the Community's Structural Funds* (Luxembourg, 1989).

TABLE 2.2. *EC structural-fund objectives (Regulation EEC 2052/88)*
Objective

1. Development of structurally backward regions. ERDF + ESF + EAGGF (Gu.).
2. Conversion of regions in industrial decline. ERDF + ESF.
3. Combating long-term unemployment. ESF.
4. Increasing youth employment. ESF.
5. (A) Adjustment of agricultural structures (*vis-à-vis* reform of CAP). EAGGF (Gu.).
   (B) Promoting the development of rural areas. ERDF + ESF + EAGGF (Gu.).

dimension is only one of many dimensions of the effects of economic integration.

As can be seen from Table 2.2, three objectives were overtly 'regional' in nature. These were objective 1, the 'development of structurally backward regions'; objective 2, the 'conversion of regions in industrial decline'; and objective 5(B), 'promoting the development of rural areas'. In no case was the ERDF left to try to achieve an objective unilaterally. In all cases other structural funds were combined with the ERDF in achieving the objective. A coordinated approach is clearly what was called for.

Identifying Regions in Need of Priority Assistance

The structural fund objectives effectively identified the types of region on which ERDF and other structural funds help was to be focused. In order to begin to put into operation the new policy, it was necessary to identify the regions to be eligible for help under each of the three 'regional' objectives. For the very first time, therefore, the EC in 1989 abandoned its use of member states' own maps of eligible areas and drew up its own map of areas to be eligible for EC help under the new policy (Map 2).[15]

[15] *Objective 1* regions are defined in terms of EC Commission NUTS Level 2 regions, for an initial five-year period. They comprise regions with GDP per capita under 75 per cent of the EC average. N. Ireland is included as a special case. *Objective 2* regions are defined in terms of NUTS Level 3 regions, for an initial three-year period. Regions must have (*a*) above EC average unemployment for the previous three years; (*b*) industrial employment (as a percentage of total employment) in excess of the EC average in any of the previous fifteen years; (*c*) an

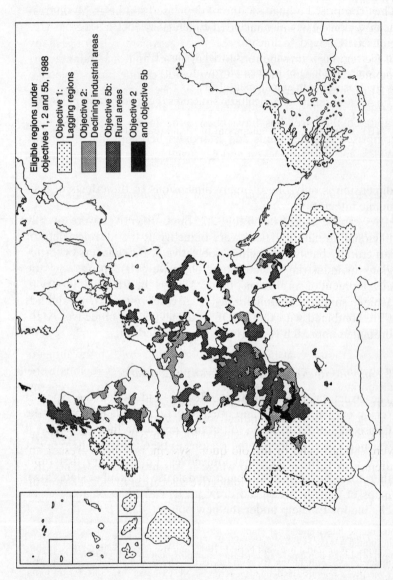

MAP 2. Eligible regions under objectives 1, 2, and 5(B) 1988.

Eligible regions under
objectives 1, 2 and 5b, 1988

Objective 1:
Lagging regions

Objective 2:
Declining industrial areas

Objective 5b:
Rural areas

Objective 2
and objective 5b

As can be seen from Map 2, the structurally backward (objective 1) regions formed the major category of problem regions in the EC. They comprised a huge swathe of depressed southern, Mediterranean regions. They also included Ireland. Objective 2 regions (regions in industrial decline) were less extensive and comprised many of the regions facing the run-down of their traditional manufacturing industries in the face of EC and world competition. Objective 5(B) regions formed a very minor category of problem regions in terms of absolute size, although structural-fund expenditures per capita in these regions have been quite large. In the UK they comprised the Highlands and Islands of Scotland, parts of rural Wales, and parts of Devon and Cornwall.

Concentrating Assistance in the Most Disadvantaged Regions

The map of eligible assisted areas (Map 2) represented only the first step in a determined attempt to concentrate EC regional policy help on the most disadvantaged regions. It was the most serious effort yet to get away from the original quota system of the 1975 ERDF. It is the EC which has set up the system for designating and redesignating the areas set out in Map 2. Moreover, the 1989 reform envisaged two further changes designed to help focus ERDF money on areas in greatest need:

1. A gradual concentration of help on the most disadvantaged of the three types of region identified. Objective 1 regions were earmarked some 80 per cent of all help given. Objective 2 regions were earmarked most of the remaining 20 per cent.

2. A new system of indicative allocations for 85 per cent of the ERDF expenditure designated for each type of region. These were the last echo of the old quota system, but did represent an attempt to get assistance to where it was most needed. The UK, for example, was given an indicative allocation of 1.7 per cent of (85 per cent of) the objective 1 money, hardly surprising since

observable fall in industrial employment relative to a chosen reference year or substantial job losses in specified declining industries. *Objective 5(B)* regions must have (*a*) a high percentage of agricultural employment in total employment; (*b*) a low level of farm incomes; (*c*) low scores on indicators of socio-economic development; (*d*) evidence of depopulation, peripherality, and sensitivity to structural change in agriculture, or adverse structure of small holdings, an adverse age-structure of the workforce, or environmental pressures.

only Northern Ireland was eligible. On the other hand, the UK was given an indicative allocation of 38.3 per cent of (85 per cent of) the objective 2 funds, and 7.5 per cent of (85 per cent of) objective 5(B) funds. These were 'indicative' only, and therefore dependent on suitable proposals being put forward to the EC. They were also meant as averages for the initial budgetary period 1989–93.

Increasing the EC's Commitment to Regional Policy

One of the most noteworthy aspects of the 1989 reform was the commitment of the EC to greatly increasing its financial funding of the structural funds. The reform resulted in a doubling in real terms of EC financing of the three structural funds. Budgets rose from 7.7 billion ECUs in 1988 (approximately £5 billion) to over 14 billion ECUs in 1993 (£9.2 billion) at 1988 prices. This represented a major increase. Whether it has been anywhere sufficient to meet the challenges posed by SEM is another matter.

Changing the Methods of ERDF Involvement

As before, much of ERDF help post-1989 continued to be in the form of grants for investment purposes. The 1980s trend of a gradual switch from project assistance to programme assistance has been accelerated. No less than three billion ECUs was set aside for Community Programmes for the period 1989–93. The growth in programmes at the expense of project assistance not only weakens member states' discretionary power over the ERDF, it also broadens out the types of help given away from simple investment grants. Under the 1989 reform, priority has also being given to Integrated Development Programmes, with a renewed emphasis on closely co-ordinated initiatives, drawing in a number of EC instruments, and spanning a series of regions.

The EC also took the opportunity of the 1989 reform to tackle once more two serious long-standing problems with ERDF assistance: too much aid for infrastructure projects and not enough to productive industrial projects, and the recurring problem of how to ensure additionality. Assistance to infrastructure projects took no less than 91.1 per cent of ERDF help in 1987. The 1989 regulations tried to staunch this flow and stimulate help for industrial projects by tightening up the rules. Under objective 2 assistance, for example, only those infrastructure projects 'relating to the development of industrial sites and leading to the creation or development of economic activity' were to be allowed.

It remains to be seen whether this type of change, which has been tried before in various ways, succeeds, and whether the new checks designed to try to force member states to use ERDF in a genuinely additional manner, and not cut back their own regional spending as ERDF expands, will be effective. Such efforts have not been very successful in the past. The process will clearly be a long drawn-out one.

Revamping the System for Co-ordination

The 1989 reform undertook a major review of the system of co-ordination of EC regional policy. It is not too fanciful to describe this as a kind of embryonic regional planning system, for that is what it is beginning to resemble.

The system of two-yearly periodic reports on regional problems in the EC, which in turn form the basis of a set of EC Regional Policy Priorities and Guidelines (to provide a lead role in policy formulation) was retained in the 1989 reforms. As Table 2.3 shows,

TABLE 2.3. *Co-ordination in EC regional policy*

A. *Regional 'Planning'*
1. Regional Plans—member states/regional authorities.
2. Negotiation—with EC.
3. Community Support Frameworks (CSF)—EC (in consultation with member states).
4. Implementation (via operational programmes, project aid, global grants, part-financing).
5. Monitoring/Assessment
6. Repeat Process

B. *Regional Impact Assessment*

C. *Competition Policy*
1. Differential regional aid ceilings.
2. Legal restrictions:
   opaque/transparent
   operating/initial.

however, the EC in 1989 set up what can only be described as an iterative planning process. Member states are required to produce regional plans (covering help to be given by the member state as well as the EC). After a process of consultation and negotiation with the EC a set of Community Support Frameworks (CSFs) are drawn up. The CSFs are documents drafted by the EC, utilizing the member states' regional plans and after consultation with member states. The CSFs cover all three structural funds of the EC. They set out the framework within which the integrated programmes for tackling regional problems are to be developed. Within each CSF sets of specific operations are defined and implementation is via programmes, project aid, and so on. Integrated Development Operations are given priority. The whole process is subsequently repeated after monitoring and assessment of progress.

The CSFs are designed to be an important mechanism by which the EC's commitment to partnership in its regional policy can be achieved. The purpose of partnership is to draw local and regional authorities in with the member states and the EC itself in the planning and execution of regional policy initiatives. The CSFs represent an early opportunity for regional and local-level participation. The greater emphasis on Community-led initiatives and programmes, again drawing in regional and local authorities as well as member states, also represented a renewed commitment to co-ordination.

Mention should also be made of two other pre-1989 EC co-ordination policies which were retained in the 1989 reforms. Regional Impact Assessment, designed to analyse the regional effects of all major EC policies, was retained. In addition, 1989 saw the complete revamping of the EC competition policy regulations[16] designed to control member states' use of their own regional industrial subsidies. These comprised a new set of differentiated regional ceilings on assistance to industry, together with a renewal of EC restrictions on the use by member states of continuing (as distinct from initial-only) aid to firms and non-transparent (as distinct from easily calculable) aid to industry. The 1989 new regulations represented an updated version of a long-standing policy of the EC to use competition policy to co-ordinate assistance given to firms by

---

[16] Commission of the European Communities, Commission Communication on the Method of Application of Article 92(3) (a) and (c) to Regional Aid, *Official Journal* OJ C212/2 of 12 Aug. 1988, Brussels.

member states and regional and local authorities. The regionally differentiated aid ceilings, expressed in net grant-equivalent values as a percentage of initial investment costs, are designed firstly to ensure that more prosperous regions do not offer significant aid schemes in competition with more depressed regions, and secondly to prevent member states from aggressively using regional subsidies to 'competitively bid' for inward investment projects against other member states. These EC powers, together with the rest of the competition policy regulations, represent a significant intervention by the EC in member states' regional policies. The powers have been quite actively applied in recent years.

The 1993 Amendments to the 1989 Regulations

The 1991 Maastricht Summit of heads of state has proved to be one of the most momentous in the whole history of the EC. The EMU sections of the resulting European Union Treaty have been among the most controversial provisions. Immense problems have been experienced in attempting to get all of the member states to ratify the Treaty. These problems have been compounded by unusual volatility in exchange markets which has seriously weakened the ERM, a key component in the stage-by-stage implementation of monetary union envisaged in the Treaty.

Despite the continuing problems associated with the ratification and implementation of the Maastricht Treaty, the EC has chosen to push ahead with a new set of reforms to the structural funds and regional policy. These new reforms, agreed by the Council of Ministers in July 1993, are proceeding on the assumption that the Maastricht Treaty will eventually be fully ratified. At the time of writing full details of the new reforms are not available. The reforms are, however, closely based upon Commission proposals introduced in March 1993 and also build upon decisions taken at the 1992 Edinburgh Summit of heads of state.[17] The main components of the 1993 reforms are:

- An increase in the budget of the structural funds from 19.8 billion ECUs in 1993 to 27.4 billion ECUs in 1999 (both at

[17] See Commission of the European Communities, *The Community's Structural Fund Operations 1994–1999*, COM(93)67 final—SYN 455 (Brussels); Commission of the European Communities, *The Commission Adopts Proposed Amendments to Structural Fund Rules*, Information Note P(93)4 of 24 Feb. 1993 (Brussels); Com-

1992 prices). The 1999 budget represents a quadrupling (in real terms) of the budget compared with the position in 1987. Objective 1 regions have been allocated, as before, the bulk of the available money, comprising some 96.3 billion ECUs between 1994 and 1999.

- The creation of a new fund, the Cohesion Fund. This has been allocated a budget of 1.5 billion ECUs in 1993, rising to 2.6 billion ECUs in 1999. Only those countries with a GDP per capita under 90 per cent of the EC average are eligible. These are Ireland, Spain, Portugal, and Greece. The fund will concentrate on environmental and transport investment projects.
- A small, but significant redrawing of the initial assisted areas map (Map 2). The main amendments are the inclusion of the whole of East Germany as an objective 1 region, along with the upgrading to objective 1 status of parts of Belgium (Hainault) and the UK (Merseyside, Highlands and Islands). Additional flexibility has also been introduced in the criteria used for designating objective 2 regions.
- A change in the list of structural-fund objectives which effectively adds a new 'non-regional' objective: help for workers in adapting to industrial change and changes in production systems. The three 'regional' objectives (1, 2, and 5(B)) remain essentially unchanged.
- Detailed changes to the regulations designed to introduce simpler and faster decision-making by the EC. The iterative planning procedures discussed earlier have also been slightly simplified.
- Additional procedures designed to try to put greater pressure on member states to use structural-fund allocations in an 'additional' manner.

An Assessment of the New EC Regional Policy

Each new major reform of EC regional policy, of which the 1989 and 1993 reforms are the most recent examples, can be regarded as part of a process of reallocation of regional policy powers among

mission of the European Communities, *European Council in Edinburgh—11 and 12 December 1992—Conclusions of the Presidency*, Briefing Document (London).

the different jurisdictional levels of the EC.[18] The major jurisdictional levels in the EC are local government, regional authorities, member-state governments, and the EC itself. The successive reforms of EC regional policy since 1975 have been almost entirely concerned with the balance of regional policy powers between the EC itself and the member-state governments, although the EC has sought to increase the involvement of regional and local levels. In this it has been successful to a certain extent.

Viewing each successive reform of EC regional policy as a reallocation (or 'reassignment') of powers has the merit of allowing each reform to be assessed systematically. Regional policy powers, it can be argued, are exercised via three main key sets of decisions:

1. Decisions which determine the size of financial transfers between regions (from more prosperous to less prosperous regions).
2. Decisions which determine the specific manner in which regional policy assistance is given.
3. Decisions which affect the co-ordination of the regional policies of the different jurisdictional levels.

In this section the 1989 reform of EC regional policy (together with its 1993 updating) will be assessed in terms of its likely effects on these three sets of decision-powers.[19] Before this is done, it is important to recognize two crucial weaknesses which have dogged EC regional policy since its inception, and which have not been resolved by the 1989 and 1993 reforms. First, EC regional policy does not have clear long-term goals. The goal of 'economic and social cohesion' set out in the Single European Act of 1986 and discussed earlier in this chapter, is a valuable statement of intent, but as we have seen, is tantalizingly vague. It seems clear that part of the cohesion goal implies the reduction of regional inequalities.

[18] See H. W. Armstrong, 'The Assignment of Regional Policy Powers within the EC', in A. M. El-Agraa (ed.), *Britain Within the European Community: The Way Forward* (London: Macmillan, 1983), 271–98.

[19] See Armstrong, 'The Reform of European Community Regional Policy', pp. 319–43, for a similar assessment of the earlier 1984 reform package. The 'assignment' approach to EC policy powers was pioneered by F. Forte, 'Principles for the Assignment of Public Economic Functions in a Setting of Multi-Layer Government', in Commission of the European Communities, *Report of the Study Group on the Role of Public Finance in European Integration* (Brussels, 1977), ii. 319–97.

But which inequalities—income, employment, or unemployment? Is the goal partial or complete equalization, and over what time-period? Should EC regional policy be concerned with purely economic inequalities, or should it, for example, be concerned with the preservation of regional cultures and languages? Issues such as these have never been resolved. Until they are, it will never be possible to assess accurately the likely effectiveness of a given policy reform. One cannot evaluate a policy until one knows precisely what it is meant to achieve. In part, the failure clearly to specify long-term goals for EC regional policy is the result of a failure to explore properly the economic justification for having an EC regional policy. Some, for example, would argue that EC regional policy should confine itself to tackling only those regional problems which arise from the activities of the EC itself. Something of this logic seems to underlie the 1989 reform which was, after all, stimulated by the SEM process and by the fear that a widening of regional disputes might result. Others, however, would argue that EC regional policy should not only tackle regional problems directly caused by the EC, but should also help the member states to tackle regional problems which predate the EC or which would have existed even had there been no EC. These issues remain completely unresolved and yet have a crucial bearing on such things as the desirable size of the ERDF and the types of policies operated by it.

In defence of existing EC regional policy it perhaps should be pointed out that the failure to identify and specify clear objectives is by no means rare in regional policy. The UK Government's own regional policy has long suffered the same problem. Moreover, in a rapidly changing world and with member states clinging strongly to power, there may be some merit from the EC's point of view in keeping the objectives deliberately vague in order to allow the policy to be altered quietly if circumstances change and in order to allow the EC to strengthen the policy gradually over time. The weakness of this point of view is that it can be used to justify delaying for ever the need to spell out precisely what the objectives are.

The second fundamental weakness which has dogged EC regional policy since its inception has been the failure to conceive of a final or optimal assignment of regional policy powers between the EC and the other jurisdictional levels, notably the member states.

It is quite easy to define the possible extremes of, on the one hand, an EC in which the member states control all regional policy, and on the other hand an EC in which the member states hand over all regional policy powers to Brussels. Neither of these extremes is acceptable.[20] The failure, however, to come to terms with 'where regional policy is going'—the eventual balance of responsibilities between the EC and member states—has unfortunate consequences. It has meant that each side, the Community and the member states, has tended to regard reform packages as a chance to manœuvre for position. In practice, member states used their position of strength at the inception of EC regional policy in 1975 to impose a tight rein on the Commission; subsequent reforms have resembled a struggle by the EC to get greater control over its 'own' regional policy from the member states, with neither side knowing what the eventual long-term division of powers is to be. This is an unsatisfactory state of affairs.

Despite the lack of long-term goals and a failure to identify an ultimate EC–member state division of powers, EC regional policy has exhibited a remarkable ability to innovate and evolve. The 1989 and 1993 reforms are merely the later phase of this evolution. In assessing the 1989 and 1993 reform packages, each major set of decision-powers will be considered in turn.

Financial Transfers for Regional Policy Purposes

The generation of financial transfers for regional policy purposes from more prosperous parts of the EC to the depressed regions is a crucial part of EC regional policy. In this chapter we will concentrate on decisions which affect ERDF expenditures, although ideally one would need to consider simultaneously expenditures of member states on their own regional policies and expenditures of ESF, EAGGF(Gu.), the EIB, and the ECSC, all of which operate with a deliberate regional bias. Indeed, a radical feature of the 1989 and 1993 reforms is the manner in which decisions which affect the regional pattern of ERDF expenditures have been combined with decisions being taken simultaneously for the other two structural funds—the ESF and EAGGF(Gu.).

---

[20] The economic logic for a division of regional policy powers between the EC and the member states is set out in Armstrong, 'The Assignment of Regional Policy Powers within the EC'.

ERDF financial transfers to less prosperous regions are the outcome of three sets of decisions: (a) decisions on the size (i.e. budget) of the ERDF; (b) decisions concerning the distribution of ERDF money amongst member states; and (c) decisions on the distribution of ERDF money amongst regions within each member state. The first of these (the size of ERDF) is a distinct decision. Decisions (b) and (c) are hard to separate in practice since they are simultaneously the result of the distribution of ERDF spending across EC regions. The 1989 and 1993 reforms have had a major effect on all three of these decision-powers.

Prior to 1989 the budget of the ERDF was set separately and annually as part of the EC budget process. As such, decision-powers were shared by the EC, acting via the Commission and European Parliament, and the member-state governments, acting via their representatives on the Council of Ministers. Under the 1989 reforms, the budget process has been given a longer planning horizon (initially 1989–93 and subsequently 1994–9), and the ERDF allocation has been consolidated with those of the other two structural funds, indicating a determination to use the structural funds in a more closely co-ordinated manner. Total structural-fund allocations were initially set at:

	Million ECUs
1989	8.98
1900	10.28
1991	11.58
1992	12.90
1993	14.466

These figures are in constant (1988) prices. In an interesting development, the precise annual budget for the ERDF was not fixed in advance. Instead, 'it was left to member states and the Commission meeting within the partnership to determine, after fixing priorities, which Funds [i.e. ERDF, ESF, and EAGGF(Gu.)] would be mobilized to achieve . . . the . . . objectives.'[21] The figure of 14.466 million ECUs (at 1988 prices) for the year 1993 was double the budget for the three structural funds in 1987, the start-point of the SEM process. As we have seen earlier, the 1994–9 budget envisages a further doubling in real terms of structural-fund expenditures.

---

[21] Commission of the European Communities, *Annual Report on the Implementation of the Reform of the Structural Funds: 1989* (Brussels, 1991), 31.

The longer budget-planning horizons, the consolidation of the three structural-fund budget decisions, the increase in the size, in real terms, of EC regional policy expenditure, and the linking of the level of spending to the process of economic integration are all radical and welcome departures from previous practice. It is to be hoped that any future developments of the EC, such as the entry of new members, will also attract new funding for the ERDF. The link between further integration and regional disparities requires a policy response.

There is, however, a negative aspect to the 1989 and 1993 reforms. As in previous reforms, no attempt is made to: (a) try to identify just how large the budget would have to be to have a significant effect on EC regional disparities; or (b) define an appropriate balance of EC and member-state government expenditures on regional policy. All that can be said about the former is that existing spending levels are almost certainly too low. The Commission has argued that member states benefiting from objective 1 assistance will have received structural funds' transfers amounting to perhaps 1.6 per cent of GDP, rising to 2.5–3.5 per cent of GDP for countries such as Ireland wholly covered by the objective 1 classification (see Map 2). However, the corresponding figures for member states benefiting under objectives 2 and 5(B) were much lower. Moreover, in a recent report of the EC[22] it was estimated that a mere 1 per cent increase in GDP of the less favoured regions of the EC would require extra investment of between 55 and 76 billion ECUs. By comparison the combined structural funds in 1993 amounted to only 14 billion ECUs. Moreover, this 14 billion ECUs itself amounted to only 7 per cent of the expected gains from SEM.[23] Calculations such as these are useful and interesting but fall well short of estimations of what the policy budget should be. Some attempts are currently under way to try to estimate the expenditures which would be necessary if the infrastructure of lagging regions, including transport, energy, and human skills, is to be brought up to EC averages and thus allow these regions to compete on equal terms. This is certainly a step in the right direction.

[22] T. Padua-Schioppa, *Efficiency, Stability and Equity: A Strategy for the Evolution of the Economic System of the European Community* (Brussels, 1987).

[23] D. Mair, 'Regional Policy Initiatives from Brussels', *Royal Bank of Scotland Review* (1990).

When we turn to the balance of expenditures on regional policy between the EC and member states, the 1989 and 1993 reforms are almost wholly silent. Indeed, the only parts of the 1989 and 1993 reforms which touch on this issue are those relating to the thorny question of additionality. In a series of measures, the 1989 reforms attempted to try to force member states to use the extra EC funds in a complementary manner to their own regional policy budgets and not as a substitute source of funds. Article 9 of the Co-ordinating Regulation, for example, required that member states must ensure that any extra EC help within their borders be genuine, meaning that their own expenditures remain at least constant in real terms. Attempts are also being made when Community Support Frameworks are agreed, and later at the implementation stage, to ensure that additionality occurs. Whether or not these measures will be successful remains to be seen—previous attempts have not had a happy history. What is interesting, however, is that the 1989 and 1993 reforms have not been used to expand EC regional policy at the expense of the regional policies of the member states. The additionality reforms nevertheless fall well short of an attempt to define an appropriate balance of EC and member-state regional policy budgets.

In addition to decisions on the annual size of the EC's regional policy budget, the extent of financial transfers between regions is determined by decisions on how funds are allocated among member states and among regions within each member state. In respect of these two sets of decision-powers the 1989 and 1993 reforms represent a continuation of the process set in motion in 1979 and continued in the 1984 reforms: a process in which the EC has been able gradually to win a greater degree of control from the member states over its 'own' regional policy. No attempt, however, has been made to wrest complete control from the member states. Indeed, the 1989 and 1993 reforms explicitly set out a system where many of the decisions are made by the EC, member states, and regional or local authorities acting in partnership.

It is interesting to contrast the post-1989 EC regional policy with the original 1975 ERDF. In 1975 the whole of the ERDF budget was allocated among member states on the basis of predetermined national quotas. Member-state governments exerted a major influence on the quotas via the Council of Ministers. They also exercised strong control over the distribution of ERDF expenditure among regions within their national frontiers by influencing the flow of projects put up to the EC for ERDF help. The post-1989 situation is very different. Under the 1989 reforms the initial allocation of finance (of all three structural funds), is by objective and not by member state. Priorities were established by the Council of Ministers in the reform package, and were translated by the Commission into the following 1989–93 allocations:

	Million ECUs (at 1988 prices)
Objective 1	38.300
Objective 2	7.205
Objectives 3 and 4	3.450
Objective 5(A)	3.415
Objective 5(B)	2.795
Transitional and innovatory measures	1.150
TOTAL:	60.315

The ERDF comprises about 50 per cent of these expenditures. In addition, some 80 per cent of ERDF expenditures were earmarked for objective 1 regions.

Only at a second stage were member-state allocations involved. How much of the money set aside for each of the 'regional' objectives listed above (objectives 1, 2, and 5(B)) goes to each member state and each region depends on a series of decisions, namely:

1. The maps of areas eligible for assistance under objectives 1, 2, and 5(B). As we have already seen, the Commission now produces the maps (see Map 2) on the basis of detailed indicators of regional disadvantage.

2. Member-state 'indicative allocations'. These are the last echo of the old quota system. Under the 1989 reforms, the Commission was asked to determine 'indicative allocations', for a five-year period, for 85 per cent of ERDF appropriations under objectives 1, 2, and 5(B). These were done in 1989 (see Table 2.4) and were based partly on the population in affected regions in each member state and partly on relative economic disadvantage. Notice that unlike the 1975 ERDF, these indicative allocations applied only to 85 per cent of ERDF appropriations for objectives 1, 2, and 5(B). Moreover, the allocations were 'indicative' and not rigid quotas. They vary from year to year depending on the quality of

TABLE 2.4. *ERDF indicative allocations, 1989–1993*

Country	Objective 1: structurally backward regions	Objective 2: industrial decline	Objective 5(B) development of rural areas
Belgium	0.0	4.3	1.2
Denmark	0.0	0.4	0.7
Germany	0.0	8.9	27.5
Greece	16.2	0.0	0.0
Spain	32.6	20.7	7.2
France	2.0	18.3	37.2
Rep. Ireland	5.4	0.0	0.0
Italy	24.5	6.3	16.4
Luxembourg	0.0	0.2	`0.1
Netherlands	0.0	2.6	2.2
Portugal	17.5	0.0	0.0
United Kingdom	1.7	38.3	7.5
	100.0	100.0	100.0

applications for assistance from the regions. The remaining 15 per cent not allocated under the 'indicative allocation' system are funds left to one side for Community initiatives, studies, and pilot projects. Clearly these are much more under EC than member-state control.

3. The flow of initiatives, programmes, and projects put forward for ERDF assistance. Under the 1989 reforms these are now very much jointly agreed between the EC or member states, with regional and local jurisdictional levels also having an input. Notice again the great contrast with the original 1975 ERDF.

The Specific Manner in Which Regional Policy Assistance is Given

The second main set of decisions through which EC regional policy powers are exercised are those relating to the specific manner in which EC regional policy assistance is given. Within this category of decision-power it is possible to distinguish between decisions concerning what types of assistance can be given, for example grants, loans, business and technical advice; what categories of projects and initiatives can be given help, for example the types of industry or infrastructure projects favoured; and the precise terms on which assistance is given.

The 1989 and 1993 reforms can best be viewed as another significant step towards greater flexibility in the specific manner in which EC regional assistance is given. Once again a comparison with the original 1975 ERDF is instructive. In its early years the ERDF was constrained by tightly drawn regulations which greatly limited its flexibility. Types of assistance were limited (notably to investment grants towards individual industrial and infrastructure projects). Eligible areas were limited to those designated by the member states. Moreover, the terms in which assistance could be given were tightly drawn, with regulations on ceilings for aid given, and on matching aid by member-state authorities. In the years since 1975 many of the detailed constraints on the ERDF have been lifted. Of particular significance has been the switch from project-by-project assistance, on which discretion has been tightly constrained, towards programmes of help agreed in partnership between the EC, member states, and regional and local authorities. Programme assistance has been allowed much greater freedom of action in terms of the areas eligible for help, the range of types of help given, and freedom from restrictive regulations in the manner in which help is made available. The 1989 and 1993 reforms have given an additional fillip to this ongoing process by further stimulating programme assistance at the expense of project-by-project help.

The trend towards greater flexibility and discretion in the way in which ERDF help can be made available has also been enhanced by three other features of the 1989 and 1993 reforms. The first of these was the additional encouragement given in the reforms designed to stimulate the indigenous development of regions. In practice this involves help targeted largely on small and medium-sized enterprises (SMEs). The ERDF had steadily increased its help for SMEs during the 1980s, and the 1989 and 1993 reforms have given this process a further boost. Help for SMEs must, by necessity, be more varied and must be more flexible than, say, help for big investment projects. SMEs need special types of help and advice such as consultancy; better access to new technology and information; and preferential access to capital investment. The second new feature of the 1989 and 1993 reforms has been a provision to allow the ERDF to provide global grants. This type of help involves giving grants to intermediaries such as a private-sector bank or a regional development agency, which then acts as the ERDF's agent in disbursing the assistance within its local area. This type of help, long used by the EIB and ECSC, is particularly useful for giving aid to small firms, where direct assistance to individual firms would be costly for the ERDF to provide. The third feature of the 1989 and 1993 reforms worthy of comment is the decision to make ERDF assistance available as part-financing of member-state regional aid schemes. Once again, schemes helping SMEs were singled out for particular mention.

In only one respect do the 1989 and 1993 reforms try to restrict the flexibility which now characterizes the ERDF's operations. In recent years the EC has become alarmed at the tendency for infrastructure projects to be the main recipients of ERDF aid. Productive investment in industry and services took only 9 per cent of ERDF help in 1987, the remainder accruing to infrastructure projects. The 1989 reforms attempted to increase the share of help targeted on infrastructure investment by tightening up the regulations on eligible categories of productive industrial investment.

Co-ordination initiatives

The third main set of decisions through which EC regional policy powers are exercised are those which concern the co-ordination of the regional policy activities of all of the parties involved. As we have already seen, the EC, from the inception of the ERDF in 1975, has taken the lead role in attempting to achieve better co-ordination, which is of two types:

1. Co-ordination of ERDF activities with those of other parts of the EC (ESF, ECSC, EIB, EAGGF(Gu.), and EC competition policy).
2. Co-ordination of EC regional policy with the regional policy efforts of member states and regional and local authorities.

Each of the successive reforms of EC regional policy in 1979, 1984, 1989, and 1993 has attempted to improve co-ordination further. The 1989 and 1993 reforms represent an ambitious attempt to create an effective system for co-ordination. The reforms tackle head-on both types of co-ordination mentioned above. Type (1) co-ordination (i.e. of different EC activities) was most radically strengthened by a common framework and set of objectives for the structural funds, in which the ERDF, ESF, and EAGGF(Gu.) were expected to work in close harmony. New regulations also tied in EIB and ECSC activities more closely with the three structural funds. Type (2) co-ordination (i.e. with different jurisdictional levels) was strengthened by a combination of the new planning system examined earlier in this chapter, together with the renewed emphasis on collaborative programmes of regional assistance. The theme of partnership runs right through the 1989 and 1993 reforms.

How successful the new co-ordination framework will be remains to be seen. There is no doubt that the EC is the only organization capable of taking the lead in co-ordination. Bilateral co-ordination by member states would be a clumsy alternative. Formidable obstacles remain, however. Different member states have widely differing regional policy philosophies. Their bureaucratic arrangements for administering regional policies also differ greatly. The magnitude of the co-ordination task should not be underestimated.

Conclusion

In this chapter an attempt has been made to review the 1989 and 1993 EC regional policy reform packages and to make an initial assessment of their main features. It has been argued that the 1989 and 1993 reforms jointly represent a significant package of changes. These changes must, however, be viewed as part of an ongoing process. They strengthen changes to EC regional policy begun in earlier reforms in 1979 and 1984. The EC now has a much greater degree of control over its own regional policy than when the policy was introduced in 1975. Member states hold less of a grip than was previously the case. The extent of this shift of power should not be overstated. In essence, EC regional policy remains a collaborative venture between the EC, member states, and, to a lesser extent, regional and local authorities.

The 1989 and 1993 reforms are by no means the last step in EC regional policy reform. The size of the EC regional policy budget remains inadequate for the tasks which currently confront it.

Further EC integration, notably the admission of new member states, would require a major new increase in the regional policy budget if regional disparities were to be prevented from widening. In terms of the manner in which assistance is given, the flexibility now visible in EC regional policy is welcome, but further evolution must occur as the regional problems themselves change.

Finally, the 1989 and 1993 reforms represent the most ambitious attempt yet to improve the co-ordination of regional policy in the EC. The success of the reforms cannot yet be judged. Only the EC can take the lead in co-ordination and, at a time of budget constraint, co-ordination is vital if regional policy is to be efficient or effective in the years to come.

MAP 3. The regions of Italy.

3

Italian Regions in the European Community

CARLO DESIDERI

Does the European Community have an impact on Italian regionalism? If so, to what extent and with what effects? While it would be untrue to say that everything which is presently happening in relation to regionalism is a result of European integration, this process is giving significant momentum to change. The strong tensions and currents sweeping across the country do not seem to be inimical to regionalism or Europe. While 'the beauty of the EC in Italy is that it is almost universally popular',[1] national institutions are found generally wanting. Yet although at first sight Europhilia and regionalism seem to go hand in hand, such a partnership may not be enough to achieve an efficient and reliable regional system.

The first section of this chapter looks at how the regions came into being and how they function within the Italian political and institutional system. The second looks at the demands of the new regionalist movement, the growth of the leagues, and the reactions of the traditional parties. The third section examines the tools the regions are giving themselves to deal with Community affairs and what leeway the State is allowing them, while the fourth analyses the implementation of the Community's regional policies. The last section points to the north–south gap as the limiting factor in Italian regionalism's ability to face the European challenge.

The Italian Regional System

In the last few years the regions have shown a greater willingness to formulate innovative proposals on their role and powers. Other

[1] A Survey of Italy, *The Economist*, 26 May 1990.

proposals have been put forward by the political parties as well as by major business associations. New hopes and expectations seem to be converging on bodies which were often criticized in the 1980s and which many believed to be going through an irreparable crisis.

Only a brief mention can be made here of the main factors which produced such weak regions in Italy. The legislators drawing up the 1948 Constitution saw the regions—conceived as an elective political body with legislative and administrative powers—as a safeguard for the democratic system against the risks of a return to totalitarianism.[2] Accommodating economic, cultural, and geographical differences was believed to be less important and the boundaries of the regions were determined on the basis of statistics dating from the nineteenth century. Only when there were specific ethnic and cultural concerns, often compounded by economic backwardness and isolation in mountainous regions or on islands, did the legislators recognize the need for special-status regions. Initially these comprised Trentino Alto Adige, Val d'Aosta, Sardinia, and Sicily. In 1963 Friuli Venezia Giulia was added and in 1972 as a result of negotiations between Austria and Italy the two provinces of the Trentino Alto Adige region were granted special status to allow a certain degree of self-government to the German-speaking Tirolese community of Bolzano.

As a response to the backwardness of the Mezzogiorno the 1948 Constitution provided for special resources to be given to regions for development programmes. In the early 1950s an *ad hoc* agency, the *Cassa per il Mezzogiorno*, was set up for the development of southern Italy. Only at the end of the 1960s, twenty years after the Constitution had been enacted, were regions set up throughout the national territory (see Map 3). The regions were set up from above through the agency of the major national parties. Their purpose was the reform and modernization of the administrative system, the diversion of social and political pressures on the central government, the development of the welfare system in order to strengthen the control of politicians over administration.[3]

The regions are therefore artificial constructions. Apart from the special-status regions they had no local roots and their boundaries

[2] E. Rotelli, *L'avvento della regione in Italia* (Milan: Giuffré, 1967).

[3] S. Cassese and L. Torchia, 'The Meso Level in Europe: The Italian Case', in L. J. Sharpe (ed.), *Between Locality and Centre: The Rise of the Meso in Europe* (London: Sage, 1993).

did not match territorial diversities, communities of interests, or social and economic systems.

The subsequent political life of the regions was equally strongly influenced by the political parties. Regional politicians are prevalently chosen from among party officials and members.[4] Political alliances and regional policies tend to reflect those of the central government. This has adversely affected the political salience of regions. Regional elections are seen by parties and voters alike as a stage of the national political confrontation in which a region's specific issues hardly matter. The lack of alternation of power in central government has not favoured the political growth of the regions as an important power base for the opposition of the day.[5]

Only Sardinia, Val d'Aosta, and the autonomous province of Bolzano have their own regional parties, the *Partito Sardo d'Azione*, *Südtirolervolkspartei*, and *Union Valdotaine*. These have experience of government in the region and also succeed in getting representatives elected to the national parliament.

If the regions are politically weak, they are similarly weak when it comes to formulating and then implementing policies. Their sphere of action is defined in the Constitution only in general terms. Details are filled in by national laws which may extend their scope but more often limit it. As the Constitution limits the regions to certain specific areas, including agriculture, tourism, artisan trades, vocational training, health, territorial organization, regional transport, and infrastructure, they do not supersede the regional administration of central government. The regions must also co-exist with local government without the ability to control it. Local government retains its own exclusive functions and direct links with central government, notably through the Ministry of the Interior.[6] Regional staff amount to 80,000 whereas the central administration employs over 2,000,000 civil servants (excluding State agencies and companies controlled by the State), while municipalities and provinces have 600,000 staff.[7] Regional expenditure is around 100,000

[4] C. Tassara, La classe political regionale', in M. Fedele (ed.), *Autonomia politica regionale e sistema dei partiti* (Milan: Giuffré, 1988).

[5] M. Keating, 'Does Regional Government Work? The Experience of Italy, France and Spain', *Governance*, 1/2 (1988).

[6] V. Santanonio, 'Italy', in E. Page and M. J. Goldsmith (eds.), *Central and Local Government Relations: A Comparative Analysis* (London: Sage, 1987).

[7] CINSEDO, *Rapporto sulle regioni* (Milan: Franco Angeli, 1989). ISTAT, *Annuario statistico italiano* (Rome: ISTAT, 1990).

billion lire, about a fifth of all expenditure by central and sub-central governments and more or less equal to that of provinces and municipalities. Transfers, mostly automatic, to other authorities (mainly provinces and municipalities) account for about 70 per cent of regional expenditure.[8]

The fact that the regions were set up by political parties which champion the supremacy of politics over administration and the entrusting of many executive tasks to political bodies, especially to the elective assembly, prevented the regions from developing sound administrative organizations. Legislation on regional responsibilities since the late 1970s has tended to provide for joint policy-making and administration with central government, often through joint bodies formed by representatives of the ministries and the regional authorities. Central government's predominant role in policy-making is reinforced by the fact that regional funds are almost entirely derived from national level.

Simultanously with the regionalization process in the early 1970s, Italy launched a tax reform providing for an almost total centralization of the tax-levying power. In ordinary-status regions, own-source revenues account for less than 2 per cent of the total.[9] Unconditional transfers on the basis of fixed criteria account for another 10 per cent. The remainder is derived from specific grants under sectoral programmes, subject to detailed constraints on its use.

In the five special-status regions, accounting for 16 per cent of the population, 7 per cent of revenues are raised through their own taxes and half from the assignment of national taxes raised in the region. However, as tax rates are set by national legislation, and national government collects the taxes, it is likely that tax-payers in the special-status regions do not even realize that they are paying taxes to the regional authorities.

There is thus little link between representation and taxation in regions. The result is a double shedding of responsibilities, by the central administration, which controls finance but not the implementation of policies; and by the regions, which use resources but do not feel accountable to citizens for their use. This pushes up public expenditure and adversely affects policies and public services. In 1993 the tax-raising power of ordinary-status regions was

---

⁸ CINSEDO, *Rapporto sulle regioni*.   ⁹ Ibid.

increased considerably, as the national government sought to limit its own expenditures.

The New Regionalism and the Parties

Since the late 1980s there has been a stream of initiatives and proposals on the regions' roles and powers from central and northern regions. The latter have played a leading role in the development of a series of proposals put forward by all the regions.

The most important proposals of the 'regional front', in a 1991 paper, 'Per un nuovo stato regionale', approved by the *Conferenza dei Presidenti dell'Assemblea e dei Consigli delle Regioni e delle Province Autonome*, include: the demand for wider and 'modernized' responsibilities; a clear-cut distinction between central and regional responsibilities with links in areas of overlapping responsibility; a safeguard of regional prerogatives ensuring the direct participation of regional representatives in the policy- and law-making process at national level through a chamber of the regions or a parliamentary committee; greater financial autonomy including a partial but significant freedom to impose taxes with mechanisms aimed at protecting disadvantaged regions.

In 1991 the flurry of regional proposals occurred in a turbulent climate characterized by conflicts with the State. A group of regions, though with only one southern region among them, formally submitted a demand for a referendum—as provided for by the Constitution—to abolish ministries interfering with regional responsibilities. In addition, all the regional authorities decided not to participate in the work of the *Conferenza permanente Stato-regioni*, a consultative body linking regions and central government, because of disagreements over finance and the timing of regional reforms.

Following this decision the minister responsible for regional affairs urged the regional representatives to respect the institutions and to confine the dispute within their parties.[10] However, these recent developments show how ill-suited the parties are to manage and resolve these new conflicts. Moreover, the wide agreement among Government and opposition forces on the reform proposals

[10] *Il Sole 24 Ore*, 6 Oct. 1991.

put forward by the regions shows that this new regionalism is a *trasversale* movement that cuts across all boundaries of the regional political forces much more than the earlier regionalism of the 1960s and 1970s.

Conflicts between the regions and central government continued throughout 1992 and 1993, not only for financial reasons. Although they sent a deputation to make the request for membership, the regions were excluded from a parliamentary commission set up in 1992 to consider constitutional reform. In March 1993, the *Conferenza dei Presidenti delle Regioni e delle Provincie Autonome* declared its deep dissatisfaction with the Commission's report and approved a document, the *Carta delle Regioni d'Italia*, demanding the introduction of the subsidiarity principle into the Italian Constitution. A further success for the regions occurred in the referendums of April 1993 which approved the abolition of the ministries of Agriculture and Tourism, although widespread popular disaffection with central government was the main factor at work here.

The late 1980s and early 1990s saw a resurgence of that current of Italian regionalism in which ethnic, linguistic, or cultural aspects play an important role. In 1991 both the press and public opinion followed the emergence of separatist trends in the Tirolese community and the federalist stances adopted by a large *trasversale* majority in the councils of the special-status regions Trentino Alto-Adige, Val d'Aosta, and Friuli Venezia Giulia. Even the resolve with which Friuli Venezia Giulia diverged from the official stance of the Italian Government during the break-up of Yugoslavia can be seen as a signal of this new assertion of regional sentiment.

However, the main reason why regionalism became the focus of attention of politicians, experts, and public opinion can be found in the spectacular victory won in the 1990 regional election by newly formed political forces, the 'leagues', based on rejection of the traditional parties. Particularly impressive was the victory won with 19 per cent of the vote by the Lombard League in Lombardy, the most developed among Italy's regions.

The League offensive is part of a more general phenomenon which also includes a loss of interest in the traditional political parties. Their combined vote fell from 90 per cent in 1975 to 65 per cent in 1990.[11] Several referendums on institutional reform have been carried against their opposition by another *trasversale* coalition, and new political forces have emerged in addition to the Leagues.

A peculiarity of the Lombard League and an absolute novelty in Italian politics is the fostering of regional identity as an attempt to cater to the need for identity and allegiance created by the crisis of the traditional political subcultures, especially the Christian-democratic and the Communist ones. This is done by means of populist gestures[12] such as the use of the Lombard dialect, an emphasis on language and the 'common sense' of 'ordinary people', and the idea of Lombard identity. It is sometimes accompanied by hostility to immigration and romantic appeals to a distant past. Lombard League was the name of the League led by Alberto da Giussano, which defeated Emperor Federico Barbarossa in the twelfth century.

However, the strength of the League, in the absence of a sense of ethnic identity in Lombardy, derives from combining an emphasis on Lombard identity and its values of efficiency, industriousness, and pragmatism, with radical criticism of an enemy increasingly despised by the population, 'the parties and government in Rome'.[13] The League blames the parties for the partitocracy and patronage, for the inefficiency of public services, and for the diversion to the south of tax revenues raised mainly in the north. According to the League these revenues have been used to finance inefficient welfare policies to the benefit of political parties and their clients, and even organized crime. The League does not call for a strengthening of the existing regions, which it sees as hopelessly sunk in party power politics and Roman centralism. It wants to escape this political straitjacket[14] to fulfil its national mission against the political parties.

One of the main arguments expressed by League leader Umberto Bossi is that 'the public hand rakes in taxes and hands out

---

[11] R. Mannheimer, 'La crisi del consenso per i partiti tradizionali', in R. Mannheimer (ed.), *La Lega Lombarda* (Milan: Feltrinelli, 1991).

[12] R. Biorcio, 'La Lega come attore politico: Del federalismo al populismo regionalista', in Mannheimer (ed.), *La Lega Lombarda*.

[13] Manheimer, 'La crisi del consenso'.

[14] C. Galli, 'Un paradosso di cattiva Lega', *Il Mulino*, 4 (1990).

the money to the parties. This chain can only be broken by the federal state.' That is why the League wants Italy to become a confederation of three northern, central, and southern republics or 'super regions'. Although this proposal is viewed with some scepticism even in circles favourable to the leagues, in February 1991 the leagues of six Northern regions (Lombardy, Piedmont, Liguria, Veneto, Emilia-Romagna, and Toscana) founded the Northern League, which immediately became the fourth largest party in those regions, with about 9 per cent of the vote.

Some leagues, associated with the Northern League, have also been set up in the centre and the south, but their electoral prospects are doubtful. The ruling parties seem to be better rooted in the south and regional and local election results since the late 1980s suggest they may be strengthening their position there. This was confirmed by the national elections of April 1992. In the north, the parties of the outgoing coalition Government obtained 40 per cent of the vote, compared with 60 per cent in the 1987 elections, while the League secured over 17 per cent, thus becoming the second largest party in the area. In the south, by contrast, the League failed to make significant inroads, while the coalition parties won 64 per cent of the vote, a gain of 4 per cent. The League argued, with some justification, that this was a result of the old parties' control of the public purse and the extensive patronage system in the south.[15] The effect was a growing political divide between north and south, matching the existing socio-economic differences. Worries even began to surface about the solidity of national identity, and the risk of the country splitting became a subject of political debate. In several interviews, Bossi denied the accusation that he wanted the north to secede, and reaffirmed the League's aim of gaining power at the central level; but he conceded that the country could divide for economic reasons, if the south were unable to make significant progress in five or six years. The League considers the existing regions inadequate to manage important tasks and proposed the formation of new mega-regions (*macroregioni*). Bossi quotes approvingly a study from the Fondazione Agnelli, which proposes a reduction from twenty to twelve regions, in the interests of financial viability and coherent development planning.

[15] P. Feltrin and M. Morisi, 'La politica locale attorno al sei maggio', *Regione e governo locale*, 2 (1991).

Faced with the success of the leagues and of regionalism in 1990–1, both Government and opposition parties briefly turned into regionalist zealots, organizing meetings, making statements, and putting forward proposals to resume regional reforms.[16]

A strengthening of regional responsibilities and greater financial autonomy were included in the programme of the Andreotti Government formed in April 1991. Meanwhile, a proposal for a constitutional reform, drawn up by the Committee on Constitutional Affairs of the Chamber of Deputies, envisaged a division of responsibilities between central government and the regions with the balance strongly tilted in favour of the latter. Central responsibilities would be clearly defined and all the remaining responsibilities entrusted to the regional authorities. However, towards the end of 1991 the regionalist counter-offensive of the parties ran out of momentum. Discussion of the draft reform had come to a standstill; nor, at least by summer 1993, did anything result from the deliberations of the parliamentary commission on regional reforms. This did not reflect a reduction in pressures from the League,[17] whose support in opinion polls and local and national elections continued to rise. In June 1993 it captured the mayoralty of Milan. However, the increasingly radical nature of the League offensive probably convinced the parties that a solution pivoting on the strengthening of the regions was useless. At a time when there are fewer resources available the parties know they cannot rely on the regions as a means to gain support, as they did in the late 1960s. Rather than reforming Italian politics, the parties seem to be waiting for the League to make a political mistake or to be weakened by internal strife. However, the success of the April 1993 referendum forced the parties into changing the electoral system. After laborious debates and compromises, new legislation in August 1993 introduced a variant of the British-style first-past-the-post system for most seats in the national parliament. There was, however, no consideration of the position of regions.

Some autonomist demands are nevertheless emerging within traditional parties too, as a result of impatience with the national leadership and the need to respond to local demands. Especially in

---

[16] See the articles in *Regione e governo locale*, 1 (1991).
[17] G. Pasquino, 'Una lega contro i partiti', *La rivista dei libri*, May 1991.

central and northern regions and in Sardinia, this represents a response to competition from the leagues or other local forces, but it also indicates the emergence at regional level of a new class of politicians not so interested in a *cursus honorum* leading up to the national political scene.[18] This trend is undermining the traditional system of centre–periphery relations dominated by the national parties and is setting the stage for the growth and development of a new regionalism.

European Integration and Regional Initiatives

At least until the end of the 1970s, the existence of a Community policy on matters falling within the competence of regional governments meant that the central government would limit the powers of the regions and where possible would take back functions it had entrusted to them. For many years the regions' main worry was how to handle disputes with central government over their respective responsibilities. Central government for its part treated Community matters as a branch of international relations, an area in which it has exclusive competence. Hence the extremely rigid position which not only excluded any participation of the regions in the Community's policy-making process, but gave central government responsibility for the implementation of Community policies in areas where the regions are constitutionally competent.[19]

Regions were later given wider responsibilities in policy implementation. Central government limited itself to setting general guidelines, while retaining the right to take over regional responsibilities in case of failure to act on the part of the regions. However, this did not put an end to the disputes between the two levels of government over their respective responsibilities.[20]

More critically, the regions are increasingly aware that a good part of decision-making power has now shifted from both central government and the regions, to the Community. Hence the focus on participation by the regions in the Community's policy- and

[18] R. Putnam, R. Leonardi, and R. Nanetti, *La pianta e le radici* (Bologna: Il Mulino, 1985). Tassara, 'La classe politica regionale'.

[19] F. Merloni, 'Italian Regions in the European Community', in M. Keating and B. Jones (eds.), *Regions in the European Community* (Oxford: Clarendon Press, 1985).

[20] A. Ferrara (ed.), *Le regioni nell'ordinamento comunitario: La legge Pergola e la sua attuazione* (Rome: Istituto di Studi sulle Regioni, 1991).

rule-making process; a participation, even in the form of observer-status, which the regions are still formally denied. To deal with Community institutions on issues for which they are responsible, the regions have to turn to the relevant national ministries.

When matters falling within the regional responsibilities are discussed, the regions are granted a domestic consultative role concerning the development of positions which the Italian Government will then try to carry through within the Community decision-making process. The instruments, however, seem to be quite weak and so far have not given satisfactory results.[21] Regions may submit to the Government comments on draft regulations, directives, and recommendations by the Community, which the Government itself sends to them, but they do not seem to use this opportunity. Often the regions receive Community documents too late, when their passage is already at an advanced stage. Moreover, how these comments may affect the Government's position is not specified. The regions have shown little interest and trust in an instrument whose effectiveness depends on the Government's good will. The *Conferenza Permanente Stato-Regioni* has rather loosely defined powers as to Community matters and meets too randomly to allow a continuous and effective participation on the part of the regions. It has so far devoted only few meetings to the implementation of Community policies.

For the time being the regions' capacity to play an effective role seems to depend mainly on their establishing good relations with the relevant ministries which participate in the Community policy-making process. What complicates matters further here is that there is a whole series of ministries the regions can turn to, with roles that occasionally overlap. These include the Ministry of Foreign Affairs within which there is a standing representation to the Community, acting as a link and information centre as well as a unit for negotiating and organizing Italy's participation in the relevant Community's institutions; the Department for the Co-ordination of Community Policies; and the relevant functional ministries, which tend to operate individually in their relations with Brussels. Finally there is CIPE (Interministerial Committee for Economic Planning), whose task is to set the general trend of Italy's action within the Community.

[21] E. Buglione and C. Desideri (eds.), *Le regioni nell'ordinamento comunitario: Stato di attuazione e prospettive della partnership* (Rome: Istituto di Studi sulle Regioni, 1991).

At present the regions are insisting on obtaining the right formally to establish direct relations—both jointly and separately—with the Community's institutions.[22] In the new statute adopted by Emilia Romagna and approved in 1990 through an Act of Parliament, as provided for in the Constitution, mention is made of links with the Community's institutions. This provision was opposed by the Government during the parliamentary debate. In the end it was passed thanks to the approval of a statement which rules out the use of the provision by the regions to set up offices within the Community's institutions.

In practice, the regional authorities do maintain relations with the Community's institutions, a situation which the Government now tolerates. This, however, is more important during the implementation stage rather than in the policy- and rule-making process. Some regions have appointed a senior official to deal with Community affairs, usually combining this with other responsibilities. Some have set up offices to maintain relations with Community institutions, co-ordinate regional projects aimed at obtaining and using Community funds, see to the adjustment of regional rules to EC regulations, and check on the progress of projects financed by the Community. In practice, however, especially in the south, these offices are quite small and short-staffed, lacking especially skilled personnel. As a regional official once said: 'whether we talk about Europe or not depends largely on the presence and good will of one or two Europhiles (*Uomini-Europa*).'[23] Nor do the co-ordination offices have much influence over the functional departments, which retain their own direct links with the corresponding central government officials.

Some regions have set up specialized committees of elected members, with official support, to give advice, carry out studies, and pinpoint problems. The idea is to strengthen political control over regional administration and its links with the Community.

[22] Conferenza dei Presidenti dell'Assemblea e dei Consigli delle Regioni e delle Provincie autonome, *Per un nuovo stato regionale* (Bologna, 26 June, 1991). Conferenza dei Presidenti dell'Assemblea e dei Consigli delle Regioni e delle Provincie Autonome, Document presented to Parliament on the Maastricht Treaty, 7 Oct. 1992; *Carta delle Regioni de' Italia* (Milan, Mar. 1993).
[23] E. Buglione and C. Desideri (eds.), *Le regioni nell'ordinamento comunitario.* See also C. Sacchetti, *Le regioni nell'ordinamento comunitario: L'organizzazione regionale per la gestione degli affari comunitari* (Rome: Istituto di Studi sulle Regioni, 1993).

Some regions have established consultative bodies, formed by representatives of the local authorities, universities and other institutions, pro-Europe movements, business associations, and unions. These are intended to point out needs and submit proposals on European integration to the regional authorities, to give advice, to undertake education and information initiatives on Community issues for the citizens of the region. They may also deal with specialized matters such as how to use the Community's intervention instruments. The regions' claim to a specific role within the Community also comes as a result of relations with other regions or similar organizations in other countries. These developments have recently been given new momentum by a ruling of the constitutional court allowing 'promotional activities abroad' as well as activities 'of lesser international importance' on the part of regions in so far as they do not require any international obligations on the part of the State and do not in any way interfere with the Government's foreign policy. Transboundary co-operation initiatives dating back to the 1970s between Italian regions and regions of other countries, such as the working community Alpe Adria, are now being strengthened and extended. New initiatives are being undertaken, such as the recent participation of Lombardy, along with Catalonia, Baden-Württemberg, and Rhône Alpes, in the 'Four Motors of Europe', a co-operation initiative on economic, cultural, technological, and educational issues.

A further contribution to the extension of relations between Italian regions and similar organizations in other countries within a Community setting is made by development agencies, in which a region usually participates along with other private and public bodies. These represent an important instrument for regional action in the local business world, especially that of small and medium-sized enterprises. A number of initiatives have been taken by individual companies as well as associations to promote an exchange of information with similar agencies in other EC countries, to help small and medium-sized enterprises to operate in larger markets, to find resources in international financial markets, to promote the regions' and firms' relations with Community institutions.

In the last few years regions have improved their arrangements for dealing with Community affairs and have brought the regional community into discussion on issues concerning European integ-

ration. For the time being, the Government still seems to be applying to Community relations the principle whereby the State has
exclusive powers over foreign affairs. The regions, in a document
drafted in Trento before the Maastricht Conference, have demanded special relations with the Community as, they claim, they
are better suited than national government to provide the Community with a detailed picture of the multi-faceted economic and
cultural reality of the country. To this end they hope the Community will entrust tasks to them directly and they say they are even
prepared to form associations so as to meet the requirements set by
Community policies.

However, although this new regionalism as a whole seems to be
advocating European integration enthusiastically, many of the initiatives mentioned so far were proposed by central and northern
regions which play a leading role in the formulation of proposals
and seem to be willing to lobby for local economic interests and
expectations within the relevant Community institutions. In many
regions there is a lot of brave talk, but very little action when it
comes to implementing Community policies.

The Regions and Community Regional Policies: A Mixed Blessing

Recent Community regional policies have provided Italian regions
with the opportunity to play a role in the Community, but they
have also shown the difficulties besetting Italian regionalism.

In the past the Community showed indifference towards the
regional authorities. Their involvement in the implementation of
regional policies was a result of a division of responsibilities between national government and the regions and as such a wholly
domestic matter. As central government prevented the regions
from having direct relations with the Community, the result was
that the regions had no clear perception of Community policies
even though they were directly affected by them, and showed
indifference to their goals and requirements. The Community for
its part could hardly understand the regions' special needs.

In this connection the Integrated Mediterranean Programmes
(IMPs) and the reform of the structural funds which, unlike IMPs,
was coupled with a significant increase in Community funds for

interventions, were interpreted by the Italian regions as a radical change of attitude on the part of the Community. Regional authorities, which are involved in the formulation of programmes as well as in their implementation and monitoring, now feel they have to deal with the Community directly. On the other hand, central government's role is ever more uncertain. First, it cannot insist on being the only authority that has direct relations with the Community, when it is the Community itself that is asking and formalizing direct relations with regional authorities through partnerships. Second, central government finds it difficult effectively to co-ordinate initiatives. There is evidence that in the past the Government was not able to select the initiatives in programmes for the use of European Regional Development Funds and IMPs and this had to be done by the Community.[24] Despite the formalization of partnerships, central government was still trying to limit the regions' role. According to the 1989 Report of the EC Commission on the implementation of the reform of structural funds, this could be one of the reasons why the Italian Government had chosen to prepare only one regional development programme for objective 1, rather than a series of individual plans for each region or group of regions.[25] However, the report stresses that the Commission had direct relations with the regions in the drawing-up of Community Support Frameworks. For the first time central government feared being bypassed. The Minister responsible for co-ordinating Community policies complained about 'the partnership whose requirements are not met by the Commission which insists on an unacceptable tendency to take initiatives directly involving regions, a procedure which, while it might appear faster, unbalances the contractual relationships and so in practice gives the Commission more freedom of manœuvre and choice.'[26]

The most recent developments in regional policies, besides showing the new opportunities for regional initiatives, also shed light on the difficulties and limits besetting Italian regionalism,

[24] C. Buresti and G. E. Marciani, 'L'esperienza del Programi Integrati Mediterranei', *Revista economica del Mezzogiorno*, 1 (1991).
[25] Commisione delle Comunità Europee, *Relazione annuale sull'attuazione dei fondi stutturali*, Com. (90), 516 def. (Brussels, 1990).
[26] Ministro per il coordinamento delle politiche comunitarie, *Relazione sulla partecipazione dell'Italian al processo normativo comunitario e sul programma di attività presentato dalla presidenzia di turno del Consiglio dei Ministri delle Comunità Europee*, submitted to Chamber of Deputies, 7 Dec. 1989.

especially in two aspects. The first is that implementation of Community policies, passing through the existing system of intergovernmental relations, is inevitably affected by it. One only needs to think of the predominant role of the sectoral ministries, which maintain special relations with the relevant regional bodies. This unfortunately happens at a time when structural policies are heading towards ever more integrated intervention. The corrective measure introduced by setting up a Department for the Co-ordination of Community Policies, with a consultative committee of representatives of the relevant ministries and the regions, has so far proved insufficient. As some regional officials put it, partnership works only vertically, with no communication between sectors.[27] Another limit is the uncertainty in financial relations between central government and the regions as to the national quota to finance IMPs, with subsequent delays in starting the programmes.

The second aspect is the wide gap in performance between northern/central regions and those of the south. Most northern and central regions have succeeded in using Community funds and have also shown a positive response to innovative impulses and the exchange of experience that the relations with the Community provided. They have also responded positively to the partnership approach and the application of new patterns and means of intervention.[28] There is a willingness to apply these kinds of approach— such as the integrated intervention by means of territorial schemes—to other policies, such as the agricultural policy, which so far have followed a more traditional course.[29]

In the southern regions there is a different situation. Paradoxically, these regions which need intervention most do not succeed in implementing Community policies and end up losing the funds allotted to them by the Community. According to a report from the Senate Committee on EC Affairs, by 31 December 1989 Italy had paid 40 per cent of the sums she was supposed to pay (as against 82 per cent for Greece and 73 per cent for France).[30] The worst delays

[27] E. Buglione and C. Desideri, *Le regioni nell'ordinamento comunitario.*
[28] Ibid.
[29] A. Picchi, 'Le politiche comunitarie', in Ente di Svillupo per l'Emilia Romagna, *L'agro industria in Emilia Romagna: Situazione e prospettive. Rapporto 1990* (Bologna, 1990).
[30] Senato della Repubblica, Giunta per gli affari delle Comunità Europee, *Stato di attuazione dei Programmi Integrati Mediterranei,* 3 July 1991.

were those registered in the southern regions, with the exception of Molise. The widest gap is between 97 per cent of the expected outlay in the case of Emilia-Romagna and 7 per cent in the case of Campania. By 31 December 1990 a slight improvement in some regions was accompanied by a worsening of the situation in others. Campania could not manage any expenditure commitment at all and this time the widest gap was between 72.5 per cent of the expected outlay in Tuscany and 4 per cent in Sicily. This situation of course may have been determined by a number of factors, not least the difficulty with which Italy has introduced innovations such as the programme contract IMPs and the limits of the relations between central government and the regions. However, the Report of the Senate Committee on EC Affairs noted that, in southern regions, which unlike other regions could rely on the allocation of special-intervention funds to contribute to the share of national financing, the problem was caused by the lack of properly trained staff or efficient offices. Political factors, such as political inter- ference in administrative questions and interruption of activities following a political crisis of the regional government, also con- tributed. In addition, as some regions entrusted the elaboration of IMPs to external consultants, programmes were not thoroughly discussed within regional offices and when it came to implementing them, regional officials had to deal with things with which they were totally unfamiliar. Finally, one should not overlook the fact that the EC financial transfers to southern regions have been very small compared with national government aid and that EC proce- dures have proved harder to comply with than national ones.

The difficulties of implementing the Community's regional poli- cies in the disadvantaged regions of the south are a further symp- tom of the uncertain role of the national government. Difficulties arose despite the fact that national agencies responsible for the special intervention played a major role in the orientation and implementation of policies. National government has not used its override powers to take action in case of failures to act on the part of the regions, probably because it deemed them to be politically too dangerous. Only in the spring of 1991, faced with the threat of losing IMP Community funds to other countries because of the delay in using them, did the Government and regions adopt a support scheme involving programme contracts with individual re- gions. This was intended to streamline procedures and co-ordinate initiatives and financial matters. Should these provisions fail to produce the expected result, there is provision for alternative action by the central government as a last resort. A similar support scheme has been adopted for interventions financed through structural funds under Regulation 2052 of 1988. Although these show better performance levels than IMPs, they are also difficult to implement, as pointed out in the 1990 Report of the EC Commission on the implementation of the reform of structural funds.[31]

It is uncertain whether these mutual-consent formulas will become the normal pattern of relations between central government and the regions when dealing with Community policies, with a new role for the central government, less jealous of its prerogatives and more willing to provide support where needed. As to the performance of these formulas it is too early to pass judgement, though experience of early programme contracts with Calabria and Campania is not encouraging. Recent data show continued large differences in performance between the regions of the north and those of the south. Further requests were made by the EC Commission that the Italian Government adopt measures to speed up the use of the funds in the southern regions.

The Italian Regions and Europe: The Regionalist Wind from the North and the 'Southern Question'

The first form of regionalism emerged as a result of pressures from above through the activities of the major national parties. Today a new regionalism is developing from below. The regions, or at least some of them, have now taken root.[32] A new class of regional politicians is emerging and the regional authorities are increasingly seen as bodies to turn to when lobbying for economic and social interests. The regions are therefore requesting a number of changes to allow them to use their experience to meet the needs of their communities. Most of this reforming activity comes from northern regions, which feel more closely related to the European economic and political dimension and whose economies have become internationalized.

[31] Commisione delle Comunità Europee, *Relazione annuale sull'attuazione della riforma dei fondi strutturali*, Com (91) 400 def. (Brussels, 1991).
[32] Putnam, Leonardi, and Nanetti, *La pianta e le radici*.

In this context the appeal to autonomy and sometimes identity is only apparently an appeal to tradition. It is really an attempt to gather strength to engage in a competitive struggle. This is a challenge facing not only firms but also regional systems whose effective operation largely depends on efficient institutions. It also explains the emergence and development of the League and the support it finds among craftsmen, small and medium industrialists, and businessmen in general as they protest against the nation's political and administrative system which they see as a burden.

As Piero Bassetti, former president of the regional council of Lombardy and now president of the Union of Chambers of Commerce, said in an interview: 'Behind the leagues there lies Europe. The north is not heading south, but it is heading for Europe.'[33] The outcome of the referendum which was held in Italy together with the 1989 European Parliament election, in which people were asked to vote on whether to entrust the European Parliament with the task of drawing up a European Constitution, showed that pro-Europe enthusiasm is quite widespread, but that it is mainly in the northern regions, where regionalism is strongest, that people show interest for European integration. Votes cast in favour of this proposition were more or less evenly spread among all regions, but turn-out was higher in northern regions than in the south. On this occasion, the abstention rate in the south was even higher than that in regional or general elections.

Finally, Europe opens up new prospects also to that regionalism which attaches great importance to ethnic, linguistic, cultural, and geographic peculiarities. These are now seen not only as traditions to safeguard but, especially in border regions, as a means to develop relations with neighbouring states and regions, providing a short cut to Europe.

What still remains unsolved is the problem of the economic and social backwardness of the Mezzogiorno and of the regions' role in this. While gross regional product per capita in Lombardy stood at 132 per cent of the national average at the end of the 1980s, it was below the average in all the Mezzogiorno regions, and as low as 56 per cent in Calabria.[34] Policy in the 1980s improved the purchasing power of southerners instead of promoting new investment and

[33] *La Repubblica*, 25 May 1990.
[34] ISTAT, *Le regioni in cifre* (Rome: ISTAT, 1990).

encouraging businesses to remain competitive. The result was an apparent modernization and a façade of affluence compounded by a general deterioration of local politics towards clientelist methods, corruption, and crime.[35]

The League's accusation that the south consumes more than it produces and sponges off the most productive regions may be countered by pointing out that aid has also been given to the north, that the diversion of funds to the south was not as substantial as people believe, that many transfers actually go to benefit regions that are far from being backward, such as some special-status regions of the north and Lazio, and finally that the north benefited from the policies aimed at supporting consumption in the south because the latter increased the demand for goods produced in the industrial north.[36] However, the fact remains that these policies have not produced satisfactory results and have even had an adverse effect on the south. Further, this trade-off (welfare policies for the south going to the benefit of the industrial north) no longer seems viable because of European integration and market liberalization. Italy's industrial north would no longer be the only area to benefit from policies aimed at defending purchasing power in the south. Moreover, the need to contain public expenditure, to use resources more productively, and to curb inflation make it difficult for national government to continue its traditional style of aid with aid policy.[37]

Internationalization of the economy and the process of European integration seem finally to have caused the collapse of that ingrained approach towards the north–south gap, some aspects of which date back to the nineteenth century. A proper economic policy aimed at dealing with the problems of a backward south was not pursued after Italy's unification.[38] Instead, the dependence of the Mezzogiorno, from which the north could benefit, was maintained, while stop-gap measures were used to placate tensions and conflicts through the development of welfare-for-votes policies and clientelist methods involving ever-larger sections of the population.

---

[35] SVIMEZ (Associazione per lo Sviluppo dell'Industria nel Mezzogiorno), *Rapporto 1990 sull'economia del Mezzogiorno* (Bologna: Il Mulino, 1990).

[36] N. Parmentola, 'Una spesa per tutte le regioni', *Il Mulino*, 4 (1991).

[37] M. Sarcinelli, 'Mezzogiorno e Mercato Unico Europeo: Complementarita o conflitto di obiettivi?', *Moneta e Credito*, 166 (1989).

[38] V. Castronovo, 'La storia economica', in *Storia d'Italia*, iv. *Dall'Unità a oggi* (Turin: Einaudi, 1975).

This has increased the support for Government parties, but the economic dependence of the Mezzogiorno has been compounded by political dependence. The seriousness of today's tensions and conflicts is a result of the caving-in of a pattern that had become ingrained in Italy's economic and social life.

The crisis of policies is now hitting the whole system of special intervention for the Mezzogiorno which was introduced in the 1950s and which, with a few changes, has kept its basic characteristics, including centralized guidance, unaltered. Within this framework the southern regions, once set up, played a substantially subordinate role, as authorities eligible to apply for funds to the central administration on a par with municipalities, provinces, and other authorities. The regions have not shown any willingness or ability to use those few possibilities to take action outlined and provided for by the law.[39] Nor have they shown any eagerness to acquire more powers and responsibilities, or the ability to implement policies effectively. Without much power of initiative, the regions, along with local authorities, have served merely as one of the links in the assistance policies of the last ten years.

The system of special intervention in the south has now largely been replaced by ordinary intervention, which is qualitatively and quantitatively smaller in southern regions than in the rest of the country.[40] The special intervention system is consequently losing an important element of legitimization, that of its being additional and special. In the last few years it has also become ever more inefficient. There has even been a proposal for a referendum to repeal it. In order to avoid such a referendum, a law of December 1992 and a regulation of April 1993 finally abolished the system of special intervention in the south. It was replaced by policies for assisting all the disadvantaged areas of the country, administered by the relevant ministries and co-ordinated by the Ministry of the Budget and Economic Planning, which also audits the programmes.

To what extent could regionalism make a significant contribution to solving the problems of the Mezzogiorno? The economic and social differences among the various areas of the Mezzogiorno have given rise to doubts about the wisdom of special intervention

---

[39] C. Desideri, 'Intervento straordinario e regioni', *Le regioni*, 2 (1988).
[40] Corte dei Conti, *Decisione e Relazione sul Rendiconto generale dello Stato per l'esercizio finanziario 1990*, xi (Rome: Istituto Poligrafico e Zecca dello Stato, 1991).

aimed at the whole macro-region. There is thus a case for entrusting a leading role to the regions themselves.

However, one should not forget that regionalism has been fos-
tered by regionalist forces in the more developed north and centre.
The regions of the Mezzogiorno seem to show a worse performance[41] and no particular desire for regionalism is emerging from the
grassroots. According to a number of opinion polls,[42] people in the
south show both more dissatisfaction with the regions and greater
trust in central government than those in the north and centre.
Mention has already been made of the greater support in the south
for traditional parties. In local elections in 1992 and 1993, however,
the Government parties suffered a major decline in their vote. The
results of the referendums on institutional reform of April 1993
also showed a desire for political change in the south, though the
turn-out was lower than in the north. As to regional politicians, a
paper approved in Maratea on 9 November 1991 calling for the
continuation of special intervention shows that they seem keen to
share in the initiatives taken by the central government rather than
to take on their own responsibilities. The southern regions did not
play any significant role in the reform of the special intervention
system in the south; nor is their role in the new system of intervention very clear.

Business, including the Confindustria and the Association of
Young Entrepreneurs, seems to be favourable to a strengthening of
regional authorities, which are considered strategically important
for economic development. However, it seems less prepared to
trust the regions of the south.[43] Business associations have also
presented themselves as a support, if not as an alternative to inefficient regional authorities in the south in the implementation of
Community regional policies. To this end, the Confindustria proposed in spring 1993 the creation of a new agency to manage EC
funds, governed by a board with representatives of the regions and
of business associations.

Compared to regional authorities in the centre and the north, an
average southern region is characterized by greater government

---

[41] Putnam, Leonardi, and Nanetti, *La pianta e le radici*.

[42] CINSEDO-DOXA, 'Atteggiamenti e opinioni del pubblico italiano nei
confronti degli enti regionali', *Regione e governo locale*, 5/6 (1989).

[43] P. Bassetti, *La Repubblica*, 4 Aug. 1991. A Urciuoli, *Il Sole 24 Ore*, 23 Oct.
1991.

instability, serious shortcomings in terms of technical and organizational resources, heavy political pressures of local groups mainly interested in resources being 'scattered' over the regional area, as well as by a blurring of the separation between politics and the administration and between these two and business, not to mention organized crime.

One seriously ought to wonder whether in the present situation regionalism can actually contribute to solving these problems, thereby strengthening national unity, or whether, being more firmly rooted in the north and in the centre, it is bound to widen the north–south gap.

Would there be any chances of success with an intervention scheme managed mainly by southern regions and with a more direct commitment of the Community, assuming the Community is willing to make it ? Or could it be that in order to avoid a widening of the gap it is necessary to rely on the national State to mediate the different needs? It is not clear that the political and institutional conditions exist for a new order which would satisfy the demands of northern regionalists while making the political classes of the south more responsible.

MAP 4. United Kingdom: nations and standard regions.

4

Nations, Regions, and Europe: The UK Experience

MICHAEL KEATING AND BARRY JONES

The British State

The United Kingdom is unique among the countries considered in this volume in its lack of a codified Constitution and of any clear conception of the State as an institution separate from the government of the day or the civil society. Instead, there is a single principle, parliamentary sovereignty, which allows Parliament, technically the monarch, Lords, and Commons, unlimited power to alter both the substance and procedure of government. The principle is compatible with the devolution of authority to subordinate jurisdictions, since this can always be reclaimed, but not with the division of sovereignty or its transfer upwards to supranational organs, or downwards to the nations and regions which comprise the UK. In recent years, this principle has come under considerable strain from the contemporaneous pressures of European integration and autonomist and separatist movements within the kingdom. Although these pressures were strong enough in the 1970s to produce the constitutional innovation of supposedly advisory referendums, they have not as yet altered the basic architecture of the British State.

The United Kingdom contains marked territorial differences. Scotland is a historic nation-state, united with England in 1707 by a negotiated treaty which left intact much of its existing civil society, including its own legal system, education system, religious settlement, and sense of nationality. Wales was united with England earlier, in 1536, and is more assimilated institutionally although the language, now spoken by a minority of the population, provides a badge of nationality. Religious and political traditions in Wales have developed distinctively and, like Scotland, the principality has experienced periodic nationalist revivals since the late nineteenth century. Northern Ireland is a remnant remaining within the UK after the independence of what became the Irish Republic in 1922 and its politics are dominated by the issue of whether it should belong to the UK or a united Ireland. Within England regional differences are more subtle and less politicized, based on resentment of the dominance of London, economic disadvantage, and some cultural traits.

There is no system of regional government. Instead, a variety of devices are used to manage the peripheral nations and regions. For Scotland and Wales, these are: a system of administrative devolution; privileged representation in the central parliament and executive; and a favourable method of allocating public expenditure. The Secretaries of State for Scotland (established 1885) and Wales (established 1964) are Members of Parliament from the ruling party, administratively responsible for a wide range of domestic matters which in England come under various functional departments. Their role is threefold: to manage those matters which for historical reasons or reasons of convenience are entrusted to their respective Offices; to adjust the details of policy at the margin in the light of local needs and demands; and to lobby for their respective nations within the central government.[1] Public spending in Scotland has been some 20 per cent higher than that on corresponding services in England. For Wales, the differential has been slightly lower. There is a parallel system of parliamentary standing committees for Scotland, to handle the separate legislation made necessary by the distinct legal system, though these are subordinate to Parliament as a whole and the governing party always retains a majority on them.

Northern Ireland has been externalized as far as possible from mainstream British politics. From 1922 until 1972 it had its own devolved parliament, with British governments pursuing a policy of benign neglect towards the Protestant ascendancy. Since then, it has been governed by a Secretary of State who, in contrast to his Scottish and Welsh counterpart, is not an MP elected in the prov-

---

[1] A. Midwinter, M. Keating, and J. Mitchell, *Politics and Public Policy in Scotland* (London: Macmillan, 1991). J. Kellas and P. Madgwick, 'Territorial Ministries: The Scottish and Welsh Offices', in P. Madgwick and R. Rose (eds.), *The Territorial Dimension in United Kingdom Politics* (London: Macmillan, 1982).

ince. Several attempts have been made to restore devolved government, with its sectarian basis removed. Externalization is completed by the refusal of the British parties to contest seats in
Northern Ireland.

Within England, regional institutions are less developed. Labour
governments in the 1960s put in place a system of regional planning,
including corporatist Regional Planning Councils but, despite the
hopes of some of their supporters, these did not develop
into elected regional government.[2] With the failure of national
planning, they went into decline and were abolished by the in-
coming Conservative Government in 1979. Since then, English
regional interests have had no means of political or administrative
expression.

Yet territorial politics have become more important in Britain
since the 1960s, raising questions both about substantive issues and
governing arrangements. Economic disparities between the south-
east of England on the one hand, and northern England, Scotland,
and Wales on the other, spawned a series of diversionary regional
development policies and resource transfers between the 1960s and
the 1980s. The years of Margaret Thatcher's prime ministership
saw a sharp increase in regional disparities as deindustrialization
hit traditional industrial areas and the newer service industries
benefited only selected locations, though the recession of the early
1990s hit the south rather harder. On the other side of the fence,
English Members of Parliament became aware of the Scottish and
Welsh advantages in public spending and campaigned to reduce
them.

The constitutional issue resurfaced in the 1970s, with the rise of
the Scottish National Party (SNP) and its Welsh counterpart Plaid
Cymru and the Labour Party's move back to its historic support for
Scottish and Welsh Home Rule. SNP support peaked at 30 per cent
of the Scottish vote and eleven MPs (out of seventy-one) in 1974,
forcing the Labour Government to introduce legislation for a
Scottish elected assembly. Plaid Cymru's success was largely confined to the Welsh-speaking heartlands where it elected three MPs
out of Wales's thirty-six, peaking at 11 per cent of the Welsh vote.
A Welsh assembly, with lesser powers, was included in Labour's

---

[2] M. Keating, 'Whatever Happened to Regional Government?', *Local Government Studies*, 11/6 (1985), 111–22.

devolution package. Parliamentary opposition, much of it from Labour's own ranks, hobbled the devolution legislation, which eventually passed subject to referendums in Scotland and Wales. The Welsh proposals were defeated in the referendum by a 4:1 margin. The Scottish proposals gained majority support but failed to meet a parliamentary hurdle requiring that the YES vote comprise at least 40 per cent of the entire electorate. The devolution episode failed to produce self-government for Scotland or Wales but it did leave a legacy in the form of more powers for the Scottish and Welsh Offices and regional development agencies for the two nations.

The devolution issue did not go away after the 1979 referendums but took on a new dimension with a growing discrepancy between election results in Scotland and Wales and those in England. By 1992 Scotland had in four successive elections produced a majority contrary to that of Parliament as a whole, raising serious questions about the moral, if not legal, legitimacy of the Secretary of State to speak for Scotland and impose the will of the Westminster majority. The SNP vote declined in the 1980s, but rose again to 21 per cent in 1992, while the Labour Party in Scotland, more convinced of the rightness of its own policy, pressed the issue more vigorously. Given the impossibility of progress as long as the English-based Conservative Party held a parliamentary majority, attention moved from Parliament to Scottish civil society. A Constitutional Convention was organized with support from the Labour and Liberal Democrat parties, churches, trade unions, and local government, but not from the SNP or the Conservatives. This produced proposals for a Scottish Parliament elected by proportional representation. Opinion polls showed increasingly solid majorities for a large measure of devolution within the UK and significant support for independence. In Wales, the failure of the local majority to match the overall parliamentary one was more familiar, having been the case through the 1950s, but the same tensions, albeit on a lesser scale, were visible.

Nationalism in Scotland and Wales has in the early 1990s been reinforced by economic concerns. Regional development, especially in the context of Europe, has re-emerged as a strong theme in reaction to the *laissez-faire* stance of the British Government in the 1980s. In England too, regionalism has resurfaced with demands for economic development machinery comparable to the special agencies set up in Scotland and Wales in the 1970s. There is also an open question about the future of local government following the abolition of the metropolitan counties and the Greater London Council. Labour and the Liberal Democrats are now committed to regional government, though its form remains vague. At the same time, a movement for constitutional reform has developed, focused on proportional representation, a bill of rights, regional devolution, a more positive attitude in Europe, and a written Constitution. While strongest in the political centre and among professional and intellectual groups whose functional independence was undermined during the Thatcher years, this movement has produced some responses in the Labour Party and even in sections of the Conservative Party.

In Northern Ireland, the political agenda is dominated by the search for a constitutional settlement to the sectarian and nationalist conflict, which could put an end to political violence.

The European Community and the British State

For many years, the debate on British membership of the European Community was conducted quite apart from that on the territorial constitution of the United Kingdom. Britain's governing élites saw the Community as a new external support system for the British State following the demise of Empire, not as the basis for a new constitutional order. They resisted the constitutional implications of entry including supranationalism and the surrender of national sovereignty. In the post-entry referendum of 1975, the YES side comprised the defenders of the post-war consensus, including what was later to become the SDP–Liberal Alliance. On the NO side were an assortment of Conservative right-wingers opposed to a surrender of parliamentary sovereignty; the Labour left, committed to a radical programme of national reindustrialization and protection; and representatives of the territorial periphery.

In the early years of membership, there was more hostility to EC membership in the peripheral territories of Scotland, Wales, Northern Ireland and, as far as can be judged, the north of England. One reason was the fear that their economic peripherality would be increased within the larger market. Sectoral concerns, including the steel industry, fisheries, and hill farming, further

fuelled hostility. Peripherality also had a political dimension.
Scottish and Welsh nationalists, concerned with the achievement of
national sovereignty, did not regard Brussels any more favourably
than London.

So firmly did the SNP view Scotland as a historic nation that they
refused to join the Bureau of Unrepresented Nations set up by
Breton, Welsh, Basque, and Alsatian groups in Brussels to press
their case within the Community. To the SNP, these were merely
fringe groups with little electoral support seeking representation
within the existing Community. They, in contrast, were a mature
national movement with mass support ready to assume independence. Their model was the Scandinavian democracies, only one of
which had joined the EC. They have similarly rejected the model of
a 'Europe of the Regions' put forward by some of the peripheral
movements on the Continent on the grounds that Scotland is not a
region but a nation comparable in status to the twelve member
states.[3] Plaid Cyrmu's position was more ambiguous but it was less
opposed to the Europe of the Regions idea and rather more inter-
nationalist in its outlook, though insisting on Welsh sovereignty as
an element of any new arrangement. Like the SNP, however, it
refused in the early years to see the EC as an appropriate framework for this.

To the nationalist concern was added a class and partisan bias.
The Labour Party and the trade unions tended, despite some vacil-
lating, to be opposed to EC membership from the 1960s until the
late 1980s. Labour interests were not only stronger in Scotland and
Wales but Labour and the trade unions in the peripheral nations
were more strongly anti-EC than their counterparts in England.[4] So
national, sectoral, partisan, and class biases cumulated to produce
greater opposition to the Community in Scotland and Wales than
in England.

In Northern Ireland, Community membership, like almost
everything else, is viewed through sectarian lenses. Protestants
show greater hostility to the Community, seeing it as a threat to the
British sovereignty which they treasure, as putting them in the

---

[3] Scottish National Party Research Department, *Independence in Europe* (Edinburgh: SNP, 1991).
[4] As measured by votes in Parliament on EC issues; M. Keating and N. Waters,
'Scotland in the European Community', in M. Keating and B. Jones, *Regions in the
European Community* (Oxford: Clarendon Press, 1985).

same jurisdiction as the Irish Republic, and as opening the way to what many of them see as the influence of a Catholic-dominated Continent. Catholics are more favourably inclined for precisely the opposite reasons. The 1975 referendum figures illustrate these differences (Table 4.1).

Polls in the 1970s and early 1980s continued to show hostility to the Community in Scotland, with a majority of Labour voters and the vast bulk of SNP voters in favour of withdrawal. They also showed that Scots supporters tended to see membership as benefiting England more than Scotland while opponents considered that Scotland was more severely damaged. Poll evidence from Wales is scarcer but two polls conducted in 1983 showed opinion rather fickle with no consistent majority either way. There is some evidence, too, that opinion in the north of England was more hostile than in the south.

In the late 1980s, attitudes on the British periphery started to change, and the questions of Community membership and territorial self-government began to come together. An important factor was the hostility of Margaret Thatcher, identified with southern English conservatism, to the social and political dimensions of the European project, together with the centralizing policies of her Government. For territorial, class, and partisan oppositions, anything which Thatcher so obviously detested had to have some merit. Shut out of access to the British central State, they sought other means of influence, including local government, a renewed commitment to devolution, and the European Community. The trade unions were the first to take the Community seriously, grasp-

TABLE 4.1. *European referendum results for the UK, 1975*

	Turnout (%)	YES vote (%)
UK	64.5	67.2
England	64.5	68.7
Scotland	61.7	58.4
Wales	66.7	66.5
Northern Ireland	47.7	52.1

Source: D. Butler and U. Kitzinger, *The 1975 Referendum* (London: Macmillan, 1978).

ing the Social Charter as a means of protecting the social and labour market gains of the post-war settlement against the Thatcherite onslaught. Soon the Labour Party followed suit, reversing its commitment to withdrawal and adopting the new European agenda, including the Exchange Rate Mechanism and, more cautiously, monetary and political integration.

As early as 1973, some Scottish MPs had begun to make a connection between the revived Scottish constitutional issue and European integration. Labour MP Jim Sillars founded the Scottish Labour EC 'watchdog committee', a group of MPs whose function was to monitor developments in the Community as they affected Scotland. Sillars's position at this time was that Britain should withdraw from the EC and Scotland should have a devolved assembly but that, if Britain remained in the Community, Scotland should have as much independence as would give it independent representation in Brussels. He was moving rapidly in a more nationalist direction and in 1976, after the referendum had confirmed EC membership, quit the Labour Party to form the short-lived Scottish Labour Party (SLP) with a policy of Scottish independence within the EC. The idea had little appeal outside the ranks of Sillars's party, however, and died with the SLP after the general election of 1979.

In the 1980s, Sillars joined the SNP and played a critical role in persuading them of the merits of independence in Europe. In a by-election in November 1988 the SNP rode to victory over Labour in the inner-city constituency of Govan on the new slogan. The idea is in many ways seductive. As part of the United Kingdom, Scotland can influence Community decisions only through the Scottish lobby, focused on the role of the Secretary of State in Cabinet. As an independent state, it would have its own delegation to the Council of Ministers. If major economic and social decisions are really to be transferred from London to Brussels, then it would be worth sacrificing representation in the former for the latter. Nationalists also point to the European Parliament where Scotland, with a population of five million, has just eight members (seven Labour and one SNP), while the Republic of Ireland, with three million population, has fifteen members. The SNP support Economic and Monetary Union and eventually a single currency but, true to their nationalist ideals, prefer an intergovernmental Community based on nation-states to a federal or supranational structure.

The contrast with the Republic of Ireland is also made in Wales which, with almost the same population, has only four MEPs. Plaid Cymru also argue that Wales's subordinate status within the British State means that it has no representative at the Council of Ministers and no right to nominate to the Commission. These complaints, articulated in the two Euro-elections in the 1980s, indicated the extent to which Plaid Cymru had come to terms with the Community. While there had always been a pro-Europe element in the party which had regarded British membership as a means to loosen the grip of the Westminster Parliament, the change in Plaid Cymru's stance was largely the result of the 1975 referendum which revealed a strong measure of support in rural Welsh-speaking Wales for continued membership and the benefits of the Common Agricultural Policy. Subsequently, Plaid Cymru has become more enthusiastically European, praising the Community's commitment to maintain the small family farm and welcoming the European Parliament's support for the languages and cultures of regional and ethnic minorities.

Independence in Europe carries reassurance to Scots and Welsh fearful to take a leap in the dark. Like the turn-of-the-century policy of Home Rule within the Empire, it promises an external support system in a dangerous world and allows nationalists to disclaim the separatist label. There is no doubt about the importance of this reassurance factor. Support for Scottish independence mounted steadily in the 1980s, after stagnating around 20 per cent for some fifty years. Since 1988, MORI polls have included the option of independence in Europe. This has increased support for independence to around 40 per cent. These figures must be interpreted with great caution, since close analysis reveals a substantial number of respondents who will support both independence within the EC and continued membership of the United Kingdom.[5] What they do show is dissatisfaction with the *status quo* and a desire for some form of new arrangement for Scotland in relation to both the EC and the UK.

There has been considerable debate on the legalities of Scottish independence in Europe and over whether Scotland would automatically continue as a member of the EC or be obliged to reapply. Anti-nationalists have insisted that Scotland would need to reapply

[5] A. McCartney, 'Independence in Europe', in A. Brown and R. Parry (eds.), *Scottish Government Yearbook, 1990* (Edinburgh: Unit for the Study of Government in Scotland, 1990).

and hinted that other members might not welcome this, fearing the precedent of the break-up of a member state. Against this, the SNP marshalled a variety of legal opinion, including the views of Emile Noël, former General-Secretary of the Commission, and French advocate Xavier de Roux. Noël's view was that, since there was no procedure for expulsion from the EC, Scotland would continue to be a member. De Roux argued on the basis of the 1707 Treaty of Union, that the EC was incorporated into Scottish domestic law. Since the Union created the United Kingdom, its dissolution would leave two successor states of equal standing, both of which would inherit the obligations of the old UK.[6] The SNP add for good measure that it took Greenland a great deal of time and effort to negotiate its way *out* of the EC.

The notion of independence has always been less clearly defined in Wales. Saunders Lewis, the founder of Plaid Cymru, placed greater emphasis on 'freedom' than on independence. The ambiguity was sustained by Gwynfor Evans as party president in his advocacy of Welsh self-government within a common market of the nations of Britain. The post-mortem following the overwhelming rejection in Wales of the 1979 devolution proposals not only produced a more pro-European attitude, identifying the Welsh as one of the historic peoples of Europe, but also placed Welsh independence in a European context. The phrase, 'community of nations' was used to emphasize the diversity which could be contained within the EC as compared with the rigidities of the centralized British State. Much of the impetus for this shift came from Dafydd Ellis Thomas, the former party president, who argued against nationalism within closed borders, suggesting instead that a people's rights and identity should no longer be defined by states but within a European framework. A poll published by the *Western Mail* in 1990 revealed a strong surge in support for Welsh devolution, with 56 per cent favouring a Welsh Assembly. Almost half (44 per cent) of those supporting this preferred the option 'Independent within Europe', with the strongest support coming from the Gwynedd heartland of Plaid Cymru.

Class, sectoral, partisan, and territorial oppositions have thus moved from hostility to the Community to seeing it as a means of

---

[6] Scottish National Party, *Background: The Legal Basis of Independence in Europe* (Edinburgh: SNP, 1991).

outflanking a centralizing, right-wing UK government. The drift of the Conservatives away from the enthusiastic Europeanism of the Edward Heath leadership, together with the collapse of Conservative support in the periphery, has reinforced this trend. In 1992, the opposition parties (Labour, Liberal Democrat, and Nationalist) gained 74 per cent of the vote in Scotland and 71 per cent in Wales. All were committed to remaining within the Community, opting into the Social Chapter, and to establishing elected assemblies in Scotland and Wales. The Conservatives remained adamantly opposed to elected assemblies in Scotland or Wales and deeply divided over Europe. Yet, while the dominant parties of the periphery were becoming more committed to devolution and to Europe, they were still groping for a formula to combine the two. Labour and the Liberal Democrats were increasingly talking the language of a Europe of the Regions, a notion which the Scottish Nationalists indignantly reject as an insult to their national status.[7] Nationalists taunted Labour and Liberals with their continued dependence on gaining a favourable Westminster majority before they could do anything. Yet the realism of their own position could also be questioned. While independence in Europe is a seductive way of selling the idea of independence, the Community itself is far from popular in Scotland. A 1993 poll showed 41 per cent of Scots opposed to the Maastricht Treaty as against 29 per cent in favour.[8]

In Northern Ireland, there has been less movement. In the debate on the 1992 initiative, the hard-line Protestant Democratic Unionist Party of Ian Paisley took a strongly anti-Community stance, while the mainly Catholic Social Democratic and Labour Party was firmly in favour and stressed particularly the social dimension and the structural funds. The largest party on the Protestant side, the Official Unionist Party, takes a critical line on the Community but is less resolutely opposed than Paisley. Sinn Fein, the political wing of the IRA, opposes further European integration but claims as a long-term goal the creation of a 'free Ireland in a free Europe'.[9]

[7] Scottish National Party, *Independence in Europe*. Scottish National Party, *Scotland: A European Nation* (Edinburgh: SNP, 1992).

[8] *Glasgow Herald*, 25 May 1993.

[9] P. Hainsworth, 'The Politics of 1992: The Single European Act and Political Parties in Northern Ireland', in P. Hainsworth (ed.), *Towards 1992* (University of Ulster at Jordanstown, 1990).

Patterns of Influence

The connection between the Community and the nations and regions of the UK is felt in several policy areas. Sectoral restructuring in heavy industry, agricultural and fishing policies, and transport questions have differing effects across the regions. The 1992 internal-market project potentially threatened peripheral regions, distant from the major centres of Europe. Deregulation and competition policies threaten cross-subsidization and regional-development programmes. Sectoral policies in steel, coal, agriculture, and fisheries have had a severe impact. European directives must be expressed in Scotland's distinctive legal idiom. Local governments have a keen interest in regulations about the environment, tendering, and harmonization. Great attention has been devoted to the Community structural funds but, although these are the most visible aspect of the Community's impact on the regions and nations of the UK, they are among the least important substantively.

For Scotland, Wales, and Northern Ireland, the principal channel to the decision-making instances of the Community is through the respective Secretaries of State. Their presence in Cabinet provides membership of the various ministerial committees which establish the British stance on Community questions as well as membership of the parallel committees of officials. Ministers from the territorial offices also serve on negotiating teams for meetings of the Council of Ministers, briefed by their own officials; but as in domestic politics, they remain junior partners. Between 1986 and 1988, the Scottish Office appeared at just five of the 151 meetings of the Council of Ministers.[10] Occasionally, they can make a significant impact, where they have special knowledge, as in matters of regional development policy or hill farming. In the past, the Scottish Office has sometimes served as the lead department in EC negotiations on fisheries.

In the Scottish and Welsh Offices, European Affairs divisions exist with two roles: that of co-ordinator and facilitator within the Offices and in relations with Whitehall; and as administrator of EC

---

[10] S. Mazey and J. Mitchell, 'Europe of the Regions: Territorial Interests and European Integration: The Scottish Experience', in S. Mazey and J. J. Richardson (eds.), *Lobbying in the European Community* (Oxford: Oxford University Press, 1993).

structural funds. They are consequently future-oriented, seeking to identify benefits to Scotland and Wales as EC directives are amended; they are proactive in promoting and defending the territorial interest within the framework of centrally determined policy lines. For the most part, however, the Offices must content themselves with minor modifications of the overall UK line. The tendency is less to assert distinctive policy priorities than to try to extract as much as possible from whatever initiatives are under way. The territorial Offices' influence in British domestic politics declined in the 1980s because of an English backlash to the devolution episode of the late 1970s and the weakness of the Secretaries of State who, lacking majority support at home, could no longer credibly claim to speak for their respective territories. This entailed a corresponding decline of influence in Europe, as the failure to secure a substantial share for UK regions in the new structural funds shows. Critics compare the discreet, behind-the-scenes mode of operation of the Scottish and Welsh Offices unfavourably with the high-profile lobbying of elected regional authorities in other member states, often led by politicians of the first rank. On the other hand, the Offices have been able to maintain the understanding that they should receive a certain share of the UK allocation.

Nor does Europe give them much scope for policy initiative. In the past, the Scottish and to a lesser extent the Welsh Office were able discreetly to bend UK policy initiatives or modify their implementation in areas of low political salience; where issues became politicized there was a tendency to UK-wide uniformity and for English regions to demand parity.[11] This appears to have happened with the EC structural funds which now have a higher political profile so that, ironically, the reform, intended to provide a greater regional input, has produced greater uniformity within the UK than existed before. The lead role of the Department of Trade and Industry has strengthened and all UK Community Support Frameworks must be drawn up within strict Whitehall and Treasury guidelines, leaving little room for local experimentation. Even where a distinct Scottish, Welsh, or Northern Irish interest has been established as part of the British negotiating position, there is the danger that it may be traded away in cross-functional

---

[11] Midwinter, Keating, and Mitchell, *Politics and Public Policy in Scotland.*

compromises with other member states. It is not surprising, then, that in 1991 the Scottish Office was again demanding to resume the lead role in fisheries policy.

Scotland has a larger range of interest groups than the other two peripheries, some of them branches of British groups, some independent but affiliated to British groups, and some quite separate. This is a legacy of the separate civil society preserved after the Union of 1707 but also represents a response to the gradual extension of administrative devolution since 1885. With a focus for lobbying in Edinburgh, Scottish interest groups are encouraged to organize and to seek to penetrate the governmental apparatus but the quality of their lobbying varies. The Confederation of British Industry has a branch in Scotland but, in contrast to the London headquarters, is only marginally involved in European issues. Business leaders in Scotland can be privately critical of the thrust of government policy since 1979, with its emphasis on deregulation and de-emphasis on regional development, but they are caught between their role as promoters of a Scottish interest and their instinctive loyalty to the Conservative Party. Their position is made even more uncomfortable by the Conservatives' minority position in Scottish politics. Scottish business leaders tend to be individualistic and not given greatly to collective or co-operative action, and they maintain a rather low political profile. Sectoral-interest organizations are more active, notably the Scotch Whisky Association which has an obvious interest in harmonization of alcohol taxation. Fisheries interests in the early 1990s began to make direct representations to Brussels, in frustration at the attitude of the British Government. Farmers, on the other hand, are more closely integrated into the Scottish Office system and do not seek to outflank it.

The Scottish Trades Union Congress is organizationally separate from the British TUC, with the major unions affiliating to both. While relations between government and trade unions never broke down in Scotland as they did in London, union influence declined sharply in the 1980s. This has led to an increased interest in lobbying the Community in matters such as regional policy and steel closures. Like its UK counterpart, the Scottish TUC moved from an anti- to a pro-Community stance in the 1980s. It is also strongly in favour of Scottish Home Rule, though it combines this with support for a strong central government and a return to intervention and planning.

The Scottish Council (Development and Industry) is a body set up in the 1930s to promote regional development in co-operation with industry, trade unions, and local government. It formerly received government funding to undertake investment promotion but since this function was transferred to the Scottish Development Agency and later to Locate in Scotland, the Scottish Council (D and I) has operated more as a private body, supported by industry and local government. It has promoted awareness of the European dimension of development policy since the early 1970s but in the 1980s, under a government opposed to the planning policies with which it had been associated, the Scottish Council (D and I) lost influence.

In Wales, the notion of a territorial interest distinct from the UK interest was slow to develop. The constitutional entity England-and-Wales had deep roots and the revival of Welsh nationalism in the 1960s made limited progress in the business and trade union sectors. However, the creation of the Welsh Office in 1964 encouraged a variety of organizations which did business with government to establish a Welsh institutional identity. This tendency became more pronounced with the expansion of Welsh Office functions and the establishment of a Select Committee on Welsh Affairs in 1979. Throughout the 1980s the Thatcher Government's unsympathetic attitude to government intervention and trade unions mobilized Welsh opposition groups. Rather than engage in public confrontation which might prove counter-productive, Welsh trade unions tended to seek allies in the Welsh Office in the hope of mitigating the harsher aspects of Thatcherite economic policies. At the same time, they directed attention to the EC. While the benefits to be gained by direct approaches are, as elsewhere, limited, high-profile lobbying of the Community did reinforce the idea of a Welsh interest and has not displeased the Welsh Office whose ability to argue the Welsh case with the Treasury depends upon evidence of Welsh concerns and activities.

There is a strong tradition in Scotland, with weaker counterparts in Wales and Northern Ireland, of a territorial lobby which, without attenuating class, partisan, or local differences, is able to come together in defence of national economic interests. The Offices are both the targets of these lobbies and part of them. With a unified territorial lobby, it is easier for the Secretaries of State to make a case in government for special treatment or extra resources.

Lobbying the EC has reinforced these cross-class and inter-party coalitions within Scotland and Wales. For example, in 1981 the rapid decline in the Welsh steel industry, as required by the Davignon Plan, brought into existence the South Wales Standing Conference, which encompassed MPs and MEPs, local authorities, the Wales Trades Union Congress, the Confederation of British Industry Wales, and other community organizations. Little was expected of Mrs Thatcher's Government and, apart from the presentation of its report and recommendations to the Welsh Office, the Standing Conference concentrated its efforts on the EC Commission. Thereafter, the Welsh organizations and interest groups represented on the Standing Commission have regularly lobbied Brussels. After a slight altercation with its British counterpart, the Wales TUC established the right to give independent evidence to the European Parliamentary Committee. The CBI Wales has adopted a similar role and frequently acts jointly with the Wales TUC in defence of common Welsh interests. In Scotland, a broad-based campaign was mounted in the 1980s in defence of the steel industry.

Territorial interest groups must concentrate their lobbying on their respective Secretaries of State. Direct lobbying in Brussels provides opportunities for publicity and for scoring points against the Government in London. Yet even where Scottish and Welsh organizations do have their own links to the Commission, they are aware that little can be done without the support of the Scottish or Welsh Office. The latter, in turn, know that an organized Scottish or Welsh lobby can strengthen their own hand in Whitehall and Brussels. In the early 1980s, the Scottish Office was reported to be actively working to heal a rift in the Scottish Fishermen's Federation in order to present a united front in London and Brussels.

Local government in Scotland and Wales has sought access to Europe. The Convention of Scottish Local Authorities has places on EC consultative committees, but it is a small and sparsely staffed organization. Individual local authorities, notably Strathclyde Regional Council which covers half the population of Scotland, have been very active in Brussels, although their claims to have extracted funding through their own efforts must be taken with great caution. In any case, the re-elected Conservative Government of 1992 has plans to abolish the Scottish regional councils altogether. Welsh local authorities have been active. While the district councils tend to work through the England-and-Wales Association of District Councils, the eight Welsh counties have set up their own coordinating body, the Assembly of Welsh Counties (AWC). This has assumed a Welsh regional role both in its dealings with the Welsh Office and in Europe. It is a member of the Conference of Peripheral Maritime Regions, the Assembly of European Regions, and the Consultative Council of Regional and Local Authorities. Despite the opposition of all eight counties to devolution in 1979, the AWC is now strongly supportive of an elected Welsh Assembly, arguing that only if it had one would Wales be able to match the democratic credentials and political clout of the German *Länder*, Italian regions, and Spanish autonomous communities within Europe.

Representation is also provided by the Community's various consultative forums. The British delegations to the Economic and Social Council and other consultative committees include Scottish, Welsh, and Northern Ireland members, where there are separate interest groups. The Consultative Council of Regional and Local Authorities includes representatives of Scottish, Welsh, and Northern Irish local government associations. In the Assembly of European Regions (ARE), on the other hand, Britain is seriously underrepresented since it does not possess formal regional governments. Strathclyde Regional Council, while the nearest thing to a regional authority in the UK, is really a local government and faces abolition. The Assembly of Welsh Counties, also a member of ARE, is an association of local authorities.

More nebulous but still important is the network of compatriots which the Scots, Welsh, and Northern Irish find in and around the Commission. This is perhaps most important in the case of Northern Ireland, where a culture stressing personal contacts finds the relatively open access of Brussels easy to work. The Welsh 'Tafia' also provides a network of sympathetic officials and helps open doors. Members of the European Parliament, elected on a constituency basis, provide another channel of access and occasionally act together on a regional or national (Scotland, Wales, and even Northern Ireland) basis. There is a willingness in principle to cooperate with the territorial departments but partisan differences do not always permit this.

As long as the Community remains primarily an intergovernmental organization, with power concentrated in the Council of

Ministers, the main channel of influence will continue to be national government. Scotland, Wales, and to some extent Northern Ireland are thus advantaged in having privileged access to national government. On the other hand, the limits of action are set by the governing party which, in recent years, is the minority party in the peripheral nations. English regions lack even this channel to Brussels via central government. Nor do English regions have well-organized regional interest groups or business lobbies. This puts the English regions at a serious disadvantage in responding to European initiatives and attempting to influence policy. There have been some efforts in recent years to establish regional lobbying and development organization, notably in the north and the north-west of England, but with little government support.[12] More generally, Europe has stimulated thinking about the need to improve regional organization and there has been some mobilization around the structural funds.

There have been many attempts in Britain, as in other countries, to establish direct links between regional and local institutions and Brussels. Several local authorities have established offices in Brussels or employed consultants on a joint basis, and delegations frequently arrive at the Commission with proposals and requests. A great deal of political capital is made out of these contacts by local politicians eager to establish their international credentials and their independence of national government. Receipt of funding from the structural funds is the most common achievement claimed, yet there is no evidence in Brussels that such approaches are able to unlock funds for individual projects or regions. Given the way in which funding is allocated, that is not to be expected. In reality, the influence here is more subtle. By lobbying the Commission, local governments may help influence policy proposals going to the Council of Ministers. They may learn of initiatives under way, which they can then lobby their own government to support or oppose.

By the early 1980s there was growing pressure in Scotland, Wales, and Northern Ireland for special bureaux in Brussels to co-ordinate their respective lobbying efforts. The Offices, as an integral part of British central government, were unable to do this

---

[12] M. Burch and I. Holliday, 'Institutional Emergence: The Case of the North West of England', *Regional Politics and Policy*, 3/2 (1993).

directly and officially took the line that Scottish and Welsh interests were better served by interdepartmental discussions during the preparation of the British negotiating position. It is not difficult to see the hand of the Foreign Office and the British delegation to COREPER here. On the other hand, the Government was anxious to counter or contain independent lobbying efforts by Scottish trade unions and local authorities, who would be likely to take an anti-Government line.[13] Eventually a formula was found whereby Brussels bureaux could be established through the Welsh Development Agency and Scottish Enterprise (formerly the Scottish Development Agency), semi-autonomous government agencies which in the past have been used to sponsor activities which the Offices themselves could not undertake directly. In the early 1980s, there had been a similar battle over the inward investment effort and overseas offices of the Scottish Development Agency which the Foreign Office and Department of Trade had regarded as a breach in the British diplomatic front. The Welsh Development Agency's operations have had an increasingly strong European dimension, promoting inward investment, identifying European partners for Welsh firms, and facilitating the use by Welsh industry of Eurotechnology initiatives. In view of the political sensitivity of the issue, Government insisted that the Welsh Bureau, Scotland Europa, and the NICE (Northern Ireland Centre in Europe) would be concerned purely with 'economic' as opposed to 'political' representation and with providing a service to clients rather than general lobbying. Ian Lang, Secretary of State for Scotland, stressed at the official opening of Scotland Europa that the new body did not represent Scotland in Europe, a role performed by the UK Permanent Representation in Brussels. 'After all,' he noted, 'we're not Bavaria. We are part of a unitary state.'[14] It is to be seen whether this rather tenuous distinction can be maintained. Already, the Scottish Council (Development and Industry), the Scottish Trades Union Congress, and Scottish local authorities have criticized the limitations of the brief.

Similar inhibitions limit the participation of Scotland and Wales in international regional linkages, although in March 1990 an accord was signed between the Welsh Office and Baden-

---

[13] Mazey and Mitchell, 'Europe of the Regions'.
[14] *Glasgow Herald*, 27 May 1992.

Württemburg which linked Wales to a regional alliance for technological collaboration, research, and development and economic
and cultural exchange, extending to Lombardy, Rhône-Alpes, and
Catalonia. The tensions between Scottish and Welsh interests
seeking a real presence in Brussels and the capacity to forge links
with regions in other states, and the unitary stance of the British
Government, are likely to remain as long as Scotland and Wales
lack their own political authority.

The limits of adminstrative devolution were shown up again in
the negotiations over the allocation of Britain's seats on the Committee of the Regions provided for in the Maastricht Treaty. The
Scottish and Welsh Secretaries of State were able to use their
influence in Cabinet to obtain an allocation greatly in excess of
their respective population shares; but in the absence of elected
Scottish and Welsh governments their respresentativeness must
always be in question. The haggling over seats allowed Ian Lang,
Secretary of State for Scotland, to divide the opposition forces and
cut a deal with the SNP in return for SNP votes on the crucial
Maastricht vote of 8 March 1993. This put an end, for the time
being, to co-operation among the opposition parties in Scotland.[15]
A similar deal was made for Wales, illustrating how easily even
territorial politics in the UK can be absorbed into the Westminster
tradition and subordinated to party advantage.

The Structural Funds

The European Regional Development Fund (ERDF) was introduced in 1975 precisely to accommodate British concerns that existing spending patterns provided little benefit for the UK. In the
original quota allocations, the UK was guaranteed about 40 per
cent of the total, which was in turn allocated among the nations and
regions by a system of internal quotas. The 1984 reform and the
accession of southern European countries was gradually to reduce
this share over the 1980s. The British attitude was, and has remained, that this is an intergovernmental compensation mechanism and that the moneys concerned are the property of Her
Majesty's Government. The UK operated a strict non-additionality

---

[15] P. Jones, 'Playing the Westminster Numbers Game', *Scottish Affairs*, 5 (1993).

rule under which most structural fund receipts were counted as reimbursements for national expenditures rather than extra moneys. Local governments receiving ERDF grants had to accommodate the expenditure within their existing capital expenditure ceilings. The advantage was that the ERDF money came as a grant, rather than a loan, saving them capital charges, though, as their central government support was also reduced to take account of this, the saving was marginal. Private firms awarded grants received nothing extra, central government regarding the money as reimbursement for national aid already dispensed. For many years, the English Department of the Environment, in announcing ERDF grants, included a rider to this effect. The Scottish Office, wishing to promote the benefits of ERDF membership in a territory where support has been low, included no such rider in its press releases. Indeed, even the Supplementary Measures money awarded in the early 1980s to compensate for Britain's high budget contribution, were claimed by the Scottish Office as extra regional spending in Scotland, though the money remained in the Treasury in London and the only effect in Scotland was the erection of signs on major central government infrastructure projects like the A9 highway and the Kessock bridge. The existence of the structural funds did have one important effect: it forced the British Government to retain some sort of regional development policy in the 1980s in order to qualify for the funding, so that arguably there was an indirect benefit for the regions.

The 1988 reform of the structural funds was aimed at the countries of southern Europe, with priority given to objective 1 areas, of which the UK had only one, Northern Ireland. The UK's indicative share of objective 1 was just 1.7 per cent. Objective 2 allocations were available to declining industrial areas in Scotland, Wales, Northern Ireland, and the north and midlands of England. The retention of this element is to a large extent a political gesture to keep the northern European countries on side but, while it has assumed great political importance, the amounts involved are very small. The UK share was 38.3 per cent but objective 2 accounted for only about 12 per cent of the structural funds. Parts of the UK's Celtic fringe in rural Wales, Highland and Island Scotland, western Northern Ireland, and south-west England also qualified under objective 5(B), of which the UK indicative share was 7.5 per cent. As a result, the UK indicative allocation for the funds as a whole fell to about 9.5 per cent of the total under the spatially targeted objectives 1, 2, and 5(B), compared with a range of 21.41 per cent to 28.56 per cent under the flexible quotas of the previous scheme, adopted in 1984. There is some evidence that the UK Government's continued hostility to the idea of European programmes and its insistence on regarding the funds as merely an intergovernmental compensation mechanism may have damaged its case in the allocations. It argued, for example, that the UK should be guaranteed 50 per cent of the objective 2 allocation and when the Commission insisted that it must come with specific proposals, proved uncooperative in providing the necessary information to allow the Commission to decide on priorities. It was in this way that the opportunity of gaining funds for the declining parts of London, where moreover there are several marginal constituencies, was lost. In 1993, the funds were increased again (see Ch. 2). The UK was able to extend objective 1 status to the Highlands and Islands and Merseyside, but again the main beneficiaries were in southern Europe and, on this occasion, eastern Germany.

Under the new regulation, funding is given through regional programmes with which regional governments and other interests must be associated. The association of regional governments has created difficulties in a country where there are no regional governments. The strict requirements for transparency and additionality have posed serious problems given the British Government practice of treating all public expenditure, except the small self-funded element in local government spending, as a single account, and structural-fund receipts merely as a contribution to this. The lead department in dealing with Brussels on structural-fund matters and co-ordinating the UK effort is the Department of Trade and Industry. Implementation is the responsibility of the Scottish, Welsh, and Northern Ireland Offices in their respective territories, associating local governments and Commission representatives with them in drawing up the Community Support Frameworks and funding programmes. In the regions of England, the regional offices of the Departments of Trade and Industry and the Environment convene working committees, with local government and Commission representatives, to perform the same function. This creates a system of extreme complexity, with central departments, Commission representatives, and local governments often taking differing views of their role and the way in which the system should develop. Certainly, the exposure of local governments and even field officials of central government with Commission representatives has opened new perspectives, with a stronger regional and European identity emerging and growing impatience at the centralist and *anti-communautaire* attitudes of London.

Structural-fund allocations are placing further strains on the British system of public accounting. The Treasury continues to count expected fund receipts as part of the consolidated fund and to resist the idea that any receipts should be hypothecated to specific expenditures. At most, it will claim that regional policy expenditure is higher than it would have been in the absence of the funds but that the precise allocation is done within Britain. So when Commission decisions on structural-fund allocations shift moneys from one account heading to another, or between England and Scotland or Wales, which have their own account headings, this upsets the Treasury books. Further problems arise with local government capital spending, which is controlled by central government and is usually fully committed. Local governments receiving structural-fund grants may thus find that they lack the capital cover (the ability to fund capital spending through borrowing or capital receipts) for their part of the matching grant. These problems are less serious in Scotland, Wales, and Northern Ireland, where the respective Secretaries of State have discretion to shift spending among functional totals and capital spending between central and local government. In the English regions, it can make for great difficulty in spending the European money which has been granted, although the Department of the Environment has now reserved part of its capital cover for these cases. An ironic by-product of the British Government insistence on keeping control of the structural-fund process is the exclusion of the private sector from the exercise, despite the Conservatives' rhetoric of privatization and involvement of business leaders in urban regeneration and local training initiatives. On the other hand, the Department of the Environment has at times provided capital cover for privatized agencies such as the English water authorities in order to pull in its full expected ERDF allocation.

Additionality has provoked a serious conflict between the Commission and Britain, to the point at which in 1991 the Commissioner for Regional Policy blocked allocations under the RECHAR programme for the UK until the issue could be resolved.[16] Establishment of regional governments together with a reform of the British system of public accounting, as promised by the Labour and Liberal Democrat parties, might resolve many of these problems. Meanwhile, bureaucratic and political complications out of proportion to the amount of money involved are likely to continue.

Future Prospects

Demands for regional or national autonomy and European integration have both been managed in the United Kingdom without any significant constitutional change. Parliamentary sovereignty remains the basic constitutional principle, reaffirmed in the Labour Government's abortive proposals to establish Scottish and Welsh devolved governments in the 1970s. Regional policies and Community government have been seen as extensions of Westminster politics. This is likely to be untenable in the future. Demands for Scottish self-government are too strong for any future non-Conservative government to resist. Resistance on the part of the Conservatives will likely build up further resentment. Despite its rejection of devolution in the 1970s, Wales is likely to follow, with provision in due course for the English regions. The Anglo-Irish agreement of 1985 already represents an abdication by the UK Government of its monopoly jurisdiction in Northern Ireland. There have already been proposals for more direct links between a future Scottish Assembly and the Commission, including a more politicized office in Brussels and the direct receipt of moneys from the structural funds. More difficult constitutionally are proposals for representation of the future Scottish Government in the UK delegation to the Council of Ministers, as proposed by the Labour Party and the Scottish Constitutional Convention.[17] Unlike Germany, the UK lacks a tradition of consensus and compromise between parties and levels of government which could make a delegation representing opposed parties at two levels viable. Both

[16] P. McAleavey, 'The Politics of European Regional Development Policy: Additionality in the Scottish Coalfields', *Regional Politics and Policy*, 3/2 (1993).

[17] Scottish Constitutional Convention, *Towards Scotland's Parliament* (Edinburgh, 1989). Labour Party in Scotland and Socialist Group in the European Parliament, *Scotland's Future in Europe* (London, n.d.).

major parties have been forced to confront the larger measure of European integration posed by the 1992 initiative and proposals for economic and monetary and political union. Both have at various times been deeply divided on the merits of Europe and neither has yet really come to terms with a world in which power is dispersed and the Westminster model of two-party alternation is an ever-less adequate description of political reality.

More immediately, the United Kingdom faces the problem that its regional institutions are woefully underequipped for the competitive challenge of the internal market. Compared with German *Länder* or even the French, Italian, and Spanish regions, UK regions lack institutional identity, a capacity for autonomous decision-making and planning, and networks of social and economic interests. Scotland and Wales certainly have their own offices with Cabinet representation. Scotland, and to a lesser extent Wales, has its own civil society, with a strong sense of identity and an administrative network in close touch with social and economic actors. Yet both offices are highly dependent on Whitehall for policy leadership and lack financial and policy discretion in key economic matters. They lack the political weight which elected assemblies could provide and reflect the Westminster, not the local, political majority. The private sector, too, is dominated by branch plants, having had no dynamic indigenous business class since the demise of locally based capitalism after the First World War. This may help to attract further inward investment from Japanese and American firms seeking access to the single market, but it is also a source of vulnerability.[18] The peripheral English regions lack even the advantage of their own central departments. Across the British periphery, there are concerns about the inadequacy of infrastructure or public policies to prepare the regions for the competitive challenge.[19] It is little wonder that a 1990 Report for the Commission identifies British regions as ill endowed to face it.

[18] M. Smith, 'The Peripheral Interest: Scotland, 1992 and All That', in A. Brown and D. McCrone (eds.), *Scottish Government Yearbook, 1991* (Edinburgh: Unit for the Study of Government in Scotland).

[19] A. Scott, 'Scotland and the Internal Market', in Brown and McCrone (eds.), *Scottish Government Yearbook, 1991.*

MAP 5. Spain: autonomous communities.

5

Spanish Regions in the European Community

FRANCESC MORATA

Introduction

Two tendencies have characterized the major European democracies since the 1970s—regionalism and supranationalism. Spain presents the most striking example of this. Entry into the EC in 1986 coincided with the process of decentralization under way since the re-establishment of democracy in 1978. Together with the impact of the Single European Act, these changes are putting to the test the capacity to adapt of the new institutions, the parties, the public administration, and Spanish society in general.

Despite all manner of difficulties, including the attempted *coup* of 1981, Spain passed in little more than ten years from the highly centralized authoritarian, and internationally rather isolated, state of the 1970s to a political and territorial pluralism with ever-stronger links to Europe. Certainly, political stability and economic growth have so far favoured Spanish integration into the Community. Yet, internally, the ceding of sovereignty to the EC has resulted in an implicit transfer of power to the central government, at the expense of the regions. At the same time, these have assumed an essential role in the implementation of a large number of Community policies.

This chapter analyses the way in which the Spanish regions confront the Community decision-making network. First, the impact of integration on regional governments and the attitudes of political and social élites in important regions are examined. Then the pattern of relationships with State and Community authorities in

Translated by Michael Keating.

decision-making is analysed. Thirdly, the formulation and implementation of key policies is assessed. Finally, a number of examples
of transregional co-operation are cited. As a preliminary, though, it
is necessary to review the basic principles of decentralization in
Spain.

The Devolution Process

The Spanish Constitution establishes a hybrid system, neither unitary nor federal but based on the 'unity of the Spanish nation' and
the 'autonomy of the nationalities and regions which constitute it'.
The rather complex and ambiguous division of power has been a
source of constant political and judicial controversy, leading in
many cases to the Constitutional Court.

Statutes of autonomy fall into two main categories, special and
general. The former covers the three national minorities—the
Basque Country, Catalonia, and Galicia—together with Andalusia,
which have 'full' autonomy statutes ratified by referendum. The
general form, applying to eleven regions, is intended to be transitional, since after five years the regional authorities can request
full powers. In addition, the Spanish Parliament can transfer legislative and executive functions without a reform of the statute of
autonomy, as has happened in the cases of Valencia and the Canaries. Because of the constitutional recognition of its 'traditional
rights', Navarre also enjoys a full autonomy regime.

The Constitution establishes that each autonomous community
(region) shall have a legislative assembly elected by universal suffrage, a government headed by a president, and a high court of
justice. Administrative organization is decided by each autonomous community. The distribution of functions is based on two
lists. Under section 148.2, all autonomous communities can take
responsibility for: the organization of regional administration, local
administration, urban planning, housing, public works, environment, social services, culture, tourism, small business and crafts,
agriculture, fisheries, communications, and regional development.
Those with full autonomy can take on education and health. However, section 149.1 gives the central State the power to set basic
legislation or norms in a range of these fields, including agriculture,
banking and credit, health, education, economic planning, employ-

ment, transport, environment, mass media, and local government. In some areas, such as culture and research policy, both levels are fully competent, producing a lack of clarity and the invasion by one of the other's field.

Autonomous communities maintain their own administration to carry out their functions, but central government also retains field services to deal with supraregional or 'general interest' matters.[1] However, central control over regional administration is limited to those functions delegated from the centre.

Following the precepts of federalism, there are mechanisms for the representation of regional interests at the national level. Some members of the Senate are chosen by regional parliaments and the latter have the right to propose bills in the lower chamber of the national parliament.

Regions enjoy financial autonomy within limits. Their revenue is derived from shared and assigned taxes, limited regional taxes and an equalization fund. All the main revenue sources, however, are controlled by central government.

One of the main tasks of Spanish democracy was to respond to the historic demands of the national minorities,[2] but the rapid generalization of autonomy statutes[3] took political actors by surprise.[4] The absence of an explicit model of the State led to a resurrection of the historic centre–periphery tension during the transition. The heterogeneity of the country complicated matters. Along with the three historic nationalities there are historic regions such as Andalusia, Asturias, Aragon, Valencia, Navarre, and the Balearics, purely administrative regions such as Castile-La Mancha, and autonomous communities composed of single provinces such as Cantabria, Madrid, La Rioja, and Murcia. There are major disparities in population, area, and income and substantial cultural diversity. Forty per cent of the population of Spain speaks Catalan, Gallego, or Basque. The functioning of the system is

[1] S. Muñoz Machado, *Derecho Publico de las Comunidades Autónomas* (Madrid: Civitas, 1982), ii.
[2] M. Keating, 'Does Regional Government Work? The Experience of Italy, France and Spain', *Governance*, 2 (1988).
[3] J. M. Valles and M. Cuchillo, 'Decentralization in Spain', *European Journal of Political Research*, 16 (1988).
[4] J. M. Maravall and J. Santamaria, 'Transición política y consolidación de la democracia en España', in J. F. Tezanos, R. Cotarelo, and D. de Blas (eds.), *La transición democrática española* (Madrid: Ed. Sistema, 1989). V. Perez Diaz, *El retorno de la Sociedad Civil* (Madrid: Instituto de Estudios Económicos, 1987).

further affected by institutional and political conflict, financial arguments, and the inadequate organization of the central administration.

Since 1982 an overall parliamentary majority has freed the socialist party PSOE from the need to negotiate laws defining the powers of central institutions, which has had the effect of limiting the powers of the regions, though the regions have been able to appeal to the Constitutional Court. At the same time, central government has not hesitated to oppose regional laws and administrative arrangements where these were considered to encroach on its competences. By 1989, these controversies had generated more than 800 legal cases.[5] The decisions of the Constitutional Court, in which the regions are not represented, have tended to favour central power. Moreover, the 1985 Local Government Act, which established the province as the second level of local administration, allows central government to transfer grants and other resources to provincial and local councils, bypassing the regions.

Despite appearances, the Spanish Constitution does not provide for the effective integration of regional concerns in the decision-making process. The Senate is mainly elected on a majority basis at the provincial level, where national parties dominate. Only 20 per cent of its members are elected from the regional parliaments. This weakens institutional cohesion. The role of sectoral conferences, of which more than thirty have been established since 1983, is in no way comparable to that of their German counterparts, as they serve mainly to exchange information. Political negotiation with central government is normally bilateral, making global agreement difficult. Nor is there any effective mechanism for horizontal co-ordination among the regions to enable them to formulate a common position or exchange ideas and points of view. Political domination of the devolution process has encouraged short-term political calculation at the expense of rationality and efficiency. The result is fragmentation, disparity of functions, an absence of a clear model of public administration, and consequently conflict.

Until 1991, there were two styles of intergovernmental bargaining. The first, of partisan inspiration, was found in the ten regions under socialist control. Policy-making here was based fundamentally on internal party negotiation and conflicts arose from power

[5] E. Aja (ed.), *Informe pi i sunyer sobre las autonomías* (Barcelona: Civitas, 1990).

struggles, not institutional disagreements. The second style was found in those autonomous communities governed by regionalist or nationalist forces, or by right-wing parties. Here behaviour was based on political antagonism and oscillated between the constitutional management of conflict and hard bargaining until agreement was reached. One-sided attitudes tended to prevail over the search for common values and interests which might promote consensus.

Except for the Basque Country and Navarre, the Constitution established a provisional financing system for the autonomous communities, based on the cost of central services transferred, assigned taxes, and the Inter-territorial Compensation Fund. The first involved a very complex method of calculation and the establishment of seventeen bilateral commissions. Central government was able to decide on the total transfer according to its own budget priorities, while regions avoided creating their own taxes for fear of unpopularity. The Compensation Fund failed in its double function of reducing territorial disparities and providing investment funds for all regions. So the regions simply ran into debt, amounting to 15 per cent of their total expenditure in 1990. A second financial arrangement, effective from 1987 to 1991, proved equally unsuccessful, though regions by that time accounted for nearly a quarter of public expenditure and a third of public investment.

Although the regions are supposed to be the main executors of public services, a real administrative reform has yet to take place. With not all regions enjoying the same competences, ministries have to retain headquarters functions affecting only some regions. The incomplete transfer of functions also allows the centre to retain an executive capacity in areas which should be devolved. The reluctance of central staff to be transferred has led some regions to recruit from local government or the private sector, often on a partisan basis.

The electoral losses suffered by PSOE in the 1989 general elections and the challenge of Europe have encouraged a dialogue with the nationalist forces. This bore fruit in the third financial accord, to run from 1992 until 1996. Besides providing a larger participation by the regions in State revenues, this establishes for the first time a fiscal co-responsibility, with the assignment to the region of 15 per cent of the income tax collected in each territory. There is also an agreement on budgetary collaboration, with a view to co-ordinating debt policies in accordance with the demands of European monetary union. The Government has undertaken to increase its support for the poorest regions, by channelling at least 35 per cent of new State investment through the Co-operation Fund. At the same time, agreement has been reached in principle on the transfer of functions to the regions with the lesser degree of autonomy, which will entail further financial transfer. Most parties also share the desire to broaden the basis of territorial representation in the Senate, without a full constitutional reform. This would involve a conference, attached to the Senate, of the presidents of the central government and the regions. At the same time, the functions of the Autonomy Commission, in which the four official languages can be used, would be reinforced.

The Regional Impact of the European Community

Spanish participation in the European Community has had important consequences for the regions. Their institutional position has been weakened by the transfer of internal competences to the Community without an affective agreement on co-operation in Community matters with the central government. Regions have also had to introduce changes in their political-administrative structures in order to implement European policies and manage European funds.

As in other decentralized member states,[6] in Spain the transfer of sovereignty has had negative effects on the constitutional position of the regions since they do not participate directly in Community decision-making. This affects many areas, especially after the coming into effect of the Single European Act: finance, agriculture and fisheries, industry, economic and spatial planning, transport, research, the environment, and consumer affairs.

According to the internal distribution of functions, the regions ought to implement Community policies within their own areas of

---

[6] H. H. Schwan, *Die Deutscher Bundesländer im Entscheidungs-system der Europ ischen Gemeinschaften* (Berlin: Duncker und Humblot, 1982). J. L. Veerweyen, *Les Autorités régionales dans le processus d' élaboration des politiques communautaires* (Maastricht: Institut Européen d' Administration Publique, 1985). F. Merloni 'Italian Regions in the EC', in M. Keating and B. Jones (eds.), *Regions in the European Community* (Oxford: Clarendon Press, 1985). F. Morata, *Autonomía regional i integración Europea* (Barcelona: Institut d'Estudis Autonomics, 1987).

competence. The effect of a directive would then be the displacement of the central State by the Community, thus allowing the region directly to implement the European rule.[7] Yet, despite the powers of central government to ensure that regions discharge their duties, there is no constitutional guarantee that European directives will be executed within the stipulated time-period. There has been one major conflict on this matter when in 1989 the Canaries Government initially refused to implement the tariff reduction provided for in the adhesion treaty. While this issue was resolved through political negotiation, conflicts still arise in areas where both levels of government consider themselves competent.

The integration of sub-central institutions into the Community decision-making process remains a problem in several countries. Since the treaties are silent on the matter, it has to be resolved within the member states. Comparative analysis shows that in any case the internal balance of power depends more on political negotiation and intergovernmental co-operation than on constitutional interpretation.[8] In 1986, faced with pressure from regions, the Spanish Government proposed an 'Agreement for Co-operation in Community Matters'. Negotiations continued until 1988, then came to a standstill.

The proposal was based on the procedure used in West Germany from 1980 to 1986.[9] It provided for the transfer of information affecting regional matters. Regions for their part would inform central government of their policy preferences with a view to their incorporation in the Spanish position, provided that they were compatible with the 'general interests of the State and the process of integration'. The autonomous communities would co-ordinate their own positions and co-operate with the centre through a regional committee. The committee could also propose the designation of an 'observer' and 'extra observer' as members of the Spanish Permanent Representation in Brussels. With this status, both observers could attend meetings of EC committees and working groups, 'expressing opinions coinciding with those of the official delegation'.

[7] E. Garcia de Enterria *et al.*, 'Spanish Report', in J. Schwarze *et al.* (eds.), *The 1992 Challenge at National Level* (Baden Baden: Nomos, 1990).

[8] Morata, *Autonomía regional i integración Europea*.

[9] W. Schumann and H. Hanneleck, 'Die Beteiligung der Länder an der EG Politik der Bundes: Problem und alternativen', *z.f. Parlamentsfragen* (1983).

The technical shortcomings of the proposal were rather obvious. What kind of information should be sent and how could it be evaluated? How could co-ordination and decision-making be organized among seventeen actors with unequal competences? To what extent would regional opinions be taken into account? The main problem, however, is that Catalonia and the Basque Country, the two most powerful regions, wanted their own representative to have more autonomy with respect to the official delegation. The central government's refusal to accept this has blocked any agreement.

All that has been achieved is acceptance of some basic principles and a few practical arrangements. There is a mutual compromise to accept the internal distribution of functions and the Constitution in matters relating to the EC. At a practical level, both sides have agreed to establish a telematic database linked to the Secretary of State for the European Communities, providing information for regional governments; and there is a co-ordination agreement on breaches of Community law.

Regional Attitudes to the EC

In 1989 a survey was carried out among regional élites in Andalusia, Catalonia, Galicia, and Valencia.[10] Interviewees comprised 200 politicians and 100 regional observers drawn from chambers of commerce, trade unions, employers' organizations, professional bodies, cultural and environmental associations, and local government organizations. Respondents were questioned about four matters: the level of adaptation of the socio-economic structure; the foreseen impact of 1992; the opportunities for the development of new Community functions and instruments; and the introduction of new forms of transregional co-operation.[11]

On the first item, there is clear agreement, especially among the interest groups, in emphasizing the low level of adaptation of regional economic structures to the needs of 1992. Opinions on infrastructure, health and social services, the functioning of urban areas,

---

[10] F. Morata, *Spanish Regions and the 1993 Community Challenge*, Working Paper (Barcelona: Institut de Ciències Polítiques i Socials, 1991).
[11] The survey is reported in more detail in F. Morata, 'Spain: Regions and the European Community', *Regional Politics and Policy*, 2/1 and 2 (1992).

technological innovation, and labour-force skills are rather negative in all regions. Catalonia represents the highest level of economic adaptation, at least in some key sectors. Significantly, this is
the only region which registers positive responses on levels of
associationalism, which may explain the higher levels of administrative and economic performance found there.[12]

Both regional observers and political élites have a clear idea as to
the impact of 1992 on their regions. They see it as very positive in
all matters affecting economic development. Increased unemployment is not foreseen, though observers in Catalonia, Andalusia,
and Galicia believe that production costs will increase. The politicians think that 1992 will lead to the modernization of regional
administration, though all the observers disagree. There is general
agreement on the likelihood of institutional renewal, the adoption
of new environmental standards, and the improvement of social
services, while no loss of regional identity is expected. Both sets of
respondents, however, fear the confusion of functions between the
different levels of administration or a slowing of decision-making.
As expected, Andalusian and Galician observers are more worried
about the deterioration of the position of underdeveloped areas.

There is almost unanimous agreement on the extension of Community functions in all areas, particularly in financing projects for
less developed areas, promotion of technological innovation, and
evaluation of regional investment projects. Observers and politicians agree that the financing for a European defence policy
should remain the same and that there should be a high level of
immigration control for non-EC countries. There is also support
for new Community instruments, including a Euro-environmental
agency, a European communications body, a European central
bank, agencies or consortia for regional co-operation, a Community Administrative Court, and a European Conference of
regional presidents, as well as regional offices in Brussels.

Regions are ready to support common initiatives and horizontal
projects. There is general agreement on the need to protect the
environment and to formulate and implement development
projects; plans for applied research; integrated programmes for
border regions; and policies to improve interregional communications. The regions express a clear wish to build exchange pro-

---

[12] R. D. Putnam, R. Leonardi, and R. Nanetti, 'Institutional Performance and
Political Culture: Some Puzzles about the Power of the Past', *Governance*, 3 (1988).

grammes and activities, promote products and services or joint ventures, such as improving air services and training civil servants. Regional lobbying in Brussels is generally welcomed.

So it can be said that the acceleration of European integration is generating positive expectations rather than reservations among regional élites. The expansion of Community competences is seen in a positive light, especially where it takes the form of stronger regional development policies. As we shall see, the erosion of frontiers is seen in two ways: as an opportunity to play a more active role in the Community and as an incentive to establish closer links with other European regions.

The attitude of the Catalan and Basque nationalists is clear in this respect. In both cases, they have opted for a 'realist' policy of playing the European card for all it is worth, outflanking the central authorities. From this perspective, the regions do not constitute a threat to existing states, but it is necessary for European integration to be built on the basis of historic identities if it is to have a sound foundation. In a framework ever-more conditioned by European decisions, the states will lose control of the large macroeconomic decisions necessary to guarantee Community competitiveness. Their calculation is that, in the long term, the process of political and economic union will lead to a federal system, with a consequent weakening of the State to the benefit of European and regional levels. However, the implicit support within Spain for European federalism does not translate into domestic politics, where there is a rejection of any notion of equality for the other regions. The nationalist leaders even insist that Community regional aid should not be directed only at poor regions, lest this cause disparities in the more developed regions.

Region–Community Links

In spite of the formal opposition of the central authorities, jealous of their competences, the Spanish regions have established regular, informal contacts with Community institutions. Indeed, their direct involvement in the application and management of European policies makes it inevitable that they should have contact with Commission officials interested, for their part, in following regional policies on the ground. The six regional offices established in

Brussels allow constant contacts with the main decision-making centres as well as channelling the demands of interest groups. In addition, several regional governments participate actively in the Assembly of European Regions (ARE) and the Consultative Council of Regional and Local Authorities.

Most regional administrations see the integration of interest groups into this effort, through information and consultation, as a priority. In Catalonia, the Patronat Català, a public consortium established in 1982, organizes, promotes, and co-ordinates activities linked to the Community and other European organizations. Chaired by the president of the regional government, the Patronat brings together representatives of Catalan public and private universities, savings banks, chambers of commerce, local government associations, and the municipality of Barcelona. Its council is organized in three sections: the academic; the parliamentarian; and the socio-economic, including business organizations, professional associations, and unions, as well as Catalan representatives of Community lobbies, and officials in Brussels. The main activities of the Patronat are the preparation of courses and seminars about the EC specially addressed to economic and professional audiences; the diffusion of Community research and development programmes; and a consulting service called Europa-93 to provide information about the internal market. In 1986 the organization opened a Brussels Office which supplies information and contacts with the Commission and other Community institutions. Nearly half the requests for information are from economic, social, and professional organizations.

The governments of the Basque Country, the Canaries, Galicia, Murcia, Andalusia, and Valencia have also set up Offices in Brussels, with the legal status of limited trade companies. Initially the Basque Office was established by a Basque Government decree proposing a Cabinet for European Community affairs which, among other functions, would 'co-ordinate relations between Basque public institutions on the one hand and Community bodies and the Council of Europe on the other, and manage and co-ordinate relations with European institutions in general from an office in Brussels'. This provoked the central government to lodge a 'conflict of competences' case, as a result of which the Basque Government decided merely to create a public company, Interbask, with the aim of 'ensuring direct and immediate observation of the activities of the EC, in so far as they affect matters and economic sectors of great importance to the Basque country'. Through its proximity to Community institutions, the company carries out consultancy work for public and private organizations, spreads awareness of European issues, and organizes, promotes, and co-ordinates Basque activities relating to the Community.

Also worth noting is the participation in ARE—linked to the Consultative Council of Regional and Local Authorities—in which since 1988 Spain, in the persons of the presidents of Catalonia and Andalusia, holds two of the nine vice-presidencies. The role of the president of Andalusia has been particularly important since, as the member responsible for relations both with the Community and with the Council of Europe, he has actively participated in the elaboration of a draft resolution of the assembly of the ARE on the institutional participation of the regional level in the decision-making process of the Community,[13] which in turn served as the basis of the proposal of the Consultative Council on the institution of an organ of regional representation in the new treaty on political union.[14]

During the negotiations, the Spanish Government adopted a more cautious attitude than its German counterpart, which was more sensitive to pressures from the *Länder*, and ended up supporting the establishment of a regional committee linked to the Council of Ministers with consultative functions similar to the Economic and Social Committee. It also urged respect for the principle of subsidiarity in the formulation and execution of Community policies. Nevertheless, the Spanish Government was flatly opposed to the Dutch draft treaty giving official status to the participation of regional representatives in the Council meetings. Yet representatives of the German *Länder* and Belgian communities already participate in Council meetings relating to cultural affairs.

Policy-Making and Implementation

Between 1986 and 1988, before the reform of the structural funds, the regions played a limited role in the European Social Fund

[13] Asemblea de las Regiones de Europa, *Proyecto de resolución de la ARE sobre participación institucional del nivel regional al proceso decisional de la Comunidad Europea* (Rome, 6 Sept. 1990).

[14] Conseil Consultatif des Collectivités Régionales et Locales, 'Résolution relative aux questions institutionnelles', *Europe*, no. 5368 NS (12–13 Nov. 1990).

(ESF) and a rather more important one in the Agricultural Guidance Fund (FEOGA). As for the European Regional Development Fund (ERDF), the regions have been able to manage their own projects only since 1988.

Adhesion to the Community and, especially, the reform of the structural funds, encouraged a revival of regional development policies in Spain. Even before 1986, there had been some rationalization of regional incentives, to take account of the requirements for Community entry and of the decentralization of the State. The real change, however, came in the late 1980s, facilitated by the resolution of the basic disequilibria of the Spanish economy, and stimulated by the increased role of sub-central authorities in the management of spending and the implications of the reform of the Community regional policy.

In Spain, regional disparities are a fundamental obstacle to social and economic cohesion. In 1987, Spanish GDP per capita was 69.7 per cent of the average for the four large member states. Seven autonomous communities figure among the twenty-five most underdeveloped of Europe's 166 regions and the best situated—the Balearic Islands—occupies seventy-fifth position. Not only are all the regions below the Community average, but there are also acute internal imbalances: between the industrialized north and the agricultural south; and between the more accessible and populated east and the west, which has a weaker infrastructure and is removed from the great axes of economic development. So almost the whole national territory is included in one of the objectives of the structural funds. Nine regions qualify under objective 1 and seven under objective 2, representing 80.2 per cent of the population and 85.1 per cent of the land-area of the country.

Since the introduction of the new Community regulation, preparation and supervision of the regional programmes has come under the Public Investment Committee, an informal co-ordinating body of the central government and concerned regions. Regions have been able to intervene in the policy-formulation stage but have had no say in the final decisions. Although Community regulations provide for the presentation of specific plans for the regions included in objectives 1, 2, and 5(B), the Spanish Government has opted for the presentation of three global plans. Despite pressure from Commission officials, the Ministry of Economics has persisted with this so that the Spanish Community Support Frameworks only regionalize that part of ERDF expenditure which falls to the autonomous communities.[15] This global approach gives central government more discretion in the spatial allocation of its share of the resources.

During the formulation of the Community Support Frameworks, the Commission made clear its interest in negotiating directly with the regions. The central administration rejected any attempt at negotiation without its presence and initially opposed the idea of the regions participating at all.[16] Eventually, the negotiations proceeded with the three parties and for the first time regional representatives were able to appreciate the complexity of the process, especially in relation to the definition of the criteria for allocating resources to operational programmes.

There were difficult moments, especially over the determination of Spain's share of objective 1 resources. Spain will receive through its Community Support Frameworks 9,779 million ECUs, equivalent to 27 per cent of all spending directly assigned to member states and 6.4 percentage points higher than that of the next-placed country, Italy. In proportion to population, however, Spain occupies only sixth place. Matching national expenditure is 6,728 million ECUs for the public sector and 1,901 million ECUs for the private sector.

Under objective 2, Spain, with the largest affected population, is to receive 679 million ECUs. Matching national finance is 1,085,260 million ECUs from the public sector and 92.72 million from the private sector. Objective 5(B) regions received just 225 million ECUs. The distribution of resources under the structural funds presented further problems since the Commission, as a result of conflicts among the various directorates-general, was unable to go beyond global totals. In the case of Spain, the various ministries involved had to resolve this.

The internal distribution of funds among the levels of government has generated jealousies and tensions. In particular, the assignment of funds to be managed by central government directly as well as those passed on to local government was decided without any participation by the regions. Objective 1 regions manage 33.8

[15] Comisión de las Comunidades Euopeas, *Marco de apoyo comunitario 1989–1993: España*, Objetivo num. 1 and Objetivo no. 2, Serie Documentos (Luxembourg: Office des Publications des Communautés Européennes, 1990).

[16] L. Lazaro, 'La reforma de los fondos estructurales y los marcos de apoyo comunitarios', *Hacienda Pública Española, Boletín mensual*, 9 (1990).

per cent of the Spanish ERDF allocation. Seven per cent goes to local governments. The remaining 59.8 per cent goes to central government, including the 8 per cent destined for public enterprises. Under objective 2, regions manage 40 per cent of funds, local governments 9.27 per cent, and the central authorities 50.73 per cent. The differences reflect the distribution of competences among the levels of government.

The distribution of ERDF by development priorities favoured infrastructure and in particular communications. Regions and central government agreed that the number of priorities in objective 1 was excessive, with the result that the figure for co-financing by ERDF is too low, especially for the regions. This could present management problems in the future.

Environment Policy

The environment is a shared responsibility of central government and the autonomous communities. According to the Constitution, central government is responsible for the basic legislation while the regions develop this, stipulate additional norms, and manage environmental protection. The regions also have related responsibilities in urban and regional planning, mountains, water, housing, public works, and natural habitats. Municipalities also have important responsibilities, notably in environmental quality and public health.

Decentralization has generated considerable complexity in environmental management. At the central level, a Secretary of State in the Ministry of Public Works is responsible for major projects of surveillance and control, planning and restoration, and support for regional efforts, but has few financial or technical resources and faces constant difficulties over co-ordination with other departments concerned. In some official spheres the idea still prevails that environmental protection is a drag on economic growth.

Within the autonomous communities there are a variety of organizational and managerial arrangements. Some, such as Catalonia, the Basque Country, and Madrid, have established specific ministries but in other cases responsibility is fragmented among several departments. In recent years, regional environmental agencies have been created but these frequently lack means to

act or real influence. Nor are there mechanisms for horizontal co-
ordination among regions to address common problems. The only
forum available is the irregular sectoral conference convened by
central government. This lacks decision-making powers, though
one of its roles is to inform the regions of Community norms.

All this explains the difficulty in implementing Community environmental policy in Spain. Despite the efforts of recent years at
both central and local level to transpose more than a hundred
Community directives, serious doubts remain about their effective
application, as can be seen from the numerous complaints made to
the Commission, and the warnings given to Spanish administrative
bodies, some of which have reached the European Court of Justice.
To cite only a few examples, the regional authorities, especially
Catalonia, Valencia, and the Basque Country, do not respect
the quality standards for bathing-water.[17] The situation of many
natural areas is clearly deficient if not catastrophic, especially
in Cantabria, Catalonia, Castile-La Mancha, the Canaries, and
Andalusia.[18] The majority of dangerous waste generated by industry is abandoned without treatment, as is two-thirds of urban waste.
In Catalonia, the high level of pollution in some rivers generated a
notification by the Commission.[19] The most industrialized regions
have serious difficulties in framing or implementing plans to eliminate toxic waste. Only 5 per cent of Spanish firms have informed
the authorities of the wastes which they produce.[20] The financial
cost to Spanish industry of implementing the environmental policy
is estimated at more than 10 billion ECUs. The cohesion fund
linked to infrastructure and environmental policies is therefore the
greatest Spanish achievement at Maastricht.

Transregional Co-operation in Preparation for 1993

In spite of the formal limitations of the Constitution, the autonomous communities have since their creation forged a dense
network of international relations. These include not only
participation in international organizations of regions but also bilateral or multilateral co-operation agreements, and contacts in

---

[17] *El País*, 5 Jan. 1990.   [18] Ibid., 9 June 1990.
[19] Ibid., 3 Dec. 1990.   [20] Ibid., 8 May 1990.

economic, cultural, and tourist matters. Official visits abroad, even with the blessing of the central authorities, are more and more frequent. The Catalan Government is the one which has been most active internationally, concentrating on the preparation for the single market. Two projects are especially worthy of mention, the 'Four Motors of Europe' and the Euro-region project involving Catalonia, Languedoc-Roussillon, and Midi-Pyrénées. The Four Motors was the result of an agreement signed in 1988 between Catalonia, Baden-Württemberg, Rhône-Alpes, and Lombardy and covers economic co-operation, exchange of information, technology transfer, promotion of research and design, professional training, social assistance, youth, co-operation between cities, environment, and culture. Under this agreement, the four regions can jointly use the information and business development offices which they retain abroad. The creation of this lobby of the most advanced regions stems from a recognition that, because of the diversity of their political and institutional memberships, the Assembly of European Regions and other sectoral organizations are not adequate to exercise pressure on the Community. With their combined power, the four regions are attempting to play a leading role in the construction of Europe as well as seeking incentives and aids to help them compete with countries such as Japan, the United States, and Canada.

In February 1989, the presidents of Catalonia, Languedoc-Roussillon, and Midi-Pyrénées decided on the creation of a transpyrenean Euro-region as the first stage in the creation of a macro-region of the western Mediterranean. In their joint declaration, the three regional governments undertook to use the technical resources of the three regions for combined actions in communications and telecommunications infrastructure; professional training, research, and technology transfer; culture, sport, and tourism. Apart from political and administrative co-operation and economic exchange, the Euro-region has the objective of increasing the importance of the Mediterranean fringe within the Community. It is certainly too early to evaluate the efficacy of this type of co-operation, either in its practical functioning or in its capacity for pressure on the Community. In any event, we are witnessing a new phenomenon, with implications at local level—another reflection of the possibilities opened by the single market.

Conclusion

Regional devolution and EC entry are two key aspects of Spanish institutional and political life in the 1980s. The former has resulted in the rapid construction of seventeen autonomous governments, initially with varied competences and financial resources but progressively expanding through the transfer of essential services and the implementation of their own policies or policies shared with central and local governments. The devolution process has been reinforced by the emergence of new political élites, often with strong regionalist or nationalist sentiments, and the construction of distinct party systems in Catalonia, the Basque Country, and Galicia. The establishment of clientelistic networks between the new administrations and interests operating at this level has doubtless also contributed to the consolidation of the regional system.

However, the ambiguities of the Constitution and political attitudes have fed the traditional centre–periphery conflicts. While the regions with the largest competences accuse the centre of frustrating the development of their autonomy, the latter reproaches the regions for their lack of solidarity. The remaining regions, for their part, demand the reform of their statutes to gain the same powers as larger regions. These demands coincide with the revision of the system of regional financing and the attempt to revitalize the Senate as a chamber of territorial representation.

Spanish behaviour in the Community reflects the inadequacies of domestic policy-making. Evidence of this is the fact that, in the face of the challenges of the single market and European union, the political actors have proved incapable of establishing a co-operation procedure to facilitate the framing and internal implementation of Community policies. Only in the access to information and in the elaboration of the new Community regional programmes has there been a certain degree of collaboration, in spite of the reluctance of the central authorities to countenance a dialogue between the autonomous governments and the Commission.

The integration process has also had the effect of making regional administrations part of the Community administration. All have adapted their political-administrative organization to the needs of the Community. They have also sought, through this and the establishment of Offices in Brussels, to dynamize interest groups and channel their demands. The single market has generated joint initiatives with other European regions, opening new perspectives for transregional co-operation.

Politicians and representatives of regional lobbies, while considering the socio-economic infrastructures of their respective regions inadequate, show a favourable attitude to the impact of 1993 and the increase in Community functions, especially where these involve new policies for regional development. They see devolution and regional integration not as two contradictory processes but as complementary and increasingly interdependent.

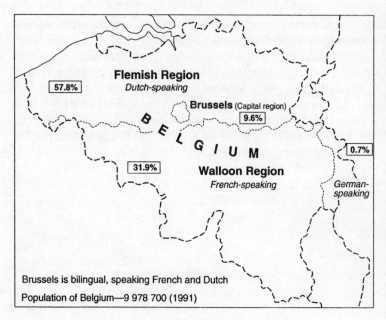

Flemish Region
Dutch-speaking
57.8%

Brussels (Capital region)
9.6%

B E L G I U M

0.7%

31.9%

Walloon Region
French-speaking

German-speaking

Brussels is bilingual, speaking French and Dutch

Population of Belgium—9 978 700 (1991)

MAP 6. Belgium: regions.

6

Belgian Federalism and the European Community

LIESBET HOOGHE

Introduction

Since the federalization of 1989 the six Belgian regions and communities have become powerful actors in domestic politics and policy-making. They have also acquired significant autonomy in their dealings with the European Community. This chapter describes the formal arrangements between governments at federal and regional/community level and the EC, and their interplay. The result is a highly complex, adaptive, but at the same time highly unstable system of intergovernmental relations. It is intermeshed with the changes in the social, economic, and cultural environment, the evolving nature of the EC, domestic politics, and the internal dynamics of the intergovernmental system. This mixture of complexity and receptivity on the one hand and instability on the other hand makes it difficult to predict future developments. The interplay has generated multiple and temporary equilibria between regions/communities, federal government, and the EC. It has multiple equilibria, because nearly each involvement of the EC with regional affairs has led to a special arrangement. The equilibria tend to hold only for a temporary period, because they are vulnerable to contradictory external pressures. The cause is the absence of an agreed set of rules or procedures between the domestic political actors.

The structure of political opportunities changed profoundly after the constitutional revisions of May 1993. The reform is an attempt to give a final definition to the transformation of the unitary state of 1970 into 'a federal state, composed of Communities and Regions' (new Article 1 of the Constitution). It deals with the outstanding issues of previous rounds of constitutional reforms in a comprehensive way. Crucial to the new construction are the arrangements on the external relations of regions and communities, which apply also to dealings with the European Community. Regions and communities are autonomous to regulate international co-operation within the scope of their competences, which include the power to participate directly in the European institutions and to conclude treaties. An elaborate machinery for co-ordination ensures the coherence with Belgian foreign policy.

The whole institutional framework becomes operational after the next general elections; that is, if the *ad hoc* political coalition for constitutional reform is able to complete its heavy programme of implementing legislation. However, it seems premature to expect soon simpler and more stable intergovernmental relations in the area of EC policy-making. Domestic and EC actors have weak incentives to give up the relative comfort of short-term and often unilaterally malleable commitments for the constraints of more durable arrangements. The Flemish community and the Walloon region especially have proved to be viable administrations, capable of organizing society and economy as effectively as the Belgian state. They could probably take care of their external relations as efficaciously as the Belgian federal State, which can command only slightly more resources within the context of the European Community. In addition, these disparate domestic practices tend to fit in well with the fragmented and volatile nature of EC policy-making.

This chapter starts out with the main socio-economic, cultural, and political factors which led the Belgian State in 1988–9 to adopt the model of jurisdictional federalism. It then considers the effects of a stronger European Community on regional and community policy-making in this constitutional framework. Next, it analyses the interplay of intergovernmental relations, from the domestic to the European level, to explain the contradictions between the apparently clear constitutional rules and the complex reality. The final sections examine the effects of EC policy on regions and communities. They look first at the impact of EC regional policy on regional/community administration, and then ask whether EC policy in general is likely to strengthen 'Eurosceptic' or 'Europhoric' tendencies in official and extra-institutional regionalism.

Trends in Society and Politics

The Belgian experience is part of a general rise of regionalism and regional government in most west European welfare societies.[1] Government has moved away from traditional models of the State, with their single centre of command, uniform channels of authority, and democratic accountability through parliamentary control. Belgium is distinctive in the degree and type of institutionalization of regionalism. Several general trends may be distinguished, whose interplay in the Belgian environment has produced a highly complex and unstable political process.[2]

A first trend concerns the policy tasks of the State. Government has grown. Total public expenditure in Belgium rose from 30.3 per cent of GDP in 1960 to 54.3 in 1980 and 51.2 per cent in 1991. At the same time, government has been faced with conflicting demands due to functional and spatial differences in socio-economic development.

Multiculturalism and interregional shifts of power against the background of nationalist conflict have caused additional strains. The growing role of government has made ethnocultural divergences more politically salient. The Flemish movement has long pressed for strict regulations on language practices.[3] The resulting language policy has helped to shape distinctive communal societies: a Flemish community of Dutch-speakers in Flanders and Brussels; a French community of francophones in Wallonia and in Brussels; and a small German-speaking community in the east of the country. Each was eager to acquire control over new government responsibilities in culture, education, and public welfare.

The economic centre of gravity shifted in the post-war period from the south to the north. Flanders overtook Wallonia in terms of Gross Regional Product per capita between 1963 and 1966 (depending on the definition of GRP). In 1963, the Flemish share in

---

[1] J. J. Hesse and A. Benz, *Die Modernisierung der Staatsorganisation. Institutionspolitik im internationalen Vergleich: USA, Gro britannien, Frankreich, Bundesrepublik Deutschland* (Baden-Baden: Nomos, 1990).

[2] See e.g. L. Hooghe, *A Leap in the Dark: Nationalist Conflict and Federal Reform in Belgium* Cornell Studies in International Affairs, Western Societies Papers N.27 (Ithaca, NY, 1991).

[3] K. D. McRae, *Conflict and Compromise in Multilingual Societies: Belgium* (Waterloo: Wilfrid Laurier University Press, 1986).

Gross Domestic Product was 49.8 per cent, while Wallonia had 31.3 per cent and Brussels 18.9 per cent. By 1988 Flanders had climbed to 58.7, Wallonia was down to 26.3, and Brussels to 15.0 per cent.[4] The economic shift was reinforced by demography as Flanders' share in the total population rose from 53.5 per cent in 1947 to 57.8 per cent in 1991.[5]

These differences gained political significance when the Government started to play a more active role in industrial policy and regional development. Wallonia has in general been more supportive of State intervention than Flanders or Brussels. But many Walloons feared that in a unitary state the restructuring of their economy would be carried out on terms dictated by Flanders (supported by Brussels), or not at all. They were, therefore, interested in economic autonomy.

Thus, government expansion helped to shape the two nationalisms. The older one centred on cultural differences and was aimed at group autonomy, whilst the other drew upon socio-economic diversity and demanded regional autonomy. In the context of the modern State, in which functions are carried out on a territorial basis, they have converged in demands for territorial autonomy, within more or less well-defined boundaries.

A second trend is that decentralized governmental actors have gained confidence. Their relations with the central authorities are now less hierarchical, less technical, and more political. The politics of policy-making has changed as open conflict has become more common.

Politics in Belgium has been deeply affected. Consociationalism failed to deal effectively with mounting nationalist pressures, partly because the traditional package-dealing became too costly. This led to a gradual 'de-Belgification' of political actors and decision-making, and a subsequent realignment of political interaction at the community and regional levels. Flemish and French-speaking actors spoke increasingly for their community or region in the first place, and began systematically to observe a Flemish–French or regional balance in national politics. A crucial step in realignment was made in 1968, when the largest political party split along linguistic lines. The other parties followed suit. Similarly, most cultural, social, and economic organizations from trade unions to

---

[4] NIS, *Statistische Studien* (Brussels: Nationaal Instituut voor de Statistiek, 1991).
[5] NIS, *Volkstelling 1947* (Brussels: NIS); *Belgisch Staatsblad*, 15 Oct. 1991 (figures for 1991 census. Calculations for the post-1963 boundaries).

employers' organizations or from the Catholic school system to the Catholic or socialist health services reorganized on linguistic or regional lines. So patterns of political interaction altered in two different ways, through balancing regional/community interests at the national level, or through the development of regional/community networks against the centre. These changes in political practice and institutions paved the way for constitutional reform. Belgium changed from a unitary state to a federal state, in all but name, between 1970 and 1989. The constitutional revisions of May 1993 put in place the full range of institutions and mechanisms typical for a modern federal state: direct election of subnational Councils, reform of the Senate, redrawing of electoral districts; rearrangement of the competences; redefinition of fiscal federalism (changes in financing mechanism and more fiscal autonomy); constitutional autonomy for each level over its own working rules; international competences and treaty power; co-ordination machinery and conflict resolution.

The input of regional interests in the current political system is extremely complex. They are recognized partly in regionalized institutions, partly in national/federal institutions. The Belgian federation has six constituent units: the Flemish-, French-, and German-speaking communities and the Flemish, Walloon, and Brussels capital regions. The communities are a response to the cultural concerns of the Flemish movement. The organizing principle is group rights for the three recognized language groups. Regional autonomy is a response to economic concerns, which have been particularly strong in Wallonia. Institutional organization rests on the principle of territoriality.

Stabilization, redistribution, and some allocation functions have remained federal. The communities have responsibility for culture, language policy, education (three-quarters of the community budget), health, and welfare, and international co-operation in these areas. Regional competences are territorially bound. They consist of regional economic development, including employment programmes and industrial restructuring; environment; nature conservation; land-use planning and urban renewal; water resources and sewage; aspects of energy policy; road building; waterways; regional airports; and public local transport, agriculture, and external trade.

The communities set the normative framework for culture and, with some exceptions, education autonomously. The greater portion of the framework outside these two domains remains federal, where it is not becoming European. The stabilization functions of budgetary, fiscal, and monetary policy will largely shift to the EC level under EMU. The net effect of this division of labour is that in 1992, 34 per cent of the overall government budget was spent by regions and communities, 29 per cent by the federal authorities, and 4.4 per cent was transferred to the European Community. The remaining 32.6 per cent was absorbed by interest payments on the public debt.

The territorial boundaries of communities and regions to a large extent coincide. The Flemish community speaks for Dutch and non-Dutch speakers alike in the Flemish region. It also speaks for Dutch-speakers in the Brussels capital region. We lack accurate figures for these since questions on language usage were banned from population censuses in 1961. Alternative measurements are often educated guesses or are contested by one side or other. Based on the proportion of the vote for Flemish parties in the first direct elections for the Brussels capital regional council in 1989, there are 15.3 per cent Flemish-speakers there, comprising less than 2.5 per cent of the total Flemish community. Hence, on the Flemish side, community and region are nearly identical and their governmental institutions have been merged. The French community has two parts: the Walloon region, excluding 67,600 in the German-speaking areas, on the one hand and the French-speakers in the Brussels capital region, one-fifth to a quarter of the French community, on the other. The German community makes decrees for predominantly German-speaking boroughs in the eastern part of the Walloon region.

Federalization has left the constitutional recognition of language-group rights at the national level unchanged. The most important provision is that the national Cabinet has an equal number of Dutch- and French-speaking ministers. As the Cabinet decides by consensus, this ensures the two largest language groups a veto at the federal level.

The Belgian Intergovernmental System

The intergovernmental system is based on competing principles of organization: unilateralism and co-operation.

Dual federalism encourages communities and regions to extend their exclusive powers to Europe, bypassing the federal government to seek direct participation in EC policy-making. The communities have had international competence, including treaty-making power, since 1980. That was extended to the regions in 1993. Cultural and economic cleavages and the decades-long nationalist competition provide additional incentives for regions and communities to act individually rather than collectively.

The dual nature of Belgian federalism is, however, misleading since the separate systems are interdependent at the level of inter-governmental relations. This involves the various actors in exchange and collaboration.

Taking Theo Toonen's paper[6] as a point of departure, one may distinguish two dimensions of interdependence. The first dimension concerns the policy tasks: the extent to which responsibility for a single policy process is divided among different governmental levels. Toonen emphasizes that a central government that depends on local or regional administrations for the implementation of public services is favourable to co-operative intergovernmental relations. Belgium is categorized as a dual federation with limited interdependence. However, while Belgian federalism does not provide for a division of legislative versus executive competences, the division of labour within the policy areas produces similar co-operative incentives. Policy areas are usually divided into thin slices and then distributed among two or three arenas (federal, community, region), each of which usually receives exclusive control over its segment.[7] The federal government is, in most cases, competent to set the general legislative and fiscal framework unilaterally, but its actions could lose considerably if the other players decided—unilaterally—not to implement them.

The second dimension concerns the actors: the degree of administrative-organizational and political interweaving of persons and institutions at all governmental levels. Toonen ranked Belgium among those systems with limited interweaving, especially because 'the administrative separation of state and regions is comp-

---

[6] See Theo Toonen, 'Europe of the Administrations: The Challenges of 1992 (and Beyond)' (paper presented at the 15th Conference of the International Political Science Association: Buenos Aires, 1991), 15.

[7] See A. Alen and P. Peeters, 'Belgie op zoek naar een co-operatief federaal staatsmodel', *Tijdschrift voor Bestuurswetenschappen en Publiek Recht*, 6 (1989), 343–71.

lemented by a situation in which national political parties have ceased to exist'.[8] However, federal and regional/community politics in Belgium are intertwined, but not in a manner which could fit into Toonen's framework. The overlapping authority of regions and communities (within and between language groups) makes some exchange unavoidable. Political processes further weaken the distinctness of federal and regional/community politics. The rigidly hierarchical regional parties are better equipped to ensure political interweaving than a loose, nation-wide party system. In each regional party, a centralized party organization monitors regional/community and federal politics. Similarly, political control is unified in the legislature: the regional and community legislative councils are composed of the members of the federal parliament.[9] Thus federal ministers, usually parliamentarians, have the right to vote on community and regional decrees. The 1993 reform introduces, however, a separate ballot for the Councils and the federal Lower House, starting from the next general elections (due by November 1995). Furthermore, the mechanisms that were introduced in 1970 to integrate language-group rights in national institutions still apply to the federal institutions and help to link federal and regional/community politics.

Regional/community civil servants maintain pre-federal networks of co-ordination. This is helped by the fact that large parts of the central civil service were reorganized along regional or language lines from the 1960s onwards and were able to develop co-ordination structures over time. The same applies at the political level. Several top ministers in the federal Cabinet were previously members of a community or regional executive, while an increasing number of community/regional ministers can offer national experience. The new institutions have gained political status at an extraordinary pace in ten years of operation. The positions of minister-president in the Flemish community and the Walloon region are second only to, and probably already on a par with, that of the federal prime minister. The small size of the Belgian political system makes it likely that this personal interweaving will continue in future.

---

[8] Toonen, 'Europe of The Administrations', 15–16.
[9] The Brussels Regional Council (1989) and the German Community Council (1990) were directly elected.

Interdependence and interweaving, despite the formal dual federalism, have led to the development of a deliberative structure modelled on German executive federalism. The result is a highly complex network of linkages between the executives of the three arenas and their bureaucracies, in which relationships are based on exchange rather than hierarchy. The central institution for federal–regional–community relations is the Deliberation Committee for the Government and the Executives (*Overlegorgaan* or *Comité de concertation*). This twelve-member committee conforms to the double parity rule between federal and community/regional levels, and between Dutch- and French-speakers. The German community takes part as a voting member on matters of concern to it. The committee takes decisions by consensus and, although its decisions are not binding, its recommendations are in practice difficult to reject.

In 1989 the Deliberation Committee established fifteen Interministerial Conferences (IMCs), which bring together functional ministers. The IMCs are authorized to conclude collaboration agreements, which are legally enforceable. Each IMC can set up working groups and commissions for preparatory activities or technical decision-making. These bodies consist of political aides of the minister or public servants, often assisted by experts. They may also include representatives from interest groups. There is also extensive informal exchange, which falls partly outside the IMCs' infrastructure. It is difficult to estimate its importance, but informal contacts seem preferred by the participants, especially civil servants, to institutionalized exchange. Informality enables them to tone down politicization and to withstand unilateral strategies.

The European Presence in the Federal System

The Belgian regions and communities have developed a keen interest in the European Community for two reasons. Spurred by the dynamics of the internal-market programme the EC moved into hitherto largely untouched areas such as environmental protection, technology, research and development, social policy, and even education and culture. The EC's role in most of these areas was strengthened in the Single European Act of 1987. Much of this new

EC activity relates to policy domains at the subnational level, especially in federal or federalizing countries such as Germany, Belgium, and Spain. The Maastricht Treaty on European Union will undoubtedly augment the EC impact on regional and community policy. In addition, certain constitutional features of Belgian federalism reinforce the interest of regions and communities in European politics and determine its outlook. The Belgian federal Constitution follows a model of dual federalism. Regions, communities, and the federal level usually have exclusive competences; a very limited number are concurrent. Legislative authority and implementation are generally on the same level, amounting to a jurisdictional rather than a functional division of powers. So federalization has attempted to create watertight compartments.

How does the increasing impact of the EC affect these constitutional features? EC policy bears upon regional/community policy-making in a direct and tangible way when it relates to exclusive competences of communities or regions. For example, EC educational policy or cultural policy has direct implications for the communities. Similarly, nearly all matters eligible for support from the EC structural funds fall under the exclusive authority of regions (mostly ERDF) and communities (mostly ESF). Since 1993 the EAGGF (Gu.) has also come under regional responsibility.

Furthermore, the impact of EC policy has many dimensions, and regions and communities must take all of them into account when designing their EC strategy. The EC affects both legislative and executive powers in the case of education or industrial policy. On the other hand, its impact is in principle limited to the executive branch in the case of public procurement, where general rule-making remains federal. Policy areas where the broad legislative framework is federal, and where more specific legislation is left to regions or communities stand midway between these extremes. Environment is an example.

The division of labour between communities/regions and the federal government—allocative tasks for the former, and redistribution and stabilization for the latter—tends to continue at the EC level. The federal government encounters the EC mainly as a rule-maker, as in the removal of internal barriers and the creation of a European normative framework. Communities/regions meet the EC administration still primarily as a source of subsidies, as is the case with the structural funds and programmes in technology, research (Esprit, Eureka), education (Erasmus, Lingua), environmental protection, and to some extent trans-European networks.

The dynamics of EC decision-making tend be different for regulation and provision. Regulatory decision-making requires extensive *horizontal* deliberation between policy-makers. Also, the more important negotiations between national actors and European institutions occur during the policy-formulation stage. Beyond that, member states can usually plan their implementing policies quite autonomously. Interactions with EC institutions in the implementation stage tend to be sparse, asymmetrical, and limited to highly specialized sections at EC level, as most contacts have to do with the supervisory control by a special unit in the EC Commission, the European Court of Justice, or a regulatory agency. With provision, the purpose is to determine the conditions under which EC funds can be released. Vertical communication between the EC bureaucracy and a particular national actor is in that case equally as important as horizontal exchange. Moreover, as most EC grants are conditional, discussions in the policy-implementation stage tend to be more intensive than in the policy-formulation stage and perhaps more symmetrical. So regions/communities and federal government have different roles in EC policy-making. The changes of 1993 will, however, lead to a greater involvement of regions and communities in EC regulatory decision-making.

Regional Participation in European Policy-Making

The Belgian federal system emerged in the middle of the European relaunch, which forced it to manage domestic and European changes at the same time.

The domestic intergovernmental system has traditionally adapted to the European Community in an incremental way. EC-related policy-making has been relatively decentralized from the beginning. Broad options were set by an interministerial committee in the national government, including the economics-related departments and the Foreign Ministry. It had a low political profile. Field departments dealt with technical affairs. The Ministry of Foreign Affairs liaised between the field departments and the Permanent Representation with the EC. High European politics was mainly a specialist's privilege until well into the 1980s. The Foreign

Office or, occasionally, a prime minister with a personal interest in European affairs, set the options relatively independently.[10]

What happened to this pragmatic approach to European politics when regions and communities became powerful actors? The combination of a formal structure of dual federalism and an elaborate intergovernmental relations system defined the context in which regions and communities attempted to extrapolate their practices in internal matters to the European arena. As in the national arena, they tempered their predominantly *cavalier seul* strategies with occasional pragmatic collaboration. In contrast to the domestic conflict, the power struggle around the international competences rarely captured the attention of public opinion.

The European Constitution seems to act as an important constraint, at least formally. The European Community recognizes only member states, which makes it difficult for the regions or communities to act officially. The Maastricht Treaty will make it possible for the five Belgian votes in the Council to be cast by a minister from the regions or communities (Article 146). Belgium, however, is not allowed to split its five votes, so regions or communities have to agree on a common position. European decision-making will remain essentially egalitarian, designed for twelve partners.[11]

This ensures the twelve a fairly predictable share but it requires the regions and communities to agree about how to distribute the Belgian vote, so ruling out an individualist strategy. Put differently, the intergovernmental Constitution at the Belgian level, which encourages regions and communities to seek direct participation, clashes with the European framework, which dissuades participation by other than member states.

How did Belgium overcome this difficulty? The principal rule of contemporary EC politics in relation to Belgium is that the Belgian Government should have the capacity for strategic intervention. In addition, the political authorities, including regions and communities, give a first priority to the implementation of European decisions in order to improve the country's mediocre performance.[12]

---

[10] See F. Standaert, *De buitenlandse betrekkingen in het federale Belgie* (Brussel: Groep Coudenberg, 1990).

[11] See M. Shackleton, 'The European Community between Three Ways of Life: A Cultural Analysis', *Journal of Common Market Studies*, 29/6 (1991), 574–601.

[12] According to the Commission's reports on the implementation of the White Paper, Belgium was at the lower end of the performance list in early 1992, with a

This demands a greater concentration of decision-making power. It also necessitates the consent of regions and communities, in return for which they would want to participate more fully in decision-making. The federal government has three additional rules to reconcile concentration and participation: federal predominance in 'high politics', a high degree of regional and community involvement in 'practical politics', and consistency between high and practical politics through federal co-ordination. Direct relations between regions or communities and European Community institutions are acceptable (and may even be preferable) as long as they concern technical rather than political issues and as long as the federal government is kept informed.

Regions and communities tried to enlarge the framework of acceptable actions and outcomes, without overtly rejecting the rules. They pushed for a greater participation in the formulation of 'high politics', they defended a liberal interpretation of 'practical politics', and tried to reduce the federal co-ordinating role. External relations remained an equivocal issue in the Constitution until 1993. The communities were made competent for international relations in 1970, but their treaty-making power remained ill defined. The reform of 1980 affected only ratification. Treaties and agreements on community matters needed to be ratified in the community councils, and not (only) in the national parliament. That is why the Maastricht Treaty, or rather its provisions on vocational training, education, youth, health, and culture, had to be ratified in the three community councils and in the joint Community Commission of the Brussels region. The revision of 1988 subsequently addressed the issue of negotiation and conclusion of treaties. The communities gained the right to conclude treaties, but the national parliament never came around to enacting the implementing legislation, which created confusing situations. Thus on education, for example, the communities would be the sole representatives of the Belgian authorities in the European student exchange programme Erasmus, but there were no clear guidelines on who would define and defend the Belgian position in the EC Council of Education and decide on the vote. The regions did not gain the same competence in external relations. The Constitution

transmission percentage of 73.6 per cent against an EC average of 77.2 per cent. By early Feb. 1993, it had climbed to the upper half of the league, with 85.5 per cent, against an EC average of 80 per cent.

of 1988 again shifted some international competence to regions and communities. Regions and communities would be consulted when preparing European decisions related to their competences. Furthermore, they would have full international competence for scientific research programmes related to their competences, but not for research policy as such. Finally, they would be involved in the management of the EC structural funds and the implementation of agriculture, both of them partly regional competences.

The constitutional landscape changed drastically in May 1993. In principle, the federal government retains a general competence to ensure the coherence of external affairs. However, the regions are now on a par with the communities, and all have become fully competent to regulate international co-operation within the scope of their competences. This includes the power to conclude treaties to be ratified in the relevant legislative assembly. Treaties that affect shared competences require the assent of all assemblies involved. A forthcoming European treaty would therefore probably require ratification in the federal parliament (Lower and Upper House), the three community councils (plus possibly the Brussels joint Community Committee) and the three regional councils.

A detailed machinery is expected to ensure the coherence of a partitioned Belgian foreign policy. The structure is the same as that of the general intergovernmental co-operative system, but more attention is paid to the operationalization. It provides in information schemes a right to appeal for the federal government on the basis of strict objective criteria (absolute veto in extraordinary circumstances), an active Interministerial Conference for external relations to discuss European policy-making, and legally binding co-operation agreements on the Belgian representation in the European Councils of Ministers and the procedure of court cases involving regions or communities before international Courts of Justice (substitution by the federal government in case of non-compliance at the cost of the miscarrying region or community).

Before as well as after the reform, the organizational structure reflects two competing philosophies on the possible role for regions and communities in EC policy and politics. The first relies more on unilateral action and links up to the intergovernmental Constitution; the other is accommodative–participative and emphasizes the interdependencies of the actors.

General Political Links between Regions/Communities and the EC

There is no *special* forum for *systematic* co-decision on European affairs. Rather, since January 1990, strategic political options have been taken in an exclusively federal body, the Ministerial Committee for European Affairs. It is chaired by the Prime Minister and the meetings are attended by the Belgian ambassador to the EC. It has a much higher political profile than the older, economics-related Interministerial Committee. This more concentrated approach to European high politics reflects the growing political significance of the EC for domestic politics. It is also proof of the federal government's determination to defend its primacy in European affairs.

Regions and communities co-ordinate their general EC policies informally, if at all. They consulted quite intensively during the Intergovernmental Conference on Political Union. The two larger communities and the Walloon region have now diplomatic representatives in the Permanent Representation. While the German *Länderbeobachter* represents all *Länder*, the Belgian regions and communities have their own diplomats. Belgian regions and communities greatly favour a Committee of the Regions, although they expect more of their participation in the Council of Ministers.

At the same time, there is a *general* forum, where *unsystematic* joint decision-making on general European affairs takes place: the Deliberation Committee of the Government and the Executives. It deals with European issues largely in a reactive manner and on an *ad hoc* basis. The Committee has a dual role. It intervenes in domestic conflicts of interests resulting from EC intervention. For example, if an IMC fails to agree on an EC file, it can bring the matter before the Committee. Such a conflict in the IMC for agriculture was resolved in the Deliberation Committee in 1991. The federal and Walloon regional ministers had been at odds on the participation of the regions in the preparation of the Community Support Framework (EAGGF).[13] In addition to its management role, the Committee discusses all matters concerning Belgian–EC relations, which one of the parties considers of national importance. For example, in 1991 the Flemish Government de-

---

[13] Deliberation Committee 1990–1, internal documents.

manded a joint strategy to resist a Commission decision on fixed book prices. In December 1990 the Committee determined the participation of the communities and regions in the Belgian negotiating party for the intergovernmental conferences. Communities and regions have regularly presented their demands in the Deliberation Committee and had them incorporated into the Belgian negotiation stand.[14] On the other hand, the important Belgian memorandum of March 1990, which launched the idea of an intergovernmental conference on political union, was apparently not discussed first with the regions and communities. The Deliberation Committee's capability to intervene strategically in EC policy seems limited, but it has proved to be a reliable reactive body. The interministerial Conference for External Affairs was resuscitated in the course of the negotiations on the 1993 constitutional reform. It is rapidly becoming the main political forum for systematic information exchange and co-decision on European affairs.

Pragmatism in Day-to-Day Policy-Making

Similar two-track developments are present at the level of day-to-day politics. On *technical* matters, regions and communities are involved directly and on the basis of equality. This involvement takes place mainly in the deliberative framework of the IMCs and their commissions or working parties. The IMCs have taken over the role of the functional ministries in EC relations before federalization. IMCs rarely lead to actual pooling of efforts or competences. Joint policy-making in a pure sense remains limited, with only the federal government showing willing. The main accomplishment of the IMCs is that they regulate and legitimize the direct presence of regions and communities at the EC level for matters of their concern. This overcomes the contradiction between the intergovernmental Constitution at Belgian level, encouraging regions and communities to seek direct participation, and the European framework, dissuading participation of those other than member states. The Commission and even the EC Council of Ministers are in general prepared to accept that regions or communities

[14] Deliberation Committee, internal documents; and interviews with participants in the federal, Flemish and French community, and the Walloon region in the course of 1991.

are actually making the decisions.[15] The European challenge stimulates the Belgian regions and communities to emphasize their common interests and to work together. It creates a kind of *Bundestreue*, which has been extremely difficult to nurture in a domestic context.

The time, the extent, and the form in which regions or communities have taken over from the federal government varies from one area to another. Federal authorities have been reluctant in agriculture or environment, but flexible in public procurement, research policy, structural funds, and economic matters. The differences are partly due to the distribution of competences, but personality clashes and political struggles between ministers or civil servants, and existing patterns of co-ordination also play a role. Four examples serve to illustrate the variety of arrangements on the eve of the rationalization effected by the 1993 reform.

The first is a successful example of federal-dominated co-ordination, largely outside the IMC infrastructure: public procurement. Liberalization of this sector is a priority in the internal-market programme. Since 1976, domestic and European public procurement policy had been co-ordinated by a special unit under the Prime Minister, and not by the department of transport, infrastructure, or economic affairs as in most other coutries. Then the constitutional reforms of the 1980s transferred several departments with high procurement expenditures to regions and communities. This increased the number of interested partners, while the tight time-schedule of the internal-market programme made co-ordination more urgent. Two new bodies were created: a mixed bureaucratic–political Interministerial Committee monitors the transmission of EC directives (1989) and a purely bureaucratic informal contact group controls conformity of the rules and responds to EC Commission complaints (1991). Both have a representation from regions and communities, and the latter was decided in the Deliberation Committee of the Government and Executives. They come under the Prime Minister's office, and have managed to retain supervision over EC policy formulation, transmission, and feedback to the Commission;[16] regions and communities are involved in the last two functions.

---

[15] Interviews with participants.
[16] Deliberation Committee, internal documents; interviews with civil servants on federal and regional level, and with a representative of an interest group.

Research policy provides a successful example of decentralized co-ordination, which makes full use of the IMC infrastructure. Most areas of research policy are the exclusive competence of regions or communities, including international co-operation; the rest is shared competence. In 1989, the Deliberation Committee established a federal–community–regional IMC for research policy, which concluded two collaboration agreements in 1990. The first agreement sets up a Commission for International Collaboration (CIS); the second regulates 'the participation of regions and communities in the activities concerning research policy of the European Community, including the organization of related domestic activities'. The CIS in turn creates working parties, which then send experts to specialized working committees at the EC level. The agreement stipulates clearly that only the parties with domestic competence *ratione materiae* are competent at EC level, that is 'either state and regions; or state and communities; or state, regions and communities; or regions; or communities; or regions and communities'. So the federal government is not present in EC working committees that deal with an exclusive competence of regions or communities. EC programmes such as CREST, CIDST, CIT, SOAC, and the programme committees fall under these rules. This decentralization is kept in balance by two co-ordination principles. First, a representative of Foreign Affairs has a suspensive veto in each working party. Second, the position of Belgium in the EC Council (Council of Ministers, COREPER, and the Council working groups) must always be a joint federal-regional-community decision of the IMC for research policy. Federal government and regions/communities concluded a comparable agreement for Eureka.[17] So the federal government has accepted extensive, direct, and exclusive relations between regions/communities and the EC in the transmission of EC decisions and the more technical aspects of decision-making. It has, however,

[17] 'Samenwerkingsakkoord tot regeling van de betrokkenheid van de gemeenschappelijke gemeenschapscommissie, de gemeenschappen en de gewesten in de activiteiten inzake wetenschapsbeleid van de Europese gemeenschappen, evenals in de organisatie van aansluitende activiteiten op binnenlands vlak' (*Belgisch Staatsblad*, 9 Feb. 1991). 'Samenwerkingsakkoord m.b.t. de inrichting van de commissies "internationale samenwerking" en "federale samenwerking" van de interministeriele conferentie voor wetenschapsbeleid' (*Belgisch Staatsblad*, 9 Feb. 1991). 'Protokol tussen de regering en de gewest- en gemeenschapsexecutieven betreffende de Belgische deelname aan Eureka' (*Belgisch Staatsblad*, 15 May 1990).

retained a role for itself, albeit not an exclusive one, in the Council of Ministers, even in matters which are the exclusive competence of regions or communities.

The third example, in education, culture, and audio-visual policy, demonstrates the nearly complete absence of federal involvement and the predominance of informal co-ordination between the communities. The three areas were almost completely transferred to the communities, which have full international competence. The IMC for education is not operative; the one for audio-visual matters is limited to technical affairs; there is no IMC for culture. Instead, community ministers and their civil servants meet informally to decide on the Belgian position at EC level, which is then communicated to Foreign Affairs and the Permanent Representation. Formally, the federal Secretary for European Affairs represents the communities' viewpoint in the Council of Ministers, and votes. However, it has happened more than once that the Belgian position has been presented by the three community ministers in concert. As the Council rarely takes a formal vote, this does not usually cause problems as long as the three ministers speak with one voice,[18] although there has been an incident involving the federal European Affairs minister on at least one occasion. Thus in education and culture, the communities have gained control of all stages of decision-making: preparation, choice, implementation, and feedback. The federal government is present only during the first two stages and then as a minor player.

In the fourth case, that of the structural funds, the federal government has disappeared almost completely. The EC Commission negotiates separately with each region or community and even occasionally bypasses them to *travailler directement au terrain* with local authorities or private actors.[19] Federal representatives are present as observers in the preparation stage of the Community Support Frameworks. The actual negotiations, within tight EC Commission criteria, the conception of the operational programme, and the follow-up in the control committee take place between the EC Commission, the regional or community executive

[18] Interviews with officials from the communities.
[19] An official of the French community referring to the European Social Fund. He made the same comment with respect to the EC Commission's policy in educational programmes, especially Tempus. See e.g. on regional policy: S. Derynck, *Bestuursverhoudingen bij het ge ntegreerd aktieprogramma voor de Westhoek* (Leuven: Lic.Th. Polit.Wet., 1991).

in question, and other public or private actors. It is the Commission which increasingly sets the rules autonomously. Thus the federal government has vacated almost the whole field of structural-funds policy, although it has tried to hold on in some areas, notably the agricultural guidance fund. There has been no serious attempt by communities and regions to co-ordinate their policies. Instead, the rules of the game are increasingly set by the Community.

Low-Key Centralization in Day-to-Day Political Co-ordination

The Ministry of Foreign Affairs attempts to play a central role in day-to-day *political* co-ordination. The Directorate for European Politics (P11) acts as the liaison body between domestic administrations and the Permanent Representation. P11 organizes co-ordination meetings on diverse subjects several times a week and with varying membership. It started to invite regions and communities, at first grudgingly, after the regionalization of 1980.

P11's main task is to monitor the 'political, institutional and horizontal side of Belgian EC politics'. It defends the official Belgian position of federalism and supranationalism against intergovernmentalist inclinations of the field ministries. Technical aspects are left to the IMCs. P11 remains hierarchically subordinate to the federal Minister of Foreign Affairs. As such, it is more likely to refer unsolved issues to the Ministerial Committee for European Affairs, an exclusively federal body, rather than the Deliberation Committee, a federal–regional–community body. Regions and communities would, therefore, prefer P11's role to be reduced to that of diplomatic post-service.

In fact, P11 plays a limited role in substantive policy-making, and co-ordination between regions and communities usually takes place outside it. The executives try to agree on a common position, which they then jointly present to the federal authorities. Moreover, the Foreign Office's general political role is constantly challenged by the IMC network, which is more intergovernmental and, therefore, in the Belgian context, more receptive to regionalist interests. Most EC decision-making is highly specialized, which makes it more acceptable to call for a greater input from technical expertise. Finally, P11 restricts itself to information exchange in areas where communities and regions deal directly with the EC, such as education policy.

A Look into the Future: Regional Participation in European Policy-Making after 1993

The need for concentration has a centralizing effect on regions and communities. It tends to strengthen hierarchical features at the national level, and it helps explain the outspoken supranationalist position on European integration of the Belgian federal government. Core institutions are the federal Ministerial Committee for European Affairs and the federal P11 agency. The need for consensus has the effect of promoting participation by regions and communities. It emphasizes the intergovernmental component at the national, and probably also the European level. The infrastructure consists of the Deliberation Committee, the IMC network, and various forms of pragmatic co-ordination.

The two trends suggest different paths for future development of the intergovernmental system of the European Community with the Belgian regions. A strengthening of the first trend would create a leaner system under unifying federal control. However, continuing Flemish–Walloon nationalist pressure is almost certain to weaken central power. If the second trend becomes dominant, regions and communities would play a more autonomous role in the EC. The system would be more open and egalitarian and would be jointly co-ordinated at the Belgian level by regions, communities, and the federal government. It would be better equipped for integrating increasingly powerful regions and communities, but it would be confederal in all but name.[20]

However, as competition between concentration and participation continues, a third scenario becomes more likely: a highly complex system featuring as co-ordinators a unilateral federal government or unilateral regions and communities, or some federal–regions–communities combination, or *ad hoc* arrangements. None of the parties concerned would get its way. The federal government would be dissatisfied with the limited federal dominance, because the P11 and other federal bodies would control only some import-

---

[20] The communities would probably disappear.

ant flows from and to the EC, and then often only in their formal aspects. The regions and communities would be disgruntled with their participation, because the system would be unclear and much would remain under formal federal control. Finally, all, including the EC institutions, would disapprove of the confusion, because co-ordination efforts would often depend on unpredictable *ad hoc* solutions.

The 1993 reform is an attempt to steer intergovernmental relations in the context of European Community policy-making between the unrealistic strong federal path and the undesirable confederal path. The core component is a co-operation agreement to be concluded in the IMC for External Affairs by the federal government, the three regional, and the three community governments. It lays down the composition of the Belgian representation in the European Councils of Ministers and the decision rules concerning negotiation strategy and voting when there is no agreement. By August 1993, the time that this research was concluded, the co-operation agreement was still at a draft stage, but seemed to be able to rely on strong political support. It was expected to be promulgated in September 1993.

First, the agreement divides the EC Councils over four categories, depending on the relative importance of federal and regional competences in a policy area. This categorization is then used to determine the representation. From type A to type D, the federal government gradually makes room for the regions or communities. Type A Councils cover exclusive federal competences, and the Belgian representative will therefore be a federal minister. The General Affairs Council, Ecofin, and the Budget Council would fall under this heading. Type B concerns share competences in which the federal level is more important than the regional level. The federal minister will be accompanied by a regional representative, but the federal minister casts the vote. Environment, health, and transport will probably end up in this group. In type C Councils, federal and regional/community ministers swap seats. The Industry Council is a strong candidate. Type D Councils deal with exclusive competences of regions and communities, and therefore no federal minister is present. This type will certainly be applied to education and culture, and very likely also to regional policy. Most discussion has focused on the grey zone between types B and C. Environment, for example, has constantly shifted back and forth between B and C.

The representation of regions and communities in the various Councils will be allocated on a six-month rotation basis. Thus, if a Flemish community minister represents Belgium in the Council of Education in the second half of 1993, either the French-speaking or the German community takes over in the first half of 1994. If the Walloon region occupies the Belgian seat in the Regional Policy Council in the last six months of 1993, the Flemish or Brussels region succeeds for the following six months.

Effective decision-making may turn out to be a problem in types C and D, where there is no leading government. The most likely solution is that Belgium will abstain if communities and regions cannot reach an agreement, as has been the practice in the past for international agreements. The problem has arisen only sporadically in the past, and never with consequences for the overall outcome. However, an abstention in EC Councils which take decisions by qualified or simple majority in fact gives support to the no-vote.

Some arrangements will be applied under the Belgian presidency of the European Community in the second half of 1993. Thus the Flemish community intends to acts as president of the Council for Education, while the French community sits in the Belgian chair— that is, as soon as the Maastricht Treaty, which would allow subnational ministers to represent their country, is ratified. With or without Maastricht, an informal Council for Culture is organized by the Flemish community, and a similar gathering for regional policy by the Walloon region.

The IMC for External Affairs is expected to nurture and guard the cohesion of the Belgian EC policy. It is therefore the core integrative institution in the new cascaded intergovernmental system. The new division of responsibilities will require a major role redefinition for the two diplomatic gatekeepers with respect to relations with the EC: the Belgian Permanent Representation and the unit P11 in the Ministry of Foreign Affairs. Under the pre-1993 system, they belonged exclusively to the federal bureaucracy, although they had already learned to incorporate community and regional concerns in practice. In the post-1993 structure, they will become genuinely intergovernmental institutions, the former on the EC scene and the latter in the national bureaucracy. The organizational implications (structure, personnel, and lines of authority) are still unclear.

The question is whether these co-ordinating bodies will succeed in steering the players towards a stable federal or confederal arrangement, or whether the new construction will turn out to be another disguise for the continuation of the third scenario. That will depend partly on the decision rules and the internal coherence of the members of the IMC. The agenda, the resources and powers of federal government, regions, and communities, the relative weight of information exchange and co-decision, the credibility of sanction mechanisms, and the cohesion of the federal government especially are to a large extent unknown factors at this stage. Success will also depend on the constellation of divergent economic, socio-cultural, and political interests in Flanders, Brussels, and Wallonia. How could these divergences be exploited or diffused by agents of mobilization: the regional and community governments, political parties, and the traditional nationalist movements?

The Impact of EC Policy on Regional Administration and Regionalism

Less than 1 per cent of the structural funds goes to Belgian regions, but this percentage rises to 3.6 per cent when the objective 1 regions (lagging regions) are excluded. The Belgian population share is about 3 per cent. The money goes almost exclusively to the regions and communities. Table 6.1 gives an overview.

This EC support was of limited direct budgetary or economic relevance until 1993. The annual funds equalled about 0.5 per cent of the French community budget, less than 1 per cent of the Flemish community's, and about 2.5 per cent of the Walloon region's. These figures do not include the funds for the Community Initiatives such as Interreg, Rechar, Stride, or Perifra. However, the 1994–9 framework has changed this situation completely for the Walloon region. The rich Flemish region does not stand to win funds, while about one-third of the Walloon region becomes eligible for structural-funds support under the most generously subsidized objective 1 criteria. The province of Hainault alone is expected to receive a total of between 780 and 800 million ECUs.

TABLE 6.1. *Distribution of structural funds by objectives* (million ECUs)

| | Objective | | | | | |
	2	3	4	5(A)	5(B)	TOTAL
Federal government	—	7.05	6.27	—	—	13.32
Flemish community	122.4	35.45	32.82		11.50	202.17
French community	—	32.57	29.04		—	61.61
Walloon region	147.5	8.82	7.86		21.00	185.18
German community	—	0.89	0.79		—	1.68
Brussels Capital region	—	2.51	2.51		—	5.02
TOTAL	269.9	87.29	79.29	119.5	32.50	588.46

Notes: Objective 2 (declining industrial areas) 1989–91, 1992–3
Objective 3 (structural unemployment) 1990–2
Objective 4 (youth unemployment) 1990–2
Objective 5(A) (agriculture) 1989–93
Objective 5(B) (rural areas) 1989–93

Source: Flemish Community, internal documents; EC Commission, Community Support Frameworks, 1989–91 and 1992–3 for converting regions affected by industrial decline (objective 2).

On top of that, Wallonia will get an increased share under the other objectives. Preliminary calculations suggest that the annual inflow under structural funds may be up to four times higher after 1993 than under the 1989–93 framework. Flanders and Wallonia have been placed at opposite ends of the support table.

The programme strategy of the EC Commission, however, has had an impact on public administration. The elaborate procedure including partnership requirements and the eligibility criteria has forced regions and communities to make planning and management more professional. The EC Commission has also been able to neutralize a national practice of fixed distributional codes. The funds for 1989–91 had been divided evenly between Flanders and Wallonia, although Wallonia should have had a larger share according to the Commission's socio-economic criteria. For the 1992–3 programmes, the Commission suggested letting the objective criteria play, which would channel 70 per cent to Wallonia. The Flemish Government defended the 1989 agreement, while the Walloon Government supported the Commission. The federal government refused to mediate. The two regional governments did not try to settle the issue amongst themselves either. The Commission shuttled back and forth, and ultimately more or less forced the two sides to settle for a 38:62 distribution. This breakthrough paved the way for the greatly enlarged influx of funding into Wallonia under the 1994–9 framework rule intended to pacify Flemish–Walloon conflict.

There has been little co-ordination between the Belgian regions and communities on structural funds or related regional policies. The EC Commission's receptive approach to regional and local participation in the structural-funds programmes partly explains this. However, co-ordination is also perceived to be less useful because of differences in administrative organization and economic structure. In the Flemish community, the role of the central administration has been passive and limited. Local private and public organizations are active in initiating programme applications, and in the negotiations with the EC Commission in the different stages of a programme execution. This bottom-up activity is co-ordinated by the political collaborators of the relevant ministers rather than by civil servants and is supervised by a political collaborator of the Minister for External Relations. The Walloon central administration has a more directive approach. Broad options are established by civil servants and not by political collaborators. The administration of the structural funds is deconcentrated to a special-purpose bureau. Bottom-up input by other actors is limited.

Furthermore, the different economic and social structures of the two larger regions make co-ordination less attractive. Wallonia is on the whole a serious problem area. It has the lowest GDP per head (83.4 per cent of EC average for 1988–90) among the regions of the northern member states apart from Northern Ireland, and the highest unemployment rate except for three other regions. The average Flemish unemployment rate in 1988–90 was only half of that in Wallonia (5.5 per cent versus 10.8 per cent); it also fell faster between 1985 and 1990 (−4.4 versus −2.1). The GDP per capita for the period 1988–90 in Flanders was higher than the EC aver-

,ge.[21] Wallonia displays the typical features of a declining industrial region. An early industrialized area, it depends heavily on three subsectors (metallurgical industry, iron and steel, and construction), all of which experienced sharp recessions in the 1970s and 1980s. Flemish industrial production is more diversified, is more often based in advanced sectors such as automobiles, chemicals, and electronics, and it did not experience comparable set-backs. Both regions experienced significant tertiary-sector growth in the 1980s, but followed somewhat different paths. In Wallonia, the expansion is most pronounced in the services category, and especially in public services and education. Tertiary growth in Flanders depends more on private initiative, and is more evenly spread over the different categories.

The different administrative approaches to EC regional policy are likely to be reinforced. The Walloon regional government has sound economic reasons for paying more attention to the Community Support Framework programmes. The highly routinized operation of the programmes and the predictable budgetary impact favour a continued centralizing approach in the regional administration. The Flemish share in the CSFs is expected to decline. This will make the other community programmes inside the structural funds, such as Stride and Interreg, and especially those outside the structural funds, such as Erasmus and Eureka, more important. This market is in constant flux, and budgetary planning is, therefore, difficult. It will give the Flemish Government few incentives to change its decentralized and more political approach.

Regional and Community Opposition to European Integration[22]

The major concern of the Flemish and French cultural communities is the potential impact of economic integration on culture (including the audio-visual sector) and education. They want full involvement in all decisions with a cultural bearing. The economic

---

[21] EC Commission, *The Regions in the 1990s: Fourth Periodic Report on the Social and Economic Situation and Development of the Regions of the Community* (Brussels, 1991).

[22] Liesbet Hooghe, 'Politics of Multi-Tiered Regionalism', in Carl Lankowski (ed.), *Europe's Emerging Identity: Regional Integration versus Opposition Movements in the European Community* (Boulder, Colo.: Lynne Rienner, forthcoming).

liberalization programme of the European Community does not arouse much opposition, although tightening controls on State aids and industrial policy may affect the traditionally more *dirigiste* Walloon Government more than the Flemish Government. The Walloon region and the French community tend also to be more irritated by the EC Commission negotiating directly with social groups or local authorities. In general, however, regions and communities do not question the existing EC decision-making structure, but they demand more formal participation. They had five major demands in the intergovernmental conferences: a Council of the Regions; a cultural and education section in the treaty that would protect the pre-eminence of member states and regions in cultural and educational policy; the right of regional/community ministers to vote in the Council of Ministers on matters in their exclusive jurisdiction; the same status for regions as for member states before the European Court of Justice; and a restrictive subsidiarity clause. All except the fourth were accepted at Maastricht.

How is this compliant attitude to be explained? First of all, European integration is attractive to regions and communities for the same political-strategic and economic reasons as it is to the Belgian Government. Moreover, the Belgian regions and communities participate in practice, if not always formally, in most EC decision-making. Finally, the fusion of regional and federal political élites ensures that national Belgian EC politics takes into account regional interests. Official regionalism is thus at this stage not a credible source of EC opposition.

The most likely breeding ground for Euro-scepticism lies in traditional Flemish cultural nationalism. Its centre lies outside the regional political establishment. An influential group fears that European integration is threatening to 'Americanize' social relations.

A salient issue is whether Brussels should become the EC capital, because this could destabilize Flemish–Francophone relations there. Cultural anxieties also have a strong social dimension. In 1989, about 19 per cent of the 1.65 million inhabitants of the Brussels urban area were foreigners, 50 per cent of whom were EC citizens.[23] Most of them speak French in public life. A sizeable

---

[23] G. Tastenhoye, *Vlaams Brabant in de wurggreep van Europa* (Leuven: Davidsfonds, 1991).

number of the EC citizens work for the EC institutions or in EC-related organizations. This is an affluent group, which according to Flemish nationalists strengthens the French character of Brussels and puts pressure on the local communities in the Flemish country-side around the capital. The second group of foreigners, from the Mediterranean countries, arrived in Brussels in the 1960s and 1970s and is concentrated in the inner city. This group is poor, but it is expanding rapidly, and is dynamic. Most Belgian Brusselers live between the predominantly non-Belgian upper and lower layers. Surveys show that anti-foreign sentiment is growing.

Opposition to Brussels as the EC capital could become linked to anti-foreign sentiment. One party in particular tries to capitalize on the issue: the *Vlaams Blok*, an extreme right-wing party, which takes a tough anti-immigrant position and promotes Flemish separatism. It obtained 6.6 per cent of the Flemish vote in the 1989 European elections, and 10.3 per cent in the 1991 national elections. Mobilization against Brussels as the capital of Europe has gone beyond the *Vlaams Blok*. The most influential participant in the Euro-sceptical coalition is the *Davidsfonds*, the largest Flemish cultural organization, related to the Christian-Democratic segment. Favouring a decentralized and humane Europe, the Flemish ecologist party *Agalev* also recommends the dispersal of the EC institutions over several European cities. But a coalition with the *Vlaams Blok* on this issue is for the Greens out of the question. An alliance with more moderate Flemish nationalist organizations remains also unlikely. So it is difficult to predict whether this issue could start a wider reappraisal of EC politics in Belgium. Much depends on the future electoral success of the *Vlaams Blok* and on the ability of other Euro-sceptical organizations to avoid an alliance with the party.

Conclusion

European institutions seem to adapt without great difficulty to the varying Belgian institutional constellations. The argument that the European Community deals only with member states finds no support in the Belgian case. Regions and communities are able to relate directly to the EC. Generally, such a situation seems to depend on a major condition: it must be tolerated by the national government of the member state. In the Belgian case, the national level has lost many resources and—equally important—incentives to prevent the regions or communities from acting on the European scene. This disintegrative process explains the unstable and, at this stage, highly complex character of the interplay between regional and EC governmental actors.

The Belgian case shows no evidence of conscious EC efforts to play the regional card. On the other hand, the EC clearly constitutes a window of opportunity for regions to strengthen their position *vis-à-vis* a weak nation-state government. But the EC offers opportunities to other actors as well. The examples of the structural funds or the Tempus programme demonstrate that EC institutions sometimes bypass national *and* regional State institutions, and work directly with other public authorities or private actors, such as mixed private–public investment corporations, chambers of commerce, trade unions, and universities.

This EC activity fits into a general trend. Society is increasingly self-organizing, various networks are set up for limited purposes, and these networks do not always coincide with State boundaries. State actors are part of some networks but not of others and their role at each governmental level is restricted. Moreover, the primary function of statehood is changing. It no longer consists of the production and allocation of basic goods, but of the promotion and co-ordination of divergent networks. The internal-market programme is seen by some as a bold manifestation of these changes. It tears down national and regional State barriers to competition, not in the first place to raise new European ones, but to put activities in the market of social actors and to define the rules for that market.[24] In this framework, intergovernmental relations *and* State–society relations are bound to be complex and fluid, and probably increasingly so. The Belgian case may therefore be an early and extreme illustration of a general trend. Its complexity and receptivity on the one hand and its instability on the other hand, are likely to last.

[24] P. Cerny, 'The Limits of Deregulation: Transnational Interpenetration and Policy Change', *European Journal of Political Research*, 19/2–3 (1991), 173–96; A. Bressand, 'Beyond Interdependence: 1992 as a Global Challenge', *International Affairs*, 66/1 (1990), 47–65.

TABLE 6.2. *Political preferences in the Flemish and Walloon regions (national and regional elections of November 1991)*

	Flemish region (188 seats)	Walloon region (104 seats)
Christian-Democrats	59	24
Socialists	42	47
Liberals	39	20
Greens	12	13
VU (moderate nationalist)	15	—
Vlaams Blok (extremists)	17	—
Others	4	—

TABLE 6.3. *Political preferences in the Brussels region and the German community (regional elections in June 1989 for Brussels, and in October 1990 for the German community)*

	Brussels region (75 seats)		German community (25 seats)
	Flemish	French	
Christian-Democrats	4	9	8
Socialists	2	18	4
Liberals	2	15	5
Greens	1	8	4
VU (moderate nationalists)	1	—	—
FDF (moderate nationalists)	—	12	—
PDB (moderate nationalists)	—	—	4
Vlaams Blok (extremists)	1	—	—
Others	—	2	—

Population (%)
Flemish region   57.8
Walloon region   32.6
   of which German community   0.7
Brussels region   9.6
(Census of 1991. Total Belgian population: 9,978,700.)

MAP 7. France: regions.

7

French Regionalization and European Integration: Territorial Adaptation and Change in a Unitary State

RICHARD BALME

Introduction

One of the most important issues in European integration is the effect of regional reforms within member states. What will be the role of regions in the future European political system, and what relationships will they establish with national governments and Community institutions? France is no stranger to these questions, as the debate on the Joxe law on the territorial organization of the republic shows. Conceived as a relaunching of the decentralization process, it is intended to prepare local governments for the internal market of 1993 and raises the question of the long-term need for a reorganization of the regions in order to compete on the European scale.

After ten years' experience of decentralization, one is tempted paradoxically to emphasize the weakness of French regions in comparison with their foreign counterparts. Their competences and financial powers remain weak. Regional politicians and their policies make little impact on public opinion. The attempt to relaunch national regional policies after several years of neglect seems to presage a reinforcement of the central administration. We would insist, however, that the regional reforms, combined with European integration, are leading to qualitative changes in centre–periphery relations. The development of the Community and the

Translated by Michael Keating.

Commission's emphasis on the 'Europe of the Regions' provide weighty arguments for seeking wider competences and more autonomy from the central state. While still relatively unfamiliar, the regions are beginning to make more impact on public opinion and are taking an active part in the making of public policies. They have also seen a political restructuring as part of the realignment of the French party system in the 1980s. Finally, new political networks have been established by transregional and transnational co-operation, undertaken to manage the effects of integration on regional economies and to express regional interests in Community programmes.

In many respects, the region appears to be the 'core' for the definition of new policies, or the institutional base for a form of meso-government. Yet the expression meso-government can be misleading, since it is not a level of government with well defined characteristics or autonomy, as in a federal system. The French region remains poorly differentiated and weakly consolidated. It is dependent from above on the legislative monopoly of Parliament and the control of planning procedures by the central administration. It is constrained from below by the influence of the departments where politicians are recruited and which provide the framework for elections, and more broadly by the other local governments which collaborate in the policies which it initiates. The region none the less provides a crucial link in centre–periphery relations and has influenced their long-term evolution since the beginning of the Fifth Republic. Their predecessors, the *Circonscriptions d'Action Régionale* under the authority of the prefects and the *Commissions de Développement Economique Régional* (CODER) in 1964, then the *Etablissements Publics Régionaux* in 1972 following the rejection by referendum of the reform proposals of 1969, first marked the end of the traditional republican rule of the notables and inaugurated the new system of planning with its complex relations between the State administration and modernizing local élites.[1] The decentralization reforms, notably the laws of 1982, 1983, and 1986, strengthened the region by increasing its competences and resources and giving it political legitimacy through direct election. More recently, the regions have allowed the French political and administrative system to adapt to the needs of European integration by providing a territorial level of

[1] P. Grémion, *Le Pouvoir périphérique* (Paris: Seuil, 1976).

management for the single market, notably through the dispositions of 1992 on interregional co-operation and the creation of new metropolitan structures in the form of 'communities of communes' and 'communities of towns'.

In the French State tradition, this takes the form of territorial administration, providing complementary forms of political legitimation and evolving in ever-more complex forms, rather than the establishment of a strictly regional type of representation, autonomous from the State and distinct from local government. It is significant that regionalization was put in place in France without a direct link with regionalism, that is, demands for autonomy impelled by ethnic or cultural factors. Such movements do certainly exist, in the peripheral parts of metropolitan France such as the Basque Country, Corsica, Alsace, and Brittany 'and, to a lesser degree in French Catalonia and Occitania, in the overseas departments (Guadeloupe and Martinique) and the overseas territories (New Caledonia). These nationalist or separatist movements have led to some violent confrontations with the State and to the adoption of reforms or special-status arrangements which, in Corsica, the overseas departments, and New Caledonia, have taken a regional form. For the most part, however, French regionalism has had little connection with regionalist demands. The striking contrast in this respect with Spain, Italy, or Belgium is testimony to the high degree of integration in the Jacobin State. The paradox is that the metropolitan regions where regionalist sentiment is weakest are the ones whose identity is most strengthened by European integration, while the peripheral regions, although benefiting from Community regional programmes, are politically little affected by integration and look to direct negotiations with the State to enhance their autonomy. Regionalism in France thus follows different logics which are in turn differently affected by the construction of the Community.

Because of the importance of recent changes, this chapter aims to present a broad picture of the evolution of the French region and the means by which it can intervene in public policy. It will show how this process is affected by European integration while, in its turn, it influences that integration. To see how the regions can shape the development of Europe, we will first examine the effects of the election of regional councils, showing that this represents a broad change in the French political system as a whole in the 1980s, rather than an example of local democratization. The weak institutional differentiation of the regions allows them very limited domestic political impact and this in turn limits their influence at the European level. However, some fundamental qualitative changes were introduced by the decentralization programme, notably the contractualization of public policy and the spread of cooperative negotiation, in which the integration of the various levels of government has proved more important than their differentiation or official hierarchy. European integration and Community programmes reinforce this type of policy-making by encouraging an expansion of policy networks, but this affects territories to varying extents, so increasing spatial differentiation and inequality.

Regional Elections and the Transformation of French Politics

The regional elections of 1986 were the first to be held by universal suffrage. This was the first time since the departure of de Gaulle in 1969 that the French had been asked to pronounce on regional affairs. Under the 1986 law which promoted the regions to full local authority status, regional councillors are elected by proportional representation from the constituent departments for six-year terms. Participation was relatively high at 77.6 per cent, equivalent to that at municipal elections and higher than that for the departments. The result was a sweeping victory for the parties of the right, with the socialists retaining only two regions, Nord-Pas de Calais and Limousin, and losing Auvergne, Languedoc-Roussillon, Midi-Pyrénées, Provence-Alpes-Côtes d'Azur. The RPR retained five regions (Aquitaine, Corsica, Île de France, Upper Normandy, and Pays de la Loire) and took Brittany from the UDF. The UDF made the largest gains of all, securing the presidencies of fourteen regions. Benefiting from proportional representation, the extreme right National Front was in a decisive position in those regions where the moderate right (RPR and UDF) held only a plurality of seats, and was able to put the right in power in four regions, Aquitaine, Languedoc-Roussillon, Franche-Comté, and Upper Normandy.

In spite of the historic character of direct regional elections, the vote was overshadowed by the national elections taking place at the same time; these were won by the parties of the right, ushering in the phase of cohabitation between President Mitterrand and Prime Minister Jacques Chirac. The highly partisan campaign was dominated by national rather than regional issues. Election posters, public meetings, and programmes were all decided from on high and national leaders supported local candidates at regional level. Regionalist movements provided some exceptions to this in Brittany, the Basque Country, and Corsica, but in general regional themes were barely touched on. National partisan divisions eclipsed any serious debate on the new functions of the regional councils.[2]

Even the high turn-out levels can be discounted as a carry-over from the legislative elections, as the similarity of the results of the two votes shows. There were, however, some differences.[3] In eight departments, participation was higher for the regional elections, usually because of the presence of regionalist lists or small parties which were unable to present two distinct lists (national and regional) in each department. So the five big parties gained 91.5 per cent of the vote for the legislative elections, against 88.3 per cent for the regional elections. Local studies of the differences between the two elections, however, reveal the existence of tactical voting and the influence of well-entrenched personalities in the regional vote.[4] In Nord-Pas de Calais the Communist Party obtained a better score in the regional elections, where voters were expressing loyalty to local leaders, than in the legislative ones, where they expressed their hostility to the national leadership of the party.[5] Allowing for differences in party candidatures, the percentage of voters expressing different choices in the two elections in this region has been estimated at 14 per cent, which merely underlines the lack of distinctiveness of the regional elections in metropolitan France.

The overseas regions (Guadeloupe, Guyana, Martinique, Réunion) each comprising a single department, must be analysed

[2] F-G. Dreyfus, 'Une campagne régionale sans voix', in P. Perreau (ed.), *Régions: Le Baptême des urnes* (Paris: Pédone, 1987).

[3] P. Perreau, 'A l'ombre des législatives... les régionales', *Revue politique et parlementaire*, 922 (1986), 19–28.

[4] P. Lehingue, 'Les Pratiques d'éclatement du vote: Vote législatif et vote rgional, l'exemple du département du Somme', in Perreau (ed.), *Régions*. C. Patriat, 'Dans un miroir déformant: Les Élections régionales de 1986 en Bourgogne, in Perreau (ed.), *Régions*.

[5] A. Laurent, 'Le Nomadisme électoral: Le Double Vote du 16 mars 1986 dans le Nord-Pas-de-Calais', *Revue française de science politique*, 37/1 (1987), 5–20.

separately. Regionalization here took a different form, with special statutes taking into account their problems of economic development and autonomist demands. Direct election of regional councils was introduced in 1983, with the 1986 elections representing a renewal. In the French Antilles and Guyana, participation was lower than in the metropole, with abstention reaching 53.5 per cent in Guadeloupe. This reflects a tradition of low turn-outs in these departments due to socio-economic factors such as the low level of education. In the Antilles the separatists called for a boycott of the elections, so that abstention here cannot be written off as mere apathy. Local and ethnic issues featured prominently in the campaign, economic development being presented by each party in various ways as a means of integration into the national community. There was a sharp division between those supporting decentralization (the socialists and independent right) and those ignoring the issue to focus on the national election issues (RPR-UDF) or to strike anti-colonialist positions.[6] It is striking that the Communist Party obtained better results here, with 29.3 per cent in Réunion, and that the left overall was in a stronger position than in the metropole, with the socialists and their allies winning four of the five regions. Only Réunion was gained by the right.

Despite the fact that it is considered part of the metropole, Corsica produced the most distinctive results. The island has a special statute under which elections were organized in 1982 and again in 1984 after the assembly had been dissolved because of its inability to approve a budget. This second election was won by a right-wing coalition including the National Front, as was the 1986 election. The special statute remained an object of contention and the target of a campaign of violence by the *Front National de Libération de la Corse* (FNLC). A new bill, increasing the powers of the regional assembly, was adopted by parliament in June 1991 after the expression 'Corsican people', inserted in the first article to placate autonomist sentiment, was declared contrary to the Constitution and deleted.

In spite of these special features, the election overall was more national than regional, with local issues confined to small groups or peripheral regions. Only six councillors belonging to regionalist movements were elected, all of them in Corsica.

[6] A.-P. Blerald, 'Le Revouvellement des conseils régionaux de Guadeloupe et de Martinique de mars 1986: Les Enjeux d'un scrutin', in *Annuaire des collectivités locales*, 1988 (Paris: GRAL), 85–105.

Although ill served by the electoral system, the region as an institution has consolidated itself over a decade of decentralization. It has first of all gained in terms of public opinion.[7] The conditions shaping attitudes to regionalization and to the construction of Europe are broadly the same. A high socio-economic status, income, and level of education and a declared interest in politics are all factors conducive to support for institutional reform.[8] The regional elections of March 1992 can be seen as a turning-point in Mitterrand's second presidential mandate, demonstrating political dealignment or realignment. Never before have the usual social determinants of voting been so weak or the volatility of the electorate so great.[9] Proportional representation revealed the loss of support for both the governing national majority and the main opposition parties, and the dispersal of votes among various single-issue movements concerned with matters such as the environment or immigration. These movements and the turnover of regional councillors have reshaped the local policy agenda, notably in relation to the environment, which is partly a regional function. The election of National Front representatives has ensured that the themes of security and above all of immigration will feature in the next municipal elections, in 1995, and this in turn will help shape the policy of the Balladur Government in the matter. The regions have thus served as a laboratory for national politics, although some of the experiments, such as proportional representation, the realignment of governing coalitions, and the new policy agenda have not had as much of a national impact after the elections of 1993 as some had expected.

Few observers have remarked on the distinctiveness of the results in the peripheral regions. In Corsica, while the RPR kept its majority, the nationalists made a significant advance. In the single-department overseas regions, despite the peculiarities of each case, there were two general tendencies. The parties of the right progressed less than in metropolitan France; they did not win a majority in any case and gained the presidency only in Guadeloupe. Local autonomist parties, however, did advance. The *Parti*

[7] A. Percheron and B. Roy, 'Le Fair régional en 1990', in *Annuaire des collectivités locales*, 1991 (Paris: GRAL), 89–104.

[8] A. Percheron, 'Les Français et l'Europe: Acquiescement de façade or adhésion véritable?', *Revue française de science politique*, 41 (1991), 382–6.

[9] P. Habert, P. Perrineau, and C. Ysmal, *Le Vote eclaté: Les Élections régionales et cantonales des 22 et 29 Mars 1992* (Paris: Presses de la Fondation Nationales des Sciences Politiques, 1992).

Socialiste Guyanais in Guyana and the *Free Dom* list in Réunion won the presidencies of their respective regions; and the independentist *Union pour l'Indépendance de la Guadeloupe* and the *Mouvement pour l'Indépendance de la Martinique* won two and nine seats respectively. These developments are noteworthy in that they show the relative isolation of these peripheral regions from the movements of opinion in metropolitan France. They also demonstrate that regionalization has not resolved the problem of economic underdevelopment nor the conflict in the local political culture between the desire for autonomy and the need for development. The 'slippery slope' argument appears to be verified here. Regionalization helped the left-wing government sustain its support better than elsewhere, but without preventing the advance of autonomist groups.

The elevation of regions to the status of full local governments by their direct election represented an important step for the whole French political system. Yet the effects have been attenuated by the national character of the regional elections, at least in metropolitan France; and by the marginal impact of the peripheral regions, where the issue of representation was most starkly posed, on the elections as a whole. Each regional election has been seen more as a new element in national political life than as a step in the localization or regionalization of the democratic debate.

A Limited Political Assertion

The region as an institution has also been reinforced by the practice of its elected members as well as by its legitimation through universal suffrage. The social composition of the new regional assemblies presents several new features. Compared with the departments, there are fewer farmers and members of the liberal professions and more industrial and commercial professionals, white-collar workers, and teachers.[10] Regions thus present a more 'modern' composition, less dominated by rural interests and more open to the new middle classes. In policy terms, their modernity is reflected in their concentration on development, with a large part of their

[10] Ministère de l'Intérieur et de la Décentralisation, cited in A. Mabileau, 'L'Élu local: Nouveau professionel de la République, *Pouvoirs*, 60 (1992), 78.

budgets devoted to investment. This logic of development is further encouraged by their staff recruitment, the reinforcement of
the executives against the assemblies and the presidentialization of
leadership, with presidents establishing their own staff 'cabinets'
and assigning key functions to vice-presidents. Although this phenomenon can also be seen in cities and departments, it takes on a
particular importance in the regions because of the proportional
composition of their assemblies and the political instability which
ensues. Their most important political feature has been the need
for party coalitions between the moderate right and the National
Front or between the left and centrists to secure the election of
their presidents and the passage of budgets. Dominated by the
right, the regions have had to undertake difficult negotiations with
the State and have at times come into open conflict with the socialist Government. The most spectacular conflict was that between
the Government of Michel Rocard and the local politicians in Île
de France, including mayor Jacques Chirac of Paris and regional
president Pierre-Charles Krieg, over planning in the Paris region.

More generally, regions act as a pressure group on national
government, especially through the activities of some of their
heavyweight politicians such as RPR notable Olivier Guichard
in Pays-de-La-Loire, Jean-Pierre Raffarin (UDF) in Poitou-
Charentes, or former president of the republic Valéry Giscard
d'Estaing in Auvergne. The last is president of the Association
of Regional Councillors and as such was consulted by the Balladur
Government on the employment bill presented to Parliament in
September 1993, obtaining an assurance that part of the new public
loan would be devoted to the renovation of high schools, for which
the regions are now responsible.

The political assertiveness of the regions nevertheless remains
limited. One indication is the pattern of accumulation of mandates
following the 1985 law which restricted the number any individual
is allowed to hold. Most politicians have chosen to give up the
regional mandate, with two consequences. It is primarily the heavyweight politicians who have abandoned the regions, giving way to
more junior figures,[11] less well established in the public mind and
with less influence in central government. At the same time, there

---

[11] A. Mabileau, 'Le Cumul des mandat's, *Regards sur l'actualité*, 169 (1991), 17–
30.

is a new pattern of accumulation, with individuals tending to accumulate the positions of mayor and parliamentarian on the one hand, or of regional and departmental councillor on the other. It is the mayor Member of Parliament who is clearly the more important. Co-ordination and regulation are provided increasingly by partisan networks, in which teams of individuals accumulate offices in a form of collective political enterprise.[12] With the development of complex systems of co-financing for projects, this produces a politicization of local public policies, whose implementation is dependent on the degree of partisan harmony among the various levels of government involved.

Another basic limitation on the political assertiveness of the regions is the electoral system. A reform proposal introduced in Parliament in the spring of 1991 which would have provided for elections on a regional rather than departmental basis was denounced by the opposition as a manœuvre to limit the socialists' expected losses. Significantly, however, it received less than wholehearted support from the president of the republic, who did not like the idea of powerful regional notables emerging. This itself is an indication of the potential for regions were they not constrained by political manœuvring at the centre.

Thus a political cleavage has been added to the expected institutional rivalry between the State and the regions. Initiated by a left-wing government, regionalization was slowed down by the rise of the right-wing parties in local and regional elections. This territorial political division obviously tempered the enthusiasm of the central government for further decentralization.

So, while opinion polls show that the public are in favour of regionalization, its political base is weak and it remains subject to powerful political constraints. Regions have provided the site for important changes in the balance of power among the parties and thus represent a prize in national political terms. The election of March 1992 produced contrasting majorities within regional assemblies which will inevitably affect public policies. It is through this policy process that the regions will negotiate their autonomy *vis-à-vis* the State and in this they may find Europe a decisive partner.

[12] P. Garraud, 'La Vie politique locale', in *Institutions et vie politique* (Paris: Documentation Française, 1991), 119–26.

The Contractualization of Public Policy

The decentralization reforms transfer new competences to the regions in the fields of planning, economic development, education, and professional training. These competences are tightly defined and must be exercised within the limits specified in the law. The task of the regions is to stimulate and co-ordinate regional development while not encroaching on the prerogatives of the communes and departments, over which they have no legal control.[13] This transfer of resources and competences has led to a spectacular increase in expenditure, with an annual growth rate of 26.3 per cent between 1982 and 1988 for the regions of metropolitan France and a more rapid increase in debt than for the departments and communes.[14] The financial situation of the regions remains healthy overall, thanks to debt management and self-financing from transferred taxes, though regional taxation remains moderate in comparison with that of the other local authorities. In spite of the increase, the budgets of the regional councils in metropolitan France represented only 7.3 per cent of public expenditure in 1990.[15] Investment accounts for two-thirds of their expenditure, reversing the proportions found in the communes and departments. The regional councils account for a third of the economic interventions of local government in the form of direct aid and loan guarantees, though strangely they are still spending less on this, their most specific function, than are the communes.[16]

Despite the increase in the regions' fiscal capacity, intergovernmental transfers remain decisive. The contractual planning system established with decentralization marks an important change from the past. For the period 1984 to 1988, the State regional planning contracts account for an expenditure of 73 billion francs, of which 60 per cent is provided by the State and 40 per cent by the regions. The Tenth Plan for 1989–93 provides a total of 100 billion francs, 55

[13] P. Sadran, 'La Région', in *Collectivités territoriales*, Cahiers français, 239 (Paris: Documentation Française, 1989), 25–32.

[14] Ministère de l'Intérieur, Direction Générale des Collectivités Locales, *Les Finances régionales en 1988* (Paris, 1990), 3.

[15] Ministère de l'Intérieur, Direction Générale des Collectivités Locales, *Les Vingt Ans des régions: Dossier documentaire*, Conseil Régional de Picardie, colloque des 17–18 Oct. 1991, Amiens.

[16] Ministère de l'Intérieur, Direction Générale des Collectivités Locales, *Les Vingt Ans des régions: Dossier documentaire*.

per cent from the State and 45 per cent from the regions. So both the relative and absolute share provided by the regions has increased. In the overseas departments, planning contracts were also renegotiated for 1989–93, with several specific features, notably in educational development. Their total is estimated at 6.6 billion francs.[17] In all, planning contracts amounted to a quarter of the 31.5 billion-franc budget of the metropolitan regions as a whole.[18]

The formulation of regional plans has two distinct phases, looking first downwards and then upwards. In the first stage the central government takes the initiative, drawing on its more or less permanent consultation through the tripartite working parties of the *Commissariat Général du Plan*, bringing together business and professional groups, trade unions, and the various ministries. In 1988, Prime Minister Michel Rocard indicated the Government's priorities as sustaining economic development and employment and relaunching an urban social policy through contracts with local governments. Regional prefects were then instructed to prepare provisional documents, in co-operation with the regional presidents and regional planning committees. Local consultation practices turned out to be very variable.[19] As an inheritance from the old system of regionalization, French regions still have two assemblies, the elected regional council and a regional economic and social council representing the major socio-economic interests. According to the region, the economic and social council could be directly involved in the formulation of the regional plan, or reduced to a formal consultation at the end, when it is too late to make any changes. The law also obliges regions to consult the departments, the chief cities of departments, and towns with a population over 10,000, but leaves the means at their discretion. In practice, it is local political circumstances which have determined the form of this consultation but the departments have been reluctant to allow the regions to take the lead in operations, requiring them to make a financial contribution, for example in highway

[17] G. Peronet, 'La Première Génération des contrats de plan Etat-Régions, 1984–88 pour l'outre-mer, in *Les contrats de plan etat-régions*, Les cahiers du CNPTF, 29, (1989), 73–5.

[18] Ministère de l'Intérieur, Direction Générale des Collectivités Locales, *Les Finances régionales en 1988*, 4.

[19] Commissariat Général du Plan, *Evaluation de la planification décentralisée* (Paris: Documentation Française, 1986). Conseil Economique et Social, La Planification Régionale, *Journal officiel de la République française* (1991).

construction. Large firms, despite their impact on employment and economic development, have tended to hold back in order to protect their margin of manœuvre in national and international strategies, which might not always be compatible with medium-term commitments at the regional level.

The provisional documents thus produced are then negotiated upwards between the regions and the State, to be inscribed in the priorities of the national plan and finally entrenched in planning contracts between the two parties. A feature of the Tenth Plan was the concentration, at the insistence of the central administration, on specific objectives, limiting the interventions of central government to specific domains. From this angle, contractual planning looks more like a means to mobilize the regions behind State policies than a mechanism to provide State support for regional policies. In a similar vein, in secondary education from 1986 and higher education from 1990 under the programme *Université 2000*, regions are providing financial support for the construction and maintenance of educational property which belongs to the State. While regional politicians complain about this tendency, they go along with it because of the urgency of their needs and the opportunity it provides for regions to enter new policy fields. Nor does their limited margin of manœuvre prevent the emergence of new relationships among regional councils, organized interests, other local authorities, prefects, and the central administration. The region, even weakly consolidated politically and institutionally, remains at the centre of an organizational restructuring whose final shape remains to be seen. There are proposals for planning contracts between the State and departments or cities, which would diminish the region's key role in the procedure. It could also provide the occasion for a reinforcement of the power of the prefects. These developments show how regionalization is still being played out. It has established an evolving system of relationships, in which the position of actors is negotiated according to political circumstances through the formulation and implementation of policies. The State retains the preponderant position, but in putting these negotiations not at the margin but at the heart of the system of centre–periphery relations, the system has experienced a major change. Planning contracts have thus been dissociated from the policy sectors in which they originated, regional and national planning, and become a mechanism for intergovernmental negotiation of public policies.[20] Local policies are now not so much the work of isolated institutional actors such as deconcentrated arms of central government, or local governments, but rather emerge from interorganizational networks adapted to political or sectoral needs. Negotiation and networks are the dominant forms of public action in regionalized France. Planning contracts provide the technical, legal, and financial framework for this.

Europe as a Three-Part Harmony

These relationships are further complicated by the development of the Community. Like their foreign counterparts, French regions are affected by the single market and the movements of capital and labour which result from it. They are also sensitive to the effects of Community policies on regional disparities, notably the effect of the Common Agricultural Policy on the least developed rural areas. The weakness of French regions compared with the German *Länder* raised concerns among regional politicians and the Government in the approach to 1993. A bill proposed by former Minister of the Interior, Joxe, provided for mergers of regions but the local government associations and the Senate proved so hostile to 'forced marriages' that the final version of the law in 1992 provided only for voluntary amalgamations.

Central government is not alone in planning for Community integration. The regions themselves have developed initiatives, at first dispersed and then more and more organized. Enlargement of the Community to the south has transformed the more peripheral French regions such as Brittany and Aquitaine from the richest of the poor to the poorest of the rich. This reclassification has cost them their eligibility for certain types of regional aid such as the Integrated Mediterranean Programmes. The changing categories for Community regional policy has led regions to compare themselves with others, to seek compensation, and to reposition themselves in the new political game.

[20] R. Balme and L. Bonnet, 'The Contractual Relations between the State and the Regions and Territorial Public Policy-Making in France', conference on Regionalization of Unitary States: France and the Netherlands in Comparative Perspective, Erasmus University and University of Leiden, Nov. 1992.

For the regions, the most important financial issue arising from European integration is the Community regional policy. Between 1975 and 1986, French regions received 1957 ECUs from the ERDF, of which 21.4 per cent was reserved for Corsica and the overseas departments. For the period 1989–93, the structural funds provided 3, 420 million ECUs for France, 5.6 per cent of the total. This is the equivalent of a quarter of the budgets for planning contracts for the period, or some 50 per cent of the regions' share of these.

How does the implementation of structural-fund programmes affect political relationships within the regions? It is clear that there has not yet emerged a system of pressure groups around the regional councils. Regions are far from being an essential link in the expression of territorial interests in Europe. These interests rather express themselves through their own channels—chambers of commerce or professional organizations—or through national government departments such as External Trade or Research and Industry. While there is some local mobilization around European questions, it is limited and takes place after the regional politicians have publicized their policies. It is thus more of a mobilization a posteriori than a pressure a priori. The publicization of policy is itself variable according to sector and there is a tendency for regional politicians to focus on ERDF credits, which have a visible product such as road construction, rather than ESF programmes whose outputs, such as training programmes, are necessarily more ephemeral. Despite this, the idea of partnership advanced in the reform of the structural funds seems to work quite well, since the experience acquired in the domestic planning contracts lends itself to the needs of the Community Support Frameworks and monitoring committees for the European programmes. It remains subject to the same limits, however, in that co-operation among partners depends on the local political situation, with the State retaining a major role. The staff of the regional prefects, through their position of neutrality in local political conflicts, often take on the role of co-ordination where local relationships are too tense. They also have an important role in monitoring and checking programme implementation. A large part of the regional fund moneys passes exclusively through the central government, which further enhances the role of the prefects. Finally, in their relations with interest groups, the regions face competition from chambers of commerce, industry, and agriculture who are deeply involved in professional training and infrastructure items such as airports. Their autonomy in the implementation of Community policies is thus limited, even if they do find plenty of opportunities for publicity in the field.

At national level, Community regional policy has produced some complex patterns of interorganizational relations. These are at once horizontal, among the different branches of French national government, and vertical, among the various directorates of the Commission, national ministries, the regions, and the national field administrations. Interministerial relations are themselves complex and marked by rivalries among bureaucrats and politicians. The key central agencies are the *Délégation à l'Aménagement du Territoire et à l'Action Régionale* (DATAR), the Ministry of Employment, the Ministry of Agriculture, the Ministry of the DOM-TOM (overseas departments and territories), the Ministry of Finance, the Ministry of the Interior, and the Secretariat of the Interministerial Committee for European Affairs (SGCI) which comes under the Prime Minister. It is the SGCI which officially works out the French position in relation to Community regional policy, which is then expressed by the ambassador to the Communities. In practice, it is more often DATAR, the Social Fund branch of the Ministry of Employment, or the Ministry of Agriculture which actually formulates the policy. Negotiations in the SGCI do not take place among sectoral interests but rather pit the Ministry of Finance against the spending agencies which have worked out the programmes. In case of deadlock, the Prime Minister decides.

Formally, the regions are excluded from this process. They are brought in later, in the preparation of the Community Support Frameworks, when regional plans have to be presented within the guidelines established by the Commission. However, they are excluded completely from the preparatory negotiations, which define the objects of intervention, the zones of eligibility, and the interregional distribution of Community funds. The regions were conspicuously absent from the preparations to implement the Maastricht accords before the ratification of the Treaty, even though it included provisions for the doubling of the structural funds.

Perhaps because of this, the regions have sought to exercise pressure directly on Community institutions. Sixteen of the twenty-two metropolitan regions now have individual or joint offices in Brussels. The association *Grand Sud* represents Aquitaine, Languedoc-Roussillon, Midi-Pyrénées and Provence-Alpes-Côtes d'Azur. *Grand Est* represents Alsace, Burgundy, Champagne-Ardennes, Franche-Comté, and Lorraine. Nord-Pas de Calais, Rhône-Alpes, and the departments of Alpes Maritimes and Lot-et-Garonne have their own offices. These offices serve to exchange information rather than engage in real negotiation. They do none the less provide regional politicians with an apprenticeship in Community procedure as well as giving them advance notice of projects on which they can then make known their views, either directly to Brussels or via the French Government. It is thus a matter of informal pressure, with a mutual learning process in which the parties acquire the knowledge necessary to progress in such a complex political and administrative environment. It seems that the Programmes of Community Interest, in which national government exercises less influence, are the most propitious for direct exchanges between the Commission and the regions.

The European Parliament is also used as a means of pressure. The Atlantic Group, bringing together members from the Atlantic fringe, is led by French MEPs. It was behind the extension of eligibility criteria for the Stride programme for regional research and technology initiatives to rural and maritime regions. It also played a role in securing the Atlantic route for the high-speed train link between Paris and Madrid. The French tradition of accumulation of European, national, and local mandates ensures that territorial interests are taken into account in European policy.

One of the most important changes affecting French regions has been the development of direct links, intra- and internationally with other local governments, bypassing the central State. While the first links, with Belgian, British, Swiss, and German local governments, were the result of interstate agreements, more recent developments have been decentralized.[21] At first, these were confined to creating enlarged frontier regions, such as the Pyrenean

---

[21] Y. Luchaire, 'Les Régions et l'Europe' in *Annuaire des collectivités locales*, 1990 (Paris: GRAL, 1990), 23–35. B. Dolez, 'Nouvelles perspectives de la coopération décentralisée', *Regards sur l'actualité*, 182 (Paris: Documentation Française, 1992), 38–47.

Working Community or the Western Alpine Working Community. Now there are efforts to establish Euro-regions, with agreements among Nord-Pas de Calais, Kent, Flanders, Wallonia, and the Brussels region; among Languedoc-Roussillon, Midi-Pyrénées, and Catalonia; among the regions of the Atlantic Arc. These regions aim to ensure that their problems as a whole are taken into account by European institutions. Such exchanges have developed into veritable international relations, as in the Four Motors initiative associating Catalonia, Rhône-Alpes, Lombardy, and Baden-Württemburg. These links break the French law limiting associations to territorially contiguous areas and have extended beyond the regions to the large cities which have joined the club of Euro-cities.

The Community encourages such initiatives, notably with the programme for cross-frontier co-operation Interreg, of whose budget 800 million ECUs in 1990–3 is devoted to French frontiers. The implementation of Interreg has caused some lively exchanges between prefects and regional politicians. The Working Community of the Pyrenees, although it lacks a legal standing, complained through its president Jacques Blanc, who is also president of the region Midi-Pyrénées, that it had not been formally associated with the operational programme. The politicians are reluctant to see the prefects control the allocation of funds to which the State has made no contribution. After the failure of attempts by the Ministry of Foreign Affairs to monitor and control the external activities of local governments, the Ministry of the Interior has set up a study group in the hope that it can at least influence if not master them. It is significant that the prefects have sought to extend their own prerogatives in controlling external activities, for example by advocating international agreements between central governments. This indicates how European integration has altered relations between the State and the regions, adding to the ambiguities and uncertainties of decentralization.

Europe has modified centre–periphery relations, which have passed from a bilateral to a trilateral mode. In this three-part harmony, each actor possesses in the duets (bilateral relations) resources acquired through its relationship with a third. The system is thus much more complex and changeable than before. At first sight, there appears to be a convergence of interests between the regions and the Commission to reinforce their power at the expense of the State. But the State is also able to use its position in the implementation of Community policies to strengthen itself against the regions, recovering some of the influence which it lost through decentralization. The result appears to be a positive-sum game in which the stakes are larger and the issues less determined than in the past.

The slogan 'Europe of the Regions' is generally given a positive connotation, but the reality may be more humdrum, or at least more variable. Analysis of the vote from the referendum on Maastricht shows a territorial polarization. The richer regions tended to be in favour while those affected by industrial decline and unemployment, as well as the more isolated rural regions, were hostile.[22] The big differences were at a more local level than can be captured by considering regions as a whole, but there was nevertheless a marked contrast between Alsace, with 65.5 per cent in favour and Picardie or Limousin, with 42.9 per cent and 46.6 per cent respectively.[23] While the overseas regions voted heavily in favour of Maastricht, the turn-out there was a mere 26 per cent of the electorate. This apathy indicates that these regions have not witnessed the politicization of the European debate which has affected the metropole. The peripheral regions, which have most to gain from the structural funds, were also the most indifferent or hostile, with the NO side gaining 56.7 per cent in Corsica. This illustrates the other side of the 'Europe of the Regions'—opposition to European integration expressed in territorial form. The most overt forms of regional mobilization are often reactions to Community decisions, over steel in the 1980s or over the Common Agricultural Policy in the early 1990s. These in turn have had a marked effect on government policy, with the efforts to relaunch regional policy and the attempted renegotiation of the Blair House Agreement by the Balladur Government. In the future they are likely to have a direct impact on local political leadership, producing a divergence between the interests of local elected politicians and the State, as well as among the regions themselves, as these are differentially affected by European integration.

[22] P. Jarreau, 'Le "Non" de la France rurale et ouvrière', *Le Monde*, 22 Sept. 1993, p. 3.
[23] Ibid.

Conclusion

After ten years of decentralization, the institutional and political status of the French region remains below its ambitions. Both in domestic politics and in Europe, its capacity for initiative is tightly constrained by the State. Practitioners and academic observers alike have emphasized its limits in comparison with the Italian regions or, *a fortiori*, the Spanish autonomous communities or German *Länder*. This should not lead us to underestimate the changes which have taken place. The State and the regions *negotiate* their relationships from day to day and Community policies are a determining element in these transactions. Even though a more precise definition of the role of the State in the regions is promised for the near future, it is already the local governments which present the visible face of implementation of Community policies and take the initiative in the exchanges to which the integration process has given rise. Because of their competences in matters such as economic development, the environment, and training, the regions are necessarily implicated in Community policy-making. The fact that these competences are rather narrow compared to those of other levels of government in France or to regions elsewhere in Europe, merely incites their political and bureaucratic leaders to be all the more active. European resources, both budgetary and political, may be marginal but, for French regions, they represent a rare opportunity.

This process has modified considerably the French model of territorial integration. Decentralization has marked the end of the *pouvir périphérique* model, in which the key figure was the prefect. The prefect's technical-bureaucratic legitimacy is now subordinated to the political legitimacy of the elected councillors.[24] Yet the reforms have not meant a return to the territorial administration of the Third Republic, dominated by the notables. Political legitimation may be more important but public policies now emerge from a territorial system which is both political and administrative. The process of decentralization thus represents more of an interlinking in the policy process rather than a differentiation. It rests on co-operation among the various levels of government and

---

[24] Y. Mény, 'La République des fiefs', *Pouvoirs*, 60 (1992), 17–24. J. Rodin, *Le Sacre des notables: La France en décentralisation* (Paris: Fayard, 1985).

State administrative agencies rather than the institutionalization of two separate levels. This is further supported by the spread of the accumulation of mandates in spite of the law of 1985 which was intended to limit it, and by the increasingly porous boundaries between politics and administration, at the local as well as at the central level. In passing from a hierarchical model to a co-operative model with several levels, French territorial government has become more complex. European integration, while destabilizing the French model of public administration,[25] also encourages the tendency for policy-making to move into networks. Community regional policy, in particular, represents a complex form of negotiation in its various stages of elaboration, implementation, and evaluation which, given the multiplication of objectives or programmes and of levels of decision, are almost simultaneous. This dense set of interactions among regional, national, and European politicians and bureaucrats produces networks of policy-making which are more sectoral than territorial and whose mechanisms of regulation and co-ordination are the more complex in that they coincide only partially with national political networks. French regions are rather well equipped to gain access to Community decision-making in so far as the process for negotiating Community Support Frameworks seems to derive from that used in the French regional planning contracts. So they have benefited from an export of their administrative procedures, especially given the presence of Jacques Delors at the head of the Commission. The degree of organization of these networks varies and they tend to be rather unstable. If there is an appropriate image it is that of a cloud formation in which the various elements interact at a distance and whose state is continually changing. This instability shows itself in the rapid changes in programmes and the continuous rotation of bureaucrats among local, regional, national, and European administrations, making evaluation particularly difficult. Although these networks are difficult to identify in a stable form, however, it is evident that politicians and bureaucrats within them do share a number of key values, such as democracy in Europe and subsidiarity, of types of expertise, notably law and European policy, and of behaviours, such as trips to Brussels and the pro-

---

[25] P. Muller, 'Entre le local et l'Europe: La Crise du modèle français de politiques publiques', *Revue française de science politique*, 42/2 (1992), 275–97. P. Muller (ed.), *L'Administration française est-elle en crise?* (Paris: l'Harmattan, 1992).

motion of a cosmopolitan image. These elements help shape the policy community and promote a common cognitive framework for European policy. The complexity and uncertainty give regional actors the opportunity to affirm their identity, to define their competences and means of intervention, to mobilize European resources in order to negotiate better with the State, and to gain an advantage on their competitors. This does not happen in the same way throughout France and there are disparities resulting from the economic impact of integration and the history of relations with the national State. The paradox is that the most peripheral regions, which have the most to gain from Community programmes but which are victims of their situation and their history, should be those where the European theme plays most weakly in political terms, no doubt because it is seen as merely reinforcing their disadvantage in the national arena.

MAP 8. Germany: *Länder*.

8

German *Länder* and the European Community

HANS-GEORG GERSTENLAUER

Introduction: EC Legislation and the Länder Competences

From a constitutional point of view the German *Länder* are autonomous states with original legislative, executive, juridical, and budgetary competences. In addition to these responsibilities the *Länder* participate via the *Bundesrat* (Federal Council) in federal legislation and administration (Article 50 Basic Law). The *Bundesrat's* members are delegated by the *Länder* governments. In practice, the *Bundesrat* has a right of veto in the last resort with respect to the majority of federal-law proposals of political importance.

The Federal Republic of Germany's membership of the EC affects both of these competences. Apart from the few provisions in the EC treaties where the Commission directly applies Community law, for example on State aids, EC legal provisions in the form of regulations and directives are in general finally decided by the EC Council of Ministers as the major decision-making institution in the EC. However, as the Community treaties before Maastricht did not take account of the respective constitutional organizations of the member states including the existence of the German *Länder*, neither the *Bundesrat* nor the individual *Länder* could formally participate in the Council: Germany was represented by the federal government.

The first problem which results from this situation is that *Länder* responsibility in federal affairs exercised via the *Bundesrat* was considerably moderated in areas where the EC is active. If during the formulation process of the national policy line the *Bundesrat* had no possibility to influence the position of the federal government to be presented in the Council of Ministers, the *Länder*'s rights laid down in Article 50 Basic Law would become obsolete.

The second problem for the *Länder* results from the fact that, in the case of the *Länder*'s constitutionally assigned exclusive competences, the federal government, through its representation in the EC Council, would gain a right of decision over subjects for which under the domestic German distribution of powers, it had no competence. Although these cases are far fewer than those referred to above, it should be noted that they have been increasing as EC integration progresses. In this respect the *Länder* have been reacting to each case with a very high sensitivity. The formulation and application of EC law interferes with specific *Länder* responsibilities in the following fields:

- Education and training, where the *Länder* still exercise their own responsibilities to a great extent. EC activities affect *Länder* competences in vocational training and mutual recognition of certificates and qualifications.
- Environmental protection, especially sea and inland-water pollution.
- Transport policy, including port traffic.
- Agricultural and regional structural policy where the Joint Task programmes (with the federal level) are subject to decisions of the Commission on State aid provisions laid down under Articles 92–4 EC.

From the beginning of the EC integration process the *Länder* recognized the problems resulting from this configuration and were apprehensive that their functions might be reduced to a purely administrative nature. So from a very early stage they have attempted to compensate for and even to counteract this development. These attempts can be divided into two periods: participation on a mainly informal basis between 1951 and 1986; and the establishment of legal provisions after 1987.

Phase I: The Informal Participation of the Länder in National and Supranational Decision-Making (1951–1986)[1]

As early as 1951 the *Bundesrat* realized that in the long term the EC integration process would cut across the federal division of

---

[1] For further details see Hans-Georg Gerstenlauer, 'German Länder in the EC', in M. Keating and B. Jones (eds.), *Regions in the European Community* (Oxford: Clarendon Press, 1985).

power and lead ultimately to a loss of its own power. On the occasion of the ratification of the Rome Treaties, two demands were made: that the *Bundesrat* should be able to send some of its members to the European Assembly, and that it should be able to participate in a significant way in defining the German position in the Community Council. From a juridical point of view, however, up to 1986 the *Bundesrat* in practice achieved little. Its only right was to be informed by the federal government about Community affairs. But a question remained concerning the degree of real participation the *Bundesrat* could achieve in EC affairs.

The *Bundesrat*, as well as the *Bundestag*, received all EC proposals on Community regulations, directives, and other documents such as reports, programmes, and memoranda, communicated by the Commission to the Council of Ministers. The EC documents were debated at length by the *Bundesrat*, usually in its committees, and the results were frequently presented to the federal government in a formal statement. In most cases the *Bundesrat*'s point of view was in accordance with the federal government's approach and the federal government often took the suggestions of the *Bundesrat* into account, particularly on technical details where the *Länder* and their bureaucracies had superior administrative expertise at their disposal. However, the extent to which the federal government accepted the opinion expressed by the *Bundesrat* has not been systematically investigated and it is difficult to assess its real power. The procedure was seen merely as a way of satisfying the formal obligation of informing the *Länder*, but the actual influence of the *Bundesrat*, through informal channels, might have been considerable.

Most of the time the *Bundesrat* meets at civil-servant level. Those federal civil servants who are members of the German delegations in the working groups of the EC Council of Ministers frequently take part on behalf of the federal ministries. At this stage the final German approach has not yet been established. Thus there is an interaction and the possibility of informal influence on the federal civil servants. In many cases, the latter will have accepted an opinion expressed by one or several of the *Länder*, and will have agreed to take it into account in negotiations with Brussels. So there is not only a detailed, mutual exchange of information and opinions on EC affairs, but also an opportunity for the *Bundesrat* to influence positions taken by the federal government.

Moreover, in 1979 the federal government specifically pledged to improve the flow of information to the *Bundesrat* so that its position could more fully be taken into account during EC Council negotiations.

Before 1979, attempts by the *Bundesrat* to nominate members to the European Parliament had failed, and the German parliamentary delegation in Strasbourg was drawn exclusively from the *Bundestag*. This pattern of representation ended with direct elections. Nevertheless, even before 1979, the European Parliament had some contacts with the *Bundesrat*. These were subsequently intensified; in particular, the *Bundesrat* Committee for EC Affairs has established links with the European Parliament, informs all German MEPs of its activities and opinions on EC matters, and communicates all European Parliament resolutions, reports, and opinions to the members of the *Bundesrat*.

By definition, the *Bundesrat* is a federal institution whose role is confined to federal affairs. For constitutional reasons, it had been considered in this period that subjects which fell under exclusive responsibility of the *Länder* could not be treated within this federal organization. This was true not only for EC but also for domestic affairs. Therefore, apart from the *Bundesrat*'s opportunities to have a say in supranational decision-making, the *Länder* had to find other ways of countering the increasing influence of the EC, especially where it affected their exclusive powers.

As early as 1956, the institution of the *Länder* Observer (*Länderbeobachter*) had been established by an *ad hoc* arrangement used during the negotiations for the Rome Treaties. The *Länderbeobachter* is a senior civil servant responsible to the governments of all of the *Länder* and nominated by the Conference of *Länder* Ministers for Economic Affairs (*Länderwirtschaftsministerkonferenz*). His main task is to collect information about Community affairs which are of interest to the *Länder* and to pass it to the *Bundesrat*, sectoral minister conferences, and to the *Länder*. In this capacity, the *Länderbeobachter* can attend the Council of Ministers as a 'non-speaking' member of the German delegation; is allowed to join in the preparatory meetings for the sessions of the Council held in the Federal Ministry for Economic Affairs; and receives the instructions to the German delegation of the COREPER.

Moreover, he obtains all documents on EC matters from the secretary of the Council and other EC institutions and distributes them to the *Länder* if they have not received them from other official channels. In 1985 negotiations between the *Bund* and the *Länder* on the integration of the *Länder* Observer into the German Permanent Representation failed as the *Länder* did not agree to the Foreign Minister's demand to subordinate the Observer to the EC Ambassador.

The participation of *Länder* representatives in German delegations at EC institutions has developed in a pragmatic way and without a formal basis. Both the *Länder* and the federal government have an interest in including *Länder* experts, especially in matters for which technical or administrative know-how is required. Thus, *Länder* representatives have been able to influence the position of the federal government as well as negotiations within the EC institutions. Despite this, the *Länder* were dissatisfied with their actual participation, the size of their representation, and their status.

EC affairs were also treated within existing institutions and procedures of the 'co-operative federalism'. The implicit inclusion of EC issues in the domestic practice of vertical co-ordination between federal and *Länder* governments gave the latter additional channels of information, participation, and monitoring of EC affairs without the creation of specific new bodies. There are fourteen sectoral minister conferences and hundreds of federal–*Länder* committees on an administrative level. Exceptionally, representatives of the EC Commission attend these meetings and in some cases the whole committee or minister conference visits Brussels to inform themselves and to exchange views with their EC counterparts.

The *Länderbeteiligungsverfahren* (procedure securing fair participation of the *Länder*) was established in 1979 after several years of negotiations between the federal and *Länder* governments. The latter had pressed for a legally binding arrangement for their participation in EC affairs after they had been confronted by increasing EC interventions in areas where they were constitutionally competent or in spheres where they had to bear financial burdens as a consequence of EC legislation. The *Länder* position was that their participation in those EC affairs which fall under their exclusive responsibility cannot be exercised via a federal body, the

Bundesrat, but only directly by the *Länder* themselves. The federal government, however, had only been willing to accept a voluntary commitment.

An *ad hoc* agreement was finally established, based on an exchange of letters between the federal Chancellor and the chairman of the conference of the Minister Presidents of the *Länder*. This stressed the obligation to co-operate closely in an atmosphere of mutual trust in EC affairs which fall under the exclusive competence of the *Länder* or which affect their essential interests. The duty to inform the *Länder* was extended to initiatives and proposals of the EC Commission even before these are put forward to the Council. The federal government stated its intention to take into account the *Länder*'s common position 'as far as possible' and it was allowed to deviate from the *Länder*'s position only 'for compelling foreign and integration policy reasons'. In this latter case, the federal government had to give an explanation for its deviation. The federal government for its part expected the *Länder* to reach a common position within a reasonable time and to take into account reasons of foreign and integration policy as well as the position of the federal government. Finally, the federal government agreed to the request of the *Länder* to allow, wherever possible, two *Länder* representatives to participate in the German delegation in EC advisory bodies dealing with those EC affairs which concerned their exclusive legal powers.

In practice, this procedure has not proved very effective. The consultation and position-finding between the *Länder* was organized on a decentralized basis, in the respective responsible sectoral *Länder* minister conferences. The agreed position of the *Länder* had to be unanimous, in contrast to the *Bundesrats-Verfahren* where majority rule is practised. The parallel existence of the *Bundesrats-Verfahren* with its well-tried procedures within the *Bundesrat* tended to cut across the new consultation procedures. The final deficiency was the lack of the necessary qualitative and quantitative capacity in *Länder* administrations to deal with the increased flow of information.The results of this procedure were not at all satisfactory for either the federal government or the *Länder*. By March 1986 1,070 EC documents had been distributed to the *Länder* but in no case had the *Länder* come to a common vote.

Besides these multilateral activities, the *Länder* established various direct and individual contacts, although until 1985 these had an exclusively informal character.

Viewed objectively, the efforts of the *Länder* to achieve a reliable legal basis for their participation in EC affairs were not very successful. In practice, however, they obtained access to a wide range of information channels and possibilities for participation in EC affairs. This is not surprising, given that the federal government is dependent on the administrative experience and the technical know-how of the *Länder* bureaucracies in the policy-formulation of EC affairs. In daily business federal and *Länder* governments and administrations co-operate closely and, generally, try to take into account their mutual interests. So while the *Länder* executives were able to compensate at least partly for their losses of competence by increased co-operation with the federal government, the *Land* parliaments were by and large excluded. Despite attempts to participate in EC affairs via extension of their control rights to EC legislation or the establishment of direct contacts with the European Parliament, they have been clear losers from European integration.

New Dynamics in EC Integration and German Federalism

In the 1980s, both EC integration and German federalism were marked by new dynamics. These trends have led to a substantial change in the participation of the *Länder* in EC affairs.

The renewed dynamics of the EC integration became increasingly visible to the public through the approval of the Single European Act, the programme for the completion of the internal market, and the signing of the Treaty of Maastricht on Economic and Monetary Union (EMU) as well as Political Union. With the further deepening of EC integration it became simultaneously evident that in many policy areas a change from classical foreign policy to European domestic policy had taken place. These developments had political implications for the political freedom of action of the German *Länder*.

Federalism in Germany also developed over the years. While the first post-war decades in the Federal Republic were characterized by a shift of power from the *Länder* to the *Bund* and subsequently by an institutionalization of the different forms of co-operative federalism, since the early 1980s this trend has stopped and, in a few individual cases, has even been reversed in favour of more *Länder*-oriented politics. From the point of view of the *Länder*, the continuing loss of competences to the more distant and EC level seems to be anachronistic.

Another important element in the development of federalism in Germany was the increase of competitive elements both horizontally between the *Länder* and vertically between the Federal level and the *Länder*. It can be best illustrated by the repeated disputes on fiscal federalism. This development is in part due to the fact that the economic crisis in the 1970s reinforced existing differences and created new ones between the *Länder*, including a south–north disparity. A second factor is the higher political weight and new self-confidence which the *Länder* governments and their Minister Presidents gained in the 1970s. This came about particularly because of the majority obtained by CDU/CSU-governed *Länder* in the *Bundesrat* during the SPD/FDP federal government, making them part of a *de facto* all-party coalition in many legal questions.

In the late 1970s and the 1980s the *Länder* also profited from the increased popularity of ecological questions and the renaissance of traditional, sometimes romantic values as well as the widespread trend for small, geographically limited, decision-making bodies to which citizens could easily relate. They used these sentiments to strengthen a regional identity for their *Länder* which had mainly been created by the allies after the Second World War without respect for established traditional links and delineations. These elements strengthened the role of the *Länder* and determined their approach in EC affairs, where significant changes can be observed. The position of the *Länder* towards European integration became more critical although they did not diminish their principled support for unification. This was reflected in the general principles approved by the Minister Presidents at their annual conference in Munich from 21 to 23 October 1987.

In the general introduction the heads of the *Länder* governments recognized the unification of Europe as the condition for a permanent European system of peace and freedom. They declared their support for the further development of the EC to a European Union. In their view the final aim of integration is a Europe with federal structures which guarantee the preservation of cultural identities, social pluralism, balanced economic development, and decision-making close to the citizens in the member states. Even though the *Länder* have increased their participation at the domestic level in EC matters, they are concerned that the ongoing centralization of responsibilities at the EC level will reduce the possibilities of action of the German *Länder*. They expect future integration developments in Europe to respect the following ten principles in order to preserve the *Länder*'s political freedom of action:

1. Each legislative act requires a concrete basis in the EC treaties; this basis is at the same time the limit of EC actions. The integration and implementation of EC law has to take into account the federal structure of the Federal Republic of Germany.

2. Realization of the principle of subsidiarity: the EC should only take over new responsibilities if absolutely necessary and if their full efficiency can only be achieved at the Community level. Apart from their implementation competence the German *Länder* should keep a core of their own responsibilities in culture, education, regional structure, and health policies.

3. Federalism instead of centralism. In order to preserve the diversity of Europe, Community policies should be based on federal principles. Community activities should merely set the framework, taking account of the federal structure of individual member states.

The other principles deal with the following specific policy fields:

4. Securing the educational responsibilities of the *Länder*: the cultural responsibility which forms the core of the *Länder* identity as individual states should not be touched in the course of transfer of sovereignity to the EC.

5. Safeguarding the broadcasting responsibility of the *Länder*.

6. Securing competitive agriculture.

7. Securing the individual regional structural policies of the *Länder*.

8. Safeguarding high-quality consumer standards, particularly in the fields of health, security, environment, and consumer protection.

9. Ensuring a European economic, legal, social, and tax framework for small and medium-sized enterprises.

10. Subsidiarity in research policy.

The heads of *Länder* governments underlined that they themselves will pursue these principles through their own participation in EC matters. The federal government was asked to present these principles in the forums of the EC.

Phase II: The Legalization of the Länder's Participation in EC Affairs since 1987

At the same time as adopting a more critical approach towards EC integration, the *Länder* have improved their participation in a relatively short time. In 1986, the long-running conflict between the federal and *Länder* governments on the latter's participation in EC affairs became publicly visible. The *Länder* used the ratification procedure for the Single European Act (SEA) to demand greater participation in the formulation of national policy in EC affairs. Because of this link and the subsequent discussion, the ratification procedure in Germany was delayed and the planned date for bringing the SEA into force (1 January 1987) was seriously put into question.

The *Länder* underlined their demands with a wide range of criticisms aimed at both the EC and the federal government. These criticisms were not only expressed with respect to the SEA but reflected also the general dissatisfaction of the *Länder* with some established Community policies. The EC, and in particular the Commission, were reproached with power presumptuousness, particularly in the fields of freshwater quality, the preservation of bird species, toy safety, education, and cultural activities. The application of State aid articles in the EEC Treaty—in force since 1958!—must, in the view of the German *Länder*, not be applied to German regional programmes as they are intended to offset specific local disadvantages and not to achieve national competitive advantages. The *Länder* demanded that the high standards of protection in the Federal Republic in the fields of health, safety, environmental and consumer protection must not be lowered to a generally poorer European level. With respect to SEA provisions on research and technology policy the *Länder* insisted on a continued guarantee for policy measures at their level. More generally, the *Länder* demanded a systematic application of the principle of subsidiarity.

The federal government was accused of having not sufficiently consulted the *Länder* concerning the negotiations on the SEA. The *Länder* regarded this as incompatible with the principle of federative loyalty (*Bundestreue*) as well as a contravention of existing arrangements for their participation in EC matters. With respect to the *Länder*'s role in EC affairs their main demand was that extended rights of participation be firmly established in the Ratification Act, and they indicated that their consent to the Ratification Act was dependent on the fulfilment of this demand.

After nearly one year of discussion the *Länder* formally received in the new *Bundesratsverfahren* the legal basis they had demanded. In substance, however, the federal government did not make significant concessions which would have gone beyond the voluntary commitment already laid down in the *Länderbeteiligungsverfahren*. The agreement led to some important institutional adjustments. In contrast to the *Länderbeteiligungsverfahren* it was now up to the *Bundesrat* to play a central role in the *Länder*'s participation. This is where the *Länder* formulate their opinions in EC affairs affecting their exclusive legislative responsibilities and other fundamental interests. This development is remarkable for two reasons. First, it is a 180-degree change in direction of the argument which had justified the establishment of the *Länderbeteiligungsverfahren*. In that case the *Länder* had asked for a new procedure because, for constitutional reasons, no federal body could become active in spheres of their responsibility. Secondly, it led to the novelty in German federalism of a federal body being used for internal *Länder* co-ordination even in fields of their exclusive competence. This new element can therefore be considered a precedent in the German federal system.

Within the *Bundesrat* a new committee exclusively for EC matters was created, the *Kammer für Vorlagen der EG*. This was considered to be necessary for EC affairs which are urgent and confidential as the normal, rigid, three-week rhythm of the *Bundesrat* might not be sufficient for a quick reaction. The *Kammer* is composed of members of the *Bundesrat*, that is the *Land* Representative to the federal level or a *Land* Minister. It decides by majority vote—another innovation for co-ordination of exclusive *Länder* responsibilities where normally a unanimous vote is required.

All these developments have enabled the *Länder* to participate more effectively in EC affairs. The SEA ratification procedure not only improved the legal status of the *Länder* in EC matters but also finished off the *Länderbeteiligungsverfahren* (which had proved impracticable) where previous efforts undertaken by the *Länder* to reform it had failed.

To the public, Bonn was regarded as responsible for the clash because it had not adequately involved the *Länder* during the relatively short period of the Luxembourg intergovernmental conference. However, the federal government argued that the time for consultation had been relatively short. It also became clear that the *Länder* themselves had not been well prepared and in consequence, the *Länder* governments improved their capacities in EC affairs on both the political and administrative levels.

Changes were also made with respect to the *Länderbeobachter*. In October 1988 a formal agreement on the *Länderbeobachter* was signed which terminated its *ad hoc* status. For the first time his tasks were defined and provisions were made with respect to staff, equipment, and budget. As a consequence, he left his host office in the Baden-Württemberg representation to the *Bund* in Bonn and moved into his own office. He also changed his office in Brussels and is now located in the German Permanent Representation but with a separate entrance and no subordinate status. For the first time, his staff in Brussels was extended by the recruitment of some secretaries.

With the abolition of the *Länderbeteiligungsverfahren* the Observer and his two collaborators are able to concentrate more on their role in the Council and the preparatory meetings—tasks which cannot be shared by the information offices of the *Länder* in Brussels. The additional staff, the improvement of technical equipment, and the discontinuation of time-consuming tasks such as dealing with information requests from individual *Länder* (now answered by the *Länder* offices) have enhanced his initial information and observer function considerably.

The most visible sign of the increased presence of the German *Länder* in EC affairs is the establishment of information offices in Brussels since 1985. Hamburg was the first *Land* to open such an office, in January 1985. Wilhelm Haferkamp, who had just terminated his mandate as Vice-President of the Commission, became head of this Hanse-Office-Haferkamp. A few months later, in May

1985, the Saarland followed with its Information and Economic Promotion Office Saarland after the *Land* government had changed and a director of the EC Commission, Ottokar Hahn, had been appointed Minister for Federal and 'Special' (including European) Affairs.

All former eleven *Länder* are directly represented in Brussels with individual offices. The five new eastern *Länder* have recently also established their own offices in a common building, the former GDR embassy in Brussels. In the first months after the political unification their interests had been represented by partner *Länder* from western Germany.

The offices differ in their status, staff, equipment, and priorities but nevertheless a common profile of tasks can be identified. Six *Länder* have organized their offices on a civil-law basis. The Hanse Office Haferkamp which also represents the north German *Länder* of Schleswig-Holstein and Lower Saxony is financed by the Hamburg Information GmbH, a state-owned civil-law society. North Rhine-Westphalia's office was established by the Westdeutsche Landesbank which pays for the head of the office, a seconded *Land* official, as its employee. Five *Länder* (Baden-Württemberg, Bavaria, Bremen, Hessen, and Rhineland-Palatinate) chose a public-law status: the offices are financed from the *Land* budget and the staff are members of the public service.

Staff numbers have increased continuously. In the beginning the Saarland had one head of office and one secretary; the Bavarian office, the biggest representation, has now reached about fifteen collaborators. The common tasks of the information offices can be characterized as follows:

- To provide the *Land* government and Parliament with information on developments in the EC, in particular projects of the Commission.
- To establish and maintain contacts with EC institutions, the Permanent Representation of the Federal Republic, the other *Länder* offices, and economic interest groups.
- To consult and promote the economy of the *Land*, providing information on possibilities and procedures of EC assistance as well as on public procurement; lobbying for private business and specific *Land* interests *vis-à-vis* the EC institutions; establishing contacts for public organizations and private businesses

of the region with the EC institutions; and giving information on *Land* politics and the contacts between the Land administration and EC institutions.

- To prepare information visits of *Land* ministers, deputies, and officials.
- To provide public information, including cultural events and exhibitions.

The priorities in these activities vary considerably from *Land* to *Land*.

The federal government, afraid of a foreign policy on the side, was not very happy about the *Länder* offices. It expressed some doubts about their constitutional legality, but it did not bring the case to the Federal Constitutional Court and tolerated their successive installation. Some *Länder* also had problems and hesitated to establish their own representation. Rhineland-Palatinate shared the opinion of the federal government and in particular of the Ministry for Foreign Affairs about the usefulness of such an institution. Some critics, while not opposing the principle, showed a preference for a common institution and would have preferred a reinforced *Länderbeobachter*.

With the passage of the years, pragmatic co-operation has developed between the Permanent Representation and the *Länder* offices. Regular meetings are held, and informal and formal information-exchanges have been established. However, the different status of the Permanent Representation and the *Länder* offices has created a certain distance between the two, which the *Länder* seem to respect and accept.

The increased activities of the German *Länder* in EC matters in recent years were also reflected by a higher personal mobility between the EC and the *Länder* level. While for the first decades of European integration such direct exchange was practically non-existent, it has become more common since the mid-1980s. A few examples may illustrate this. Ottokar Hahn was Director in the Commission, then in 1985 became Minister in the Saarland responsible for EC matters, and is now again Director in the Commission. Wilhelm Haferkamp was Commissioner until 1984 and then became head of the Brussels representation of Hamburg, Lower Saxony, and Schleswig-Holstein. Franz Froschmeier was Director-General in the Commission and became Minister for Economic Affairs in Schleswig-Holstein. At a different level, the Bavarian CSU succeeded in having 'its' Commissioner in Brussels with the appointment in 1988 of Peter M. Schmidhuber, Bavarian Minister to the federal government, alongside Martin Bangemann of the FDP. This was against the unwritten rule that one German Commissioner is nominated by the federal government and the other by the opposition. It is no exaggeration to say that during the last four years Schmidhuber's Cabinet has become a bridgehead for the German *Länder* in general and Bavaria in particular.

The Länder *and the Treaty on European Union*

The greater weight of the *Länder* became obvious at the deliberations in the intergovernmental conferences on Political Union (PU) and Economic and Monetary Union (EMU). At a request of the *Bundesrat* dated 24 August 1990[2], the federal government had agreed:

- To associate all *Länder* in the preparatory work for the intergovernmental conferences on Political Union as well as Economic and Monetary Union.
- To elaborate the German negotiation position jointly with the *Länder*.
- To include representatives of two *Länder* into the delegation at each of the intergovernmental conferences.

By decision of the *Bundesrat*, representatives of the *Länder* of Baden-Württemberg and North Rhine-Westphalia attended the Political Union conference and representatives of Bavaria and Hamburg attended the Economic and Monetary Union conference.

With respect to the political line to be taken on Economic and Monetary Union the *Bundesrat* was largely in agreement with the position of the federal government.[3] In view of the planned German unification and the progress made in economic and monetary questions the *Länder* underlined the necessity of further integration. They stated also that the merging of the two German states should not slow down European integration.

[2] Decision BR-Drs 550/90.
[3] Decision of the *Bundesrat* 220/90 on 13 June 1990.

The *Bundesrat* supported progress in monetary co-operation. But it underlined also that:

- The step-by-step realization of the EMU should be accompanied by further progress in the fields of economic and financial policy, consolidation of public budgets, and external balance.
- Stability of prices should have highest priority at the realization of monetary union.
- A European central bank should be established pursuant to federal principles and be independent from EC institutions or national governments.
- Economic and financial policy should be guided by the principle of subsidiarity, the *Länder* repeating here their demand for continued individual freedom of action in economic policies for the regions, in particular in the fields of regional structural policy, research and technology policy, education policy.

Concerning the Political Union the *Länder* interest focused on the establishment of a federal structure. They approved in the *Bundesrat* on 24 August 1990 the following demands for changes of the Community treaties:[4]

- Subsidiarity as a general principle in the Community treaties.
- Modification of Art. 2 (1) of the Merger Treaty in order to allow *Länder* and regions participation in the form of an additional representative in deliberations of the Council of Ministers in the case of EC affairs which, under domestic law, fall under their exclusive responsibilities or affect their fundamental interests.
- Creation of a special Committee of Regions through which they could participate directly in EC decision-making. This Committee of Regions should have the opportunity to take a position on all EC projects. If the Council of Ministers or the Commission did not coincide with this position, they would be obliged to communicate the essential reasons to the Committee on demand.
- By virtue of modification of Art. 173 (1) EEC and the two other Community treaties, *Länder* and regions should receive

---

[4] Decision of the *Bundesrat* 550/90.

an individual right to institute proceedings against actions of the Council and the Commission.

The *Länder* were active and successful in finding allies for their interests in the other member states of the Community. They took a leading role in the conferences on a 'Europe of Regions', the first of which was held in Munich on 18–19 October 1989 following an invitation of the Bavarian Minister President Streibl. The demands of the *Länder*, regions, and autonomous communities raised at these meetings show clearly the handwriting of the German *Länder*.[5] Their view had to be taken into account at the establishment of the European Union with regard to: the principle of subsidiarity; division of the Union into the three levels of the EC; member states; and *Länder*, regions, or autonomous communities; establishment of a regional committee on EC level; the right for the subnational entities to initiate proceedings at the European Court of Justice. The *Länder*, regions, and autonomous communities claim an individual freedom of action for certain tasks such as regional development, education, media and cultural policy, environment protection, health affairs, and internal security—exactly those policy fields which the German *Länder* have repeatedly defined as their sensitive responsibilities and which have been in particular threatened by EC integration. In the Maastricht Treaty several of the *Länder* demands were taken into account, notably the introduction of the principle of subsidiarity into the Treaty and the establishment of the Committee of the Regions.

Although the *Länder* welcomed and appreciated these results and also traced them back to their direct involvement, they were not enthusiastic about the outcome. The final result of the negotiations did not totally correspond to their ideas. The *Länder* Minister Presidents complained at their meeting on 12 March 1992 that the modification of the treaties would allow the EC to become active 'to a considerable extent' in fields of *Länder* responsibilities. Moreover, they were dissatisfied that Political Union had not made the same progress as Economic and Monetary Union. They asked the federal government to take an initiative to enhance the responsibilities of the European Parliament and to increase the number of German members by the end of 1992.

[5] See 'Resolutions of the Participants of the Conferences "Europe of Regions" in Munich, Brussels, Riva del Garda', in the Bavarian Minister for European Affairs (ed.), *Euroaktuell*, nos. 9 and 13, Aug. and Nov. 1990.

But the lack of enthusiasm was also tactical. A series of additional demands had been addressed by the *Länder* to the federal government to improve further their participation in the formulation of the domestic policy line in EC affairs. After the signing of the Maastricht Treaty this point had still to be resolved. The *Länder* made it clear that they were determined to make the required *Bundesrat* approval of the Maastricht Treaty contingent on fulfilment of these demands.

The demands of the *Länder* for domestic participation in EC affairs led to a new clash with the federal government and with deputies of the federal parliament. As a result the federal government had, even five months after the signature of the Maastricht Treaty, not been able to submit a draft for the Ratification Act to the Parliament and the *Bundesrat*.

The principal demands of the *Länder* were fourfold. First, they wanted the transfer of sovereign powers to international institutions—laid down in Article 24 of the Basic Law as an exclusive power of the federal level—to require in future the consent of the *Bundesrat*. Secondly, in fields of exclusive responsibilities of the *Länder* they wanted a *Land* representative to represent the Federal Republic at the EC level. Thirdly, they wanted a constitutional right for the *Länder* to establish individual and independent representations in particular—but not exclusively—at the EC. Finally, the *Länder* asked that their rights for participation in EC affairs be fixed in the German Constitution. This demand for independent representations led some participants at the negotiations to state that the outcome of this clash would decide if the unified Germany would remain a federal state or degenerate to a federation of states.[6]

After long, controversial negotiations in the joint constitutional commission of federal parliament and council an agreement was concluded to amend the constitution with a new Article 23. The federal government may in the future only transfer sovereignty powers with the consent of the federal council. This provision applies to federal and *Länder* responsibilities, even federal responsibilities where under domestic law the *Bundesrat* can be overruled. Such a transfer now requires a qualified majority of both *Bundestag* and *Bundesrat* while previously only a simple majority was needed. In the future the opinion of the *Bundesrat* will be

[6] 'Bundesstaat oder Staatenbund?' *Frankfurter Allgemeine Zeitung*, 21 Mar. 1992.

decisive for the German position in those areas which affect the exclusive legislative responsibilities of the *Länder*, the establishment of their authorities, or their administrative procedures. However, the *Bundesrat* is obliged to safeguard the responsibility of the Federal Republic. In other cases—including those which fall under the exclusive legislative responsibility of the federal level—the federal government has to take into account the position of the *Bundesrat*. In fields of exclusive legislative responsibilities of the *Länder*, the Federal Republic may be represented in the EC Council of Ministers by a representative of the *Länder*. The Maastricht Treaty explicitly provides for this. The *Länder* will have to agree among themselves who the representative should be on any given occasion.

Conclusion

From the beginning of European integration forty years ago, the German *Länder* pursued a policy of compensating for their loss of exclusive powers by participation in policy-formulation at both domestic and European level. They have created a series of procedures and institutions which allow them to push through their interests. Their influence on all EC matters has increased considerably, particularly in the last decade. They have made special progress in this period in upgrading the juridical basis for their participation. The largely informal basis of participation was first upgraded by a comprehensive federal law approved during the Ratification Act on the Single European Act. Now it has been agreed that the rights of the *Länder* to participate in EC affairs will be guaranteed by the Constitution.

Although the federal government has understood the *Länder* demands its main concern has been to ensure its own freedom of manœuvre at the EC level. The *Länder*, once they decided to increase their influence, showed an astonishing flexibility in adjusting the federal system. They overcame their legal reservations, had no scruples in turning from their former position by 180 degrees, and did not hesitate to reorient their most powerful institution in federal affairs, the *Bundesrat*. This body not only co-ordinates all *Länder* positions in EC affairs regardless of the responsibility under the German Constitution but has also been equipped with a special committee to allow a quick response from the *Länder* side.

Moreover, as it is in the interest of the *Länder* to reach a common position among themselves quickly so that it can be taken into account by the federal government and the EC institutions, each of them had to make another fundamental concession. They have relinquished the unanimous vote normally required in domestic co-ordination in areas of their exclusive legislative responsibilities in favour of a majority rule. So in order to make the totality of the *Länder* more powerful each *Land* lost an important right and sign of its own state identity. The increase in the number of *Länder* after German unification means that the role of each individual *Land* becomes even more marginal. However, these losses are tempered by the establishment of *Länder* offices in Brussels.

Although there have been a lot of adjustments on both sides, the potential tension between the federal government's concern to keep its policy-making manœuvrability in EC affairs as well as the *Länder* governments' concern to gain influence continues to exist. More legalization of *Länder* rights might diminish the risk of a confrontation. But also the contrary could occur. More legal provisions could tempt either side to go more often to the Federal Constitutional Court. A confirmation for this thesis could be seen in the fact that the first court case was invoked only after the legal establishment of *Länder* rights in EC affairs. In the end much will depend on the general climate between federal and *Länder* governments and the overall state and practice of the German 'co-operative federalism'.

Whether co-operative federalism is still an appropriate term for the German governmental system is open to question. The unification process has promoted serious strains which have exacerbated the patiently constructed relationship between the *Länder* and the federal government. These strains have caused German politicians and constitutionalists to examine the possibility of reform to the federal system in two specific areas: financial equalization and territorial reform.

Prior to 1990 and unification, a system of horizontal financial relations between the *Länder* had been established, but there were limits to its effectiveness. The money available for redistribution among the *Länder* was limited and a common policy could not be agreed between the contributing and recipient *Länder*. In large part this was a north–south divide. The northern *Länder*, particularly the city states of Hamburg and Bremen, have higher social expenditure per head than the states of larger areas with more balanced populations; but there were differences of opinion as to how this factor should be weighted. Attempts to resolve the problem were made after much acrimonious discussion on the structural-aid law (*Strukturhilfegesetz*) but this merely sparked appeals to the federal Constitutional Court by the beneficiary *Länder* who thought that the population weighting was unfair. The appeals were hotly disputed by the largely southern *Länder* who felt that the distribution of structural aid was an unconstitutional form of hidden financial equalization. In the opinion of one observer, 'cooperation was conspicuous by its absence'.[7]

However, the disparities of wealth between the northern and southern *Länder* in the old West Germany were minimal compared to the differences between western and eastern *Länder* after unification. While the needs of the eastern *Länder* were recognized, neither the federal government nor the western *Länder* wished to be disadvantaged by the new Unity Fund. This is a single fund administered by the federal government, which is much simpler than a multilateral arrangement with all the *Länder* involved. It is, however, a transitional arrangement; the money is not sufficient to relieve the situation in eastern Germany and the fund is producing strains in the federal structure which will continue until 1995, when fundamental questions not simply about the financial basis of German federalism but about the federal system itself will have to be addressed.

An indication of the financial difficulties precipitated by unification is the rising debate on the territorial reform of the federal system. The anomalous position of the city-state *Länder* has been a constant preoccupation of German constitutionalists, but the issue has never reached the political agenda. The accession of the economically weaker eastern *Länder* has heightened the debate on reform. The stimulus to this debate has always been the principle of equality of public services, which are mostly provided by the *Länder*. Various proposals have been suggested, such as the merger of eastern and western *Länder*, which could have both cultural and financial benefits. The federal government is also sympathetic to any move towards reducing the number of *Länder*. The western *Länder* generally support the principle, as long as it does not apply

---

[7] W. Exler, 'Financing German Federalism: Problems of Financial Equalisation in the Unification Process', *German Politics*, 1/3 (1992).

to themselves. While full-scale reorganization is unlikely in the near future, the issue of the number, size, and effectiveness of the *Länder* is on the agenda and this, combined with growing pressures of national identity and economic centralization, has, in domestic politics, placed the *Länder* on the defensive.

Ironically, the progress which the *Länder* have made in establishing a positive role for themselves in the consultative procedures of the European Community are now in danger of being undercut by the implications of German unification, which have raised doubts about the appropriate financial relationship between the federal and *Land* levels and the functional and territorial attributes of the *Länder*. There are signs that the eastern *Länder* favour a stronger German federal state and are more fearful than their western counterparts of a Europe of the Regions in which they would be rather weak players. In the longer term, the political consequences of a united Germany redefining its role *vis-à-vis* the European Union could pose even more profound problems for the ability of the *Länder* to play a fuller role in European affairs.

Is the increased influence of the German *Länder* in EC affairs a sign of more democracy? Will decisions be taken closer to the people? Can citizens now expect more regional variety? On the one hand, the *Länder*'s strengthened ability to assert their interests and to participate in EC decision-making can contribute to making Community laws more sensitive with respect to regional needs. However, it should be recalled that German federalism in concept and practice is an 'executive federalism'. Consequently, it is the *Länder* governments and, in particular, their bureaucracies which have gained influence in EC affairs. The compensation the *Länder* parliaments have achieved for their loss of responsibilities is negligible and European integration has further weakened their position. The greater participation of the *Länder* has enhanced executive power in the policy network at EC, federal, and *Länder* levels and exacerbated the 'democratic deficit'. The *Länder* have considerably contributed to the principle of subsidiarity becoming a basic element of future European Union. In this light it is surprising how firmly they have opposed the idea that the local municipalities should receive similar rights.

In order to reach their goals, the *Länder* have pursued an often contradictory approach. On the one hand, they have in the past repeatedly and unanimously supported further European integration and in this they have generally been on the same side as the federal government. The *Länder* have held campaigns to inform the public on the EC in a positive way and an important pro-EC role has been played in this context by the *Länder* offices in Brussels. On the other hand, in order to justify their demands, *Länder* have criticized the Community increasingly and more aggressively. As regional lobbyists, they were not afraid of pursuing or supporting disinformation campaigns in which they wrongly informed the public or were explicitly unclear about the real motives and objectives of Community actions.

Numerous examples for these issues can be quoted, such as the discussions on purity laws for beer and sausages or the Commission's intentions to reduce the comprehensive regional aids of the *Länder* under State aid rules. As a consequence, their general positive orientation towards further EC integration, though officially maintained, becomes less and less credible. Their insistence on constitutional change requiring a two-thirds majority in both *Bundestag* and *Bundesrat* for further transfers of power to the European Union creates a major obstacle to further integration in Europe. Given the growth of extreme political parties opposed to Europe, this could considerably limit the freedom of the Federal Republic to act in European affairs. Hence, only a few years after the completion of German unification, this could be the *de facto* end of another constitutive element of the Federal Republic's *raison d'être*.

MAP 9. The Netherlands: provinces.

9

The Dutch Province as a European Region: National Impediments versus European Opportunities

FRANK HENDRIKS, JOS C. N. RAADSCHELDERS, AND THEO A. J. TOONEN

The Dutch province may be called a 'region' in both senses of the word. First, it represents the administrative tier at meso-level in the Netherlands, that is the tier between national and local government. Second, it is the geographic entity that Dutch people refer to when they define their regional identity, their 'home-base' between nation and locality. An inhabitant of Maastricht may identify himself as a Dutchman, but it is even more likely that he calls himself a 'Limburger' (Limburg is one of the twelve Dutch provinces).

The province is not only a region in the national context. In recent times it has come to be known as a European region, assigned to the NUTS 2 category of the standard European classification scheme, along with the French region and the Spanish autonomous community. The fact that the Dutch province is assigned to a certain standard category does, however, not imply that it can play a 'standard' role as a European region. European integration does give the province opportunities for repositioning, as it does for other regions in western Europe, but the role that the province can play on the European stage is also very much influenced by its position in the national administrative system. In this chapter we want to confront the opportunities which have arisen in recent times with the constraints to provincial functioning which go back to before the European integration process. We describe the historical background of provincialism and regionalism in the Netherlands, since that is the base on which changes in Dutch meso-government are founded. We are then better able to understand the two competing concepts—'Europe of the Cities' versus

'Europe of the Regions'—discussed in the following section. Next we discuss how Dutch provinces have adopted and advocated the latter concept and its consequence for the provinces, especially in the western part of the country. In the last section we summarize the opportunities and impediments that the Dutch provinces face at the end of the twentieth century.

The Historical Background of Provincialism and Regionalism in the Netherlands

The provinces were once the building-blocks of the Dutch State. At the time of the Dutch Republic of Seven United Provinces (1588–1795), sovereignty resided with the provinces, both *de jure* and *de facto*. Compared to this glorious past, the present situation of the Dutch province presents a rather bleak picture. Neither the general public nor Members of Parliament have been impressed by the fact that the provinces have accumulated new tasks during the last century, especially in the field of public utilities, water management, regional economic planning, physical planning, environmental management, and welfare. Naturally this resulted in an absolute increase of personnel and budget. In relative terms the provincial budget has doubled and was in 1989 approximately 9 per cent of the total expenditure of subnational governments—including joint provisions, this came to 11 per cent; municipalities accounted for 80 per cent.

Neither the argument that provincial supervision, mediation, and dispute-settlement are vital for a robust and resilient administrative system, nor the point that the province has both the constitutional facility and the technical scale for regional co-ordination, has carried much weight in the debate about regional government in the Netherlands. One of the characteristics of this debate is that the province has always been handled as the 'closing-entry' of administrative thinking. As we concluded elsewhere: 'the regional question in the Netherlands has, almost without exception been defined as a supra-local question. As a consequence, the province has been set aside as a wrong answer.'[1]

---

[1] Theo A. J. Toonen, Jos C. N. Raadschelders, and Frank Hendriks, *De (randstad) provincie in Europees perspectief* (i.e.: 'The (Randstad) Provinces in European Perspective'), commissioned report for the interprovincial cooperation 'Region Utrecht—Holland', (1992).

It has been thought that the European integration process might improve the position of the province. The 'Europe of the Regions' concept regards the meso-level as the level where integration can be more easily realized than at national level. Through a direct appeal to regional government, Brussels may seek to bypass certain national sentiments that could impede further integration. *Grosso modo*, provincial governments in the Netherlands have utilized the European incentive through more intensive co-ordination between provinces, tapping into EC funds for regional development, and providing provincial representation in Brussels. A side-effect of this development has been a renewed self-confidence in the provinces. In all parts of the country provinces have expressed the desire to institutionalize the co-operation between provinces, going as far as advocating the amalgamation of provinces into three or four *landsdelen* at subnational level. In this argument, the concept of the 'Europe of the Regions' is often used as a strong selling point.

Thus, the European integration process provides the Dutch provinces with both the opportunity and symbols for a restructuring. There are, however, serious impediments to a provincial repositioning. These stem from the historical evolution of the Dutch administrative system. In order to put the present tendencies and the future opportunities into perspective, it is wise to take these historical constraints into account. We will now analyse this development in three phases: the pre-pillarization period (up to the 1880s); the pillarization era (1880–1965); and the period of depillarization (since 1965).

The Pre-Pillarization Period

During the time of the confederate Dutch Republic (1588–1795) sovereignty resided with the provinces.[2] Each province was autonomous within its own territory. Each had representatives in the Estates-General of the confederacy and in its delegated bodies (Council of State, Chamber of Accounts, and Admiralties). Seen from the confederate viewpoint the province was the most important level of government . However, within each of the provinces, the cities exercised great influence, especially in the province of

---

[2] Theo A. J. Toonen, 'Dutch Provinces and the Struggle for the Meso', in: L. J. Sharpe (ed.), *Developments at the Meso in Europe* (London and Beverly Hills, Calif.: Sage, 1991).

Holland. In other provinces the rural gentry played a role of some importance. Because of regional differences the confederacy suffered from political and administrative inertia when it came to reorganizing government. This issue surfaced in the eighteenth century when the Dutch economic and military power dwindled. With the impotence of confederate decision-making in mind, reforms during the periods of the Batavian Republic (1795–1806), the Kingdom of Holland (1806–10), and the Department of Holland (as part of the French Empire, 1810–13) were aimed at clipping the provincial tails and strengthening national and local government.

The 'State-Regulation' of 1798 (the first Dutch Constitution) stipulated that the Dutch territory was 'one and indivisible'. A unitary state was born in which the province was nothing but an administrative extension of central government. The province kept its traditional tasks regarding supervision of water boards and municipalities. For most of the nineteenth century the role and position of the province within the government system was severely limited.

The Pillarization Era

In western countries the 1880–1920 period is regarded as one in which a new type of state came into being. Industrialization, urbanization, and mass literacy resulted in greater demands for citizen participation in public decision-making. In the Netherlands this demand was channelled into professional associations and political parties. In the period indicated the Dutch pillarized system came into existence that had its 'pedestal in different "regions" of the country: the Catholics in the south and the south-eastern region, the Protestants in the north and the north-eastern region, and the smaller and ... less well-organized social-democratic and conservative ("free" or *liberale*) "pillars" in the urbanized and therefore more heterogeneous western region of Holland'.[3]

At the time that local and national governments truly expanded their service-delivery and experienced major reorganizations, the province as a government level lagged behind, since intermediate and regional governance was 'covered' by the pillars. 'While solv-

---

[3] Theo A. J. Toonen and Frank Hendriks, 'Regional Governance in the Netherlands and the Heritage of Pillarisation', unpublished paper (Leiden, 1992), 8.

ing the cultural, denominational, educational and welfare problems and conflicts between themselves, the different pillars were . . . resolving many issues which in other countries—particularly federal ones—would have surfaced as "regional" or inter-regional issues.'[4] What was left to the provinces was the more technical and legal support of the process of political will-formation which was located elsewhere in the system. In the more coherent parts of the country—almost anywhere but in the west—this division of responsibilities functioned quite satisfactorily as a system of both intra-regional and interregional governance. In the western city regions however, the consociational system of governance left a gap. There, the pillarized system contributed to the tension between mainly social-democratic core cities and mainly conservative suburbs. There also, the voluntary arrangements for inter-organizational decision-making—which would suffice for most of the country—would not do. This explains why the discussion about the 'regional gap' in the Netherlands has for so long been dominated by a concern for upper-local city management.

During the days of pillarization the provinces moved only very slowly into new areas. As late as 1884 a contemporary scholar observed no significant increase in provincial tasks. Indeed, even between 1880 and 1945 the provinces hardly developed new initiatives. Most of the expansion in tasks in government occured at the municipal level, followed by the national level.[5] During the *interbellum* (1918–40) many provinces created regional bodies for public utilities, such as electricity or water delivery, hitherto provided through municipal or intermunicipal arrangements. On the whole the provinces continued to be a rather technocratic, staff-type of organization in the period before the Second World War.

After the War the provinces seem to have gained momentum—although some observers would call that an overstatement.[6] They

---

[4] Toonen and Hendricks, 'Regional Governance', 9.

[5] J. C. N. Raadschelders, *Plaatselijk bestuurlijke ontwikkelingen 1600–1980* (i.e.: 'Local Government Administrative Developments') (The Hague: VNG-uitgeverij's, 1990).

[6] Johan P. Olson, *Analyzing Institutional Dynamics* (Norsk senter for forskning i ledestelsel, organisasjon og styring, 1992). Theo A. J. Toonen, 'Europe of the Administrations: The Challenges of '92 (and Beyond)' in: *Public Administration Review*, 52/2 (1992), 108–15. Alberta M. Sbragia (ed.) *Europolitics: Institutions and Policymaking in the 'New' European Community* (Washington, DC: The Brookings Institution, 1992).

developed agencies for physical regional planning and economic development and they enjoyed an increase in budget and personnel, both in absolute and relative terms. This development coincided with a process of depillarization, a process that transformed the political landscape.

The Period of Depillarization

In the second half of the 1960s the system of pillarization crumbled and with it evaporated an implicit system of regional governance. In theory the opportunities for regional governance by the provinces increased, which is not to say that the provinces actually made use of these opportunities. In line with the historically developed intergovernmental relationships the political and administrative élites of the cities responded more quickly to the 'regional gap' which seemed to be broadening. For reasons described above, city managers had cultivated a more aggressive and assertive way of dealing with intergovernmental relations. Regional issues were thus handled and almost monopolized by institutions that were supra-local in nature, which confirmed the historical tendency to define regional governance as a matter of big-city management. This is quite different from the way regional governance is defined in many other European countries.

However, in the late 1960s and early 1970s it appeared as if the regional gap in the Netherlands could be filled through the creation of *gewesten*, a level between the municipality and the province. Many a proposal was drafted, but none could be enacted. The idea disappeared from the public agenda in 1983. The only change that occurred at meso-level was the creation of a new province for the reclaimed polders in the IJssel lake (1982). For the rest, decision-making turned towards a traditional Dutch solution: strengthening the opportunities for intermunicipal (joint) provisions. Given the voluntary nature of joint provisions, they functioned well in the rural parts of the country where the differences between municipalities were, and are, negligible. In the urban areas the tension between central cities and adjacent smaller municipalities limited the usefulness of joint provisions. Thus, the 'regional gap' in city regions continued to demand a solution, even though the problem had temporarily fallen off the national agenda.

In the meantime the Dutch province acquired new responsibilities, even though it was still not institutionally strong. National plans in the areas of water management, environmental management, and physical planning needed translation into more concrete provincial plans that were tuned in to one another. These in turn served as a framework for local planning. The province thus assumed an important co-ordination role—both horizontally and vertically—in planning. Besides these tasks the province has developed new initiatives in public health (homes for the elderly) and culture (libraries, recreation boards). Considering the development of provincial tasks since 1945, one has to admit that the province has become more important than it had ever been during the Batavian–French period and the period of the monarchy (since 1813). Provincial expenditure has increased more than twenty times since 1960, the major increase occurring since 1980. The importance of the province within the Dutch State system, however, is not only to be judged by its nominal increase in expenditure. Relative to other levels of government, its expenditure has only doubled.

In the 1980s the debate about regional government reopened. As a consequence of the economic crisis that hit all western economies, the Dutch Government realized that revitalization of the national economy required new initiatives in what they called the 'regions', but which in fact were the big agglomerations in the western part of the country—especially the main ports of Amsterdam and Rotterdam. In 1988 the Dutch Cabinet set up a special committee to advise on the future organization of local government with an eye on the competitiveness of urban areas in an integrated Europe. This committee (named after its chairman the Montijn Committee) reported in 1989 and proposed the creation of strong regional governments in the largest urban areas. The report has largely been transformed into official Cabinet policy through the proposal to create special authorities for seven of the Dutch urban areas. The Cabinet plans *Bestuur Op Niveau I* and *Bestuur Op Niveau II* did not pay attention to the consequences of their proposals for the provinces. The four largest urban areas (Amsterdam, The Hague, Rotterdam, and Utrecht) are all situated in the three western provinces, and when they are exempted from provincial government there is little left for the traditional province. At the time of writing this chapter (December 1992–early January 1993), the Ministry of Home Affairs revealed some of the proposals to be published under the title *Bestuur Op Niveau III*. BON III was considered a sequel to BON II, and was initially aimed at the abolition of the present provinces, to be replaced by about twenty regions of a smaller scale. It seemed that national government took a position in the debate about the two rival concepts that are discussed in the next section. In reaction, the provinces attempted to rescue as much as possible of their position in the Dutch State structure. The latest news indicates that most of the provinces might be spared. First, the Dutch Senate—the First Chamber whose members are chosen by the provincial councils—has stated that it would not support the plans of the Ministry of Home Affairs. In addition, the Cabinet has distanced itself from its earlier point of view, and will now strive to create upper-local solutions only for the major metropolitan areas—beginning with the Greater Rotterdam area which will, it is intended, gain provincial status. The direct consequences of this policy-shift will be confined to the province of South Holland, keeping the other provinces out of harm's way—at least for the time being. One thing is clear at this moment: the story has not yet come to an end.

The rivalry between 'Europe of the Regions' and 'Europe of the Cities' as guiding concepts for the Dutch administrative system is bound to stay for some time and therefore deserves attention in the next section.

'Europe of the Cities' versus 'Europe of the Regions'

Various member states of the EC have seen a revival of the debate about the most appropriate governmental organization in response to European integration. Internationalization is associated with a trend towards enlargement of scale. In many European countries the local level of government is strengthened through decentralization, which in turn calls for reforms of the urban agglomerations. These reforms are further instigated by the notion that the urban motors of the economy can only compete at a European level when they are of sufficient size and competence. As far as the Netherlands is concerned the Randstad area as a whole may represent an entity of truly metropolitan and Euro-regional stature.

Strengthening the urban areas is the target of those who emphasize a 'Europe of the Cities' approach. European integration has also reinforced the position of the regional issue on the political agendas, as we can see in France, Spain, and Belgium. Regionalization, though, in most European countries refers to a scale and level that in the Netherlands is identified as *landsdeel*, being the level between provincial and central government and more comparable to, for instance, the German *Länder*.

As indicated above, Dutch Cabinet policy operated in the slipstream of the Montijn Committee. In the *Bestuur Op Niveau I and II* proposals seven urban areas are given special competences that virtually exempt them from provincial supervision. The State decentralizes certain competences to these new urban authorities. At the same time the municipalities in those territories will have to give certain tasks to the urban-regional authorities. The provinces will lose most of their tasks in those areas to the urban-regional authorities. This would leave a provincial government that is only operative for the rural areas with a limited amount of tasks. Basically that configuration leaves little room for the province.

In reaction to these ideas, the provinces have adopted since the mid-1980s a more innovative attitude toward administrative reform. Until then the provincial politicians' and administrators' attitude toward administrative reform was reactive: waiting for Cabinet and municipal initiatives upon which they voiced their own stance. European integration has opened new opportunities for the provinces and their efforts to be innovative have gained even more impetus through the 'sandwich-position' into which the pending reforms inside the Netherlands have forced the provinces. The province might even be more moulded between national and municipal levels in the Netherlands than the nation-state is between Brussels and the regions. Although some predict the end of the nation-state, most observers still expect a decisive role for national governments for a long time to come.[7] This is important since it indicates a more limited role for the 'Europe of the Regions'.

In this light, it becomes clear that subnational governments in the Netherlands cannot afford to take a reactive attitude. Certainly the integration process does provide new opportunities for prov-

[7] Toonen, Raadschelders, and Hendriks, *De (randstad) provincie in Europees perspectief*.

inces. Political-administrative adjustments at subnational level will be the result of specific initiatives based on their own history, identity, and dynamics. In the Dutch context—and for that matter, in the context of other member states as well—this means that large-scale reorganization of the basic structure of the State is an illusion and would not be in tune with prevailing political–administrative relationships.

When focusing on the question of what the role and position of the Dutch province can be in a more integrated Europe, there are a number of interrelated topics that merit attention:[8] provincial policy and EC regulation; organizational structure of interprovincial co-operation and co-ordination; provincial policy-making with regard to Europe; and the province in the (international) network.

As we have seen above the province nowadays fulfils important planning and co-ordination tasks in various policy-areas, which explains why provincial policy is still very much dominated by home affairs. With regard to European-oriented policies, the provinces were dominated by the directorates for economic affairs, not surprisingly, since the most important structural funds were available in the field of regional economic development. Indeed, a 'European orientation' of the provinces is still dominated by economic considerations. Slowly, but persistently, actors in other policy areas become aware of EC affairs (environmental planning, water management). If, indeed, the provinces aim at becoming more active in the lobby-arena then they will have to provide for a clear, co-ordinated structure and for sufficient administrative backing.

In many of the policy-areas where the Dutch provinces have taken a leading role the European Commission has developed initiatives that directly or indirectly influence policy-making and implementation in the provinces. This concerns both the adjustment of provincial regulations to EC regulations, including a more active role as influential lobbyist in Brussels; and an effective utilization of EC funds and programmes for regional development, including further development of interregional co-operation. As things stand there is no idea about the number of EC regulations

[8] Viktor Freiherr von Malchus, *Partnerschaft an europäischen Grenzen: Integration durch grenzüberschreitende Zusammenarbeit* (Europäische Geschriften des Instituts für Europäische Politik, vols. 39/40; Bonn: Europa Union Verlag GmbH, 1975).

that already affect the provinces and those that potentially can affect the provinces. Most practitioners feel that Europe is of limited importance for provincial policy-making. In so far as provincial politicians and administrators are aware of Europe, it is only in limited areas. Knowledge about EC regulations is not widespread. Also, information from Brussels is not always on time. It is not uncommon for information about regulations to be enforced or funds to be applied for to be sent shortly before the actual date of implementation. The Dutch provinces in general have not yet taken upon themselves the task of investigating systematically how many EC regulations might be or become relevant for them. This is partially because they are concentrating on the acquisition of EC funds instead of on influencing the policy and decision-making process in Brussels. A shift to the latter is all the more important given the emphasis which the EC now places on social and economic cohesion. Backward regions will be even more stimulated financially, and the regions in the richer countries might find a role in developing interregional networks, particularly with southern and eastern European countries.

There are three interregional networks developing: interprovincial co-operation in the Netherlands; interregional cooperation between regions in EC and eastern European countries; and co-operation in border regions. The three northern provinces (Groningen, Friesland, and Drenthe) have entered into a joint provision. The three western provinces have done the same and are even pursuing more intensified co-operative structures (see below). As far as provincial relations with eastern Europe are concerned the co-operation is in its preparatory phase. Finally, some of the Dutch border regions have entered into joint programmes with adjacent regions: the northern provinces with part of the north German lowland; South Limburg in the Euregion Meuse-Rhine; and North Brabant with East and West Flanders. It is perhaps in the search for solutions of cross-border problems such as water pollution and industrial development that European integration for the moment has found its most concrete manifestation.[9]

Meanwhile, tapping into the lobby-circuit appears mandatory. More and more the European Commission is playing a central role

---

[9] B. Guy Peters, 'Bureaucratic Politics and the Institutions of the European Community', in Sbragia (ed.), *Europolitics*.

in EC policy-making. Although the broad outlines of policy are decided upon within the Council of Ministers, much of the policy-making depends on bureaucratic interaction and negotiation. Because of the increasing importance of the EC's twenty-three directorates-general, policy-making is more and more characterized by differentiation and functional specialization. Policy-making has become a matter for experts and civil servants working along functional lines. No one could have foreseen the complex consultation and bureaucratic patterns that now have developed in the EC.[10]

Within various member states the subnational level of government has moved to a more active position. On the one hand this is the result of developments within a country. In countries such as Belgium, Spain, Portugal, Italy, and France the meso-level clearly has been strengthened through decentralization. On the other hand the enhanced weight of subnational governments is also the result of more direct penetration of the EC in that level, for instance through the stimulation of regional economic policies. Both national and subnational governments have become participants in the integration process.[11] This creates certain tensions within each of the member states, and has certainly done so in the Netherlands. Next to the normal competition between government departments at central level, for example foreign affairs versus the sectoral departments, we now see a competition between national and subnational levels. Regional governments and EC institutions perceive one another more and more as potential allies in the strive toward integration.[12]

Increased EC intervention in various levels of government makes it more important to have 'eyes and ears' in Brussels. Lobbying therefore has become a normal activity. Next to the permanent representatives of central government in Brussels, subnational governments (individual provinces, individual municipalities, joint representations) as well as private companies in the Netherlands have now their own representation in Brussels. Lob-

---

[10] Sbragia, *Europolitics*.
[11] Gary Marks, 'Structural Policy in the European Community', in Sbragia (ed.), *Europolitics*.
[12] Svein A. Andersen and Kjell A. Eliassen, 'European Community Lobbying', *European Journal of Political Research*, 20 (1991), 173–87. Bruno Julien, 'Euro-Lobbying Invades Berlaymont', *European Affairs*, 3 (autumn 1990), 28–33.

bying appears to be successful when attempted at the earliest possible moment; and at the lowest possible level.[13] The further a draft proposal proceeds, the less the chances are that one can lobby successfully in the EC. To that effect the three western provinces in the Netherlands have had temporary advisers in Brussels since 1990 (at first two; since March 1992 one).

Case-Study: The Western Provinces

We can illustrate the topics discussed above with developments in the three western (*Randstad*) provinces of the Netherlands. For information in this section we have drawn upon a recently published commissioned report.

The Randstad area consists of three provinces and is one of the most densely populated areas of the world. With a total of seven million inhabitants, the population density is about 800 per square kilometre. The Randstad consists of a ring of cities starting at Dordrecht and progressing via Rotterdam, The Hague, Leiden, Haarlem, and Amsterdam to Utrecht. Each of these cities has suburban municipalities around it, while smaller cities can be found in between the urban areas (Delft, Lisse, Hillegom, Hilversum). Within the city ring a 'Green Heart' is situated. It is of vital importance for the Dutch economy. Next to an important horticultural industry (flowers, vegetables, bulbs) it houses the harbours of Rotterdam and Amsterdam, Schiphol airport, and a major steel industry. Since the early 1980s the three provinces have slowly developed joint structures for policy-making in certain fields.

At about the same time a European orientation surfaced, which was to a great extent influenced by the province of South Holland. In 1981 South Holland had created a Provincial Stimulation Fund for Employment, and administrators attempted to acquire EC structural funds. During negotiations about this they heard of the Renaval project, an EC programme to revitalize harbour areas in decline. With an eye on declining employment in the Rotterdam harbour, a request for subsidy was send to Brussels. Soon it ap-

---

[13] Jos C. N. Raadschelders and Theo A. J. Toonen, 'Adjustments of the Dutch Public Administration to European Demands: Coordination without a Coordinator?', Conference on Administrative Modernization in Europe, Perugia, June 1992.

peared that South Holland alone would not be considered for a grant, so co-operation started with the province of North Holland (for the Amsterdam harbour). This resulted in a funding of 62 million guilders. The Renaval fund is considered the largest success that the Randstad provinces have achieved so far. Interprovincial co-operation intensified through the creation of the Randstad Working Group for Economic Affairs in 1983, followed by other working groups for physical planning, water, environment, and administrative organization.

Renaval was the trigger to broaden provincial efforts with regard to Europe. Two experienced advisers in Brussels (former high-ranking EC civil servants and Europarliamentarians) were contracted in 1990 in order to provide the three provinces with information about new regulations being prepared in Brussels and to train provincial civil servants. For backing of both advisers and for assurance that their work would be disseminated adequately through the provincial organization, each province created an Interagency Project group that reports to the Randstad Project Group Europe. In each of the three provinces there are at present eleven to thirteen civil servants involved for one-fifth of their time. Next to this some twenty civil servants per province are more indirectly involved. This is a very small number of people in comparison to the total size of the civil service in the three provinces, about 4,000.

On 25 February 1991 the three provinces entered a formal joint provision as the Region Randstad Holland and Utrecht to further strengthen interprovincial co-operation. It is here that the political level of the provincial organization is active. Some of the provincial politicians openly flirt with the possibility of an amalgamation of the three western provinces into a *Randstad-landsdeel*, which could exist beside two or three other *landsdelen* at subnational level. On the whole, the Randstad provinces have seen what it means to participate more actively in European issues. The Renaval project could be successfully concluded despite the resistance of the Ministry of Economic Affairs. Having their own advisers in Brussels made all the difference. By 1993 the provinces were considering whether or not to open a permanent provincial bureau in Brussels. This bureau could organize seminars and courses to update the entire civil service on Europe in general and on specific policy-areas. Hitherto this was done by their adviser(s) on an *ad hoc* basis.

In general we conclude that in a relatively short time the three provinces have been able to develop a European orientation. It is time, however, that they included the whole organization and acquired insight into the number of EC regulations that already directly influence the provinces, and those that do so indirectly. If an amalgamation of provinces became a reality it would be all the more important to have systematically collected information about the impact of European regulation at the meso-level, and to have a strong co-ordination structure with a permanent representation in Brussels.

Opportunities and Impediments for Provincial Repositioning

It appears that Europe has provided the Dutch provinces with arguments to strengthen their role and position within the Dutch State system. The emphasis used to be on acquiring EC funds, but the focus has slowly been turned to influencing EC programmes and regulations. It is in the policy-making process in Brussels that the provinces could deepen their involvement. The potential to do so is available both in terms of manpower and in terms of organization. It appears also that the provinces have predominantly acted in a planning, co-ordinating, and mediating role. Much can be said in favour of such a role. Central government is involved in the transposition of EC regulations into national law, while local governments bear responsibility for actual implementation. The province in the Netherlands is the only level of government where EC policy-making and regulation can be translated to specific regional needs from an intersectoral point of view. The provincial initiatives developed so far indicate that this is indeed an important role. We therefore hold the opinion that Europe has opened new policy-windows for the province that might even generate a repositioning of that level.

There are, however, three impediments blocking the way to provincial repositioning, which are rooted in historical and contemporary developments. First, the province never really recovered from the reorganizations that took place in the Batavian–French period. Even though it recently broadened its scope of activity, the province is still very much perceived as the least important of government levels. Needless to say that this position is most strongly taken by national and (upper-) local governments. We should add, though, that this assessment is to a large extent shared by provincial élites. Second, regional governance in the Netherlands during the pillarization period was a matter of the four societal segments called pillars (which were complexes of political parties and religious and professional associations). Despite task-expansion in the twentieth century, the political-administrative élite in the provinces has not developed an innovative *habitus* such as can be found at central and local level. The provincial politico-administrative élite is reactive instead of innovative. Indeed, the provinces are in search of a philosophy to underline their unique importance within the larger State. Even though there are ample opportunities for underlining the importance of the province both in terms of implementation as well as mediating/co-ordinating tasks, it is within the provincial bodies that self-confidence is often lacking. Third, regional problems have always been conceptualized at an upper-local level. Solutions were traditionally found in municipal annexations, amalgamations, and joint provisions. The most recent Cabinet proposals (*Bestuur Op Niveau III*, February 1993) follow in that tradition and there is still (or again) a chance that provinces, especially in the western part of the country, will lose many tasks and competences to the new urban-regional governments.

10

Regions within a Region: The Paradox of the Republic of Ireland

MICHAEL HOLMES AND NICHOLAS REESE

Introduction

Ireland has always been heavily centralized, administratively and economically. But at the European level, the Irish Government has been an enthusiastic supporter of EC regional assistance measures, welcoming their strengthening, development, and budgetary expansion. Regionalism at the domestic and European levels overlaps in practice, and there is a considerable degree of permeability between the two, so that the European Community—most especially through its own regional policy—is influencing the debate, arguments, and ideas about regionalism in Ireland. Where the Irish Government previously faced little opposition to its heavily centralized structures, the impact of European regional policies has helped to generate a far more critical domestic environment as the contradictions between what the Government preaches in Brussels and practices at home become ever more apparent. There would appear to be a Jekyll-and-Hyde-type situation—a government which is all in favour of regionalism at the Community level is opposed to any extension of regional autonomy within Ireland.

This chapter examines the extent to which this apparently paradoxical stance on regionalism in Ireland is true, and what might result from the increasing interaction between the European and domestic decision-making environments. In the first section, we present an examination of why regionalism has failed to develop in Ireland. This suggests that although the Republic of Ireland is culturally a very homogeneous society and politically an intensely centralized one, the economic and social arguments for regionalism are gaining strength. The subsequent section of the chapter places Ireland in the context of membership of the EC, and in particular the ERDF is used to explore Irish regionalism. This suggests that the example of the EC has strengthened the arguments for regionalism in Ireland. The body of the chapter then presents an analysis of the manner in which the domestic and the Community frameworks work together. Here, the intention will be to draw out the different networks of influence that have developed between local, regional, and central authorities and the Community, and to suggest the overall impact these networks have had. The prism of the Community's regional policy can thus be used to bring out fully the spectrum of Irish regionalism, from the country as a single region itself to the country composed of a number of smaller but no less valid regions. The chapter concludes by clarifying how this contrast of regions within a region has built up in Ireland, and how it demonstrates the extent to which the Community can influence the domestic politics of its member states.

Irish Regionalism

The problem of how to treat regions within a region is not exactly a new one for Ireland. The experience of being a region within a larger whole is one that the entire island went through for many years, when Ireland constituted a region within the United Kingdom, but on independence in 1922 the country was divided, with Northern Ireland remaining in the United Kingdom. The legacy left by British rule to Irish regionalism thus embraces both sides of the paradox—Ireland as a single region, and Ireland divided regionally. The legacy also extends beyond this, for the British left both a framework of local government and a centralized colonial structure. That system was intended, theoretically at least, to encourage a devolution of powers: as Chubb notes 'it was intended to be local self-government; democracy carried down to the smallest community unit practicable'.[1] What might have developed from such a system remains conjecture: what occurred on independence was a wholesale reduction in the numbers and competences of such local authorities and a vigorous centralization and concentration of government.

[1] B. Chubb, *The Government and Politics of Ireland* (London: Longmans, 1982), 287.

Centralization was undertaken through three main policies.[2] Most government functions were carried out by a small number of ministries, each responsible for a wide range of functions. In addition, certain single-function agencies were set up, the distinctive State-sponsored bodies. Finally, the competences of local government were gradually removed and the whole local government structure was subordinated to national politics. Local government, for example, had no powers of taxation and were thus dependent on the national exchequer. The logic for these policies stemmed partly from the nationalist heritage, partly from the perception of Ireland as a small, underdeveloped country. Nationalism created an ethos of unity and indivisibility. It also brought to power a new élite, anxious to assert control over their new country. The perception of that country as small and poor reinforced the logic. Ireland was seen as too small to divide into regions, and also as uniformly underdeveloped, so that arguments were less about regional imbalances within Ireland than the overall Irish imbalance in the international environment. This has been a fairly constant feature of Irish politics. Government policies have always given priority to promoting national economic development ahead of regional considerations. But that should by no means be taken to imply that there are no such regional considerations to be taken into account. On the contrary, there are marked socio-economic differences evident between areas in Ireland, and despite the State's earlier policies of centralization, these regional differences have had to be afforded official recognition. As Table 10.1 indicates, there are large disparities within Ireland on a number of key measures, such as employment, population distribution, and degrees of industrialization. The disparities add up to what has traditionally been seen as a divide between a more developed east and a more peripheral west, though it is probably more accurate to specify the south-east and north-west respectively.[3]

These differences received what amounted to official recognition in 1952, with the passing of a government act providing special-assistance grants to some western regions (the Underdeveloped Areas Act).[4] This can be interpreted as the first attempt at regional

[2] T. J. Barrington, 'Ireland: The Interplay of Territory and Function', *West European Politics* 10/4 (1987), 36–8.

[3] B. Brunt, *The Republic of Ireland* (London: Paul Chapman, 1988), 56.

[4] H. Clout, *Regional Variations in the European Community* (Cambridge: Cambridge University Press, 1986), 113.

TABLE 10.1. *Selected measures of regional variations, Ireland*

	A	B	C	D	E	F
East	37.7	85.4	3.7	16.8	20.1	149
South-west		15.2	51.7	19.0	9.4	13.6	125
South-east		10.9	40.0	22.8	8.7	12.7	108
North-east		5.6	41.5	18.3	10.5	14.7	107
Mid-west		8.9	41.3	22.0	9.0	13.2	116
Midlands		7.4	30.5	26.7	7.5	11.1	116
West	8.3	29.1	31.2	7.8	12.6	103
North-west		2.4	23.6	21.6	7.8	12.9	90
Donegal		3.7	20.8	*	*	*	*
Ireland		56.4	15.2	11.9	15.8	114

* Figure for Donegal included in north-west total.

Notes:

A: Population by region, % of national population (1986).
B: Urbanization (defined as living in a town of population 1,500 or more), % of regional population (1986).
C: Agricultural workers, % of regional labour force (1989).
D: Clerical workers, % of regional labour force (1989).
E: Professional and technical workers, % of regional labour force (1989).
F: Average weekly income IEP (1980).

Sources: Census of Population 1986; Labour Force Survey 1989; Statistical Abstract 1989, Household Budget Survey 1980.

policy in the independent Irish State. It was followed in subsequent years by further government initiatives which aimed to tackle regional disparities: a local government planning and development act in 1963, the establishment of nine planning regions in 1964, regional policy statements in 1965, 1969, and 1972, and the government-commissioned Buchanan Report on regions in 1968.

Certainly it would seem that the earlier government approach of centralization was reversed in this period, that 'the issue of regional imbalance became a major public policy concern during the 1960s and early 1970s'.[5] It is, however, worth looking at these developments in greater detail. The overall approach to national economic development in the country at that time was based on attracting foreign firms to set up plants in Ireland, and new firms preferred to

---

[5] T. Boylan and P. J. Drudy, *Towards a Regional Development Strategy for Ireland* (Dublin: Regional Studies Association, 1990), 4.

locate outside the traditional industrial centres in Ireland.[6] This in turn meant that government investment in infrastructure to attract such new firms was widely dispersed around the country. The Government favoured a strategy of economic dispersal which was deemed to be politically acceptable, though many experts viewed concentration as more economically sound.

But the reduction of internal regional imbalances remained a secondary objective, and although as Brunt rightly states 'the 1970s constitute the most highly articulated period of regional development', this was always likely to prove dependent upon the continuing success of overall industrial policy.[7] Thus, when the oil crises of the 1970s led to inflation, recession, and rising unemployment, attention became focused once more on aggregate national performance, with significantly less attention being paid to regional policy. 'By the mid 1980s it appeared as if the regional question was no longer an important national issue even though regional disparities were as acute as ever.'[8] In the late 1980s, regional issues re-emerged to an extent, but again it must be stressed that this was partly as a consequence of a shift in the emphasis behind national economic targets. Government policy moved away from encouraging foreign investment to trying to nurture indigenous small and medium-sized firms, which again, given the dispersion of such firms around Ireland, inevitably benefited regions as a by-product. Most recently in the 1990s there has emerged a new argument that regionalism may be a route to higher national economic growth.

There is thus a strong case for regional economic policy in Ireland, albeit one kept secondary to national economic priorities. But 'regions are already there and have proved necessary'.[9] What form have these regions taken? The answer is, quite a miscellany. There are statutory regional bodies for health, tourism, and fisheries, and some semi-State bodies have regional structures, such as the IDA and FAS. However, beyond these basic forms, regions in Ireland exhibit a number of weaknesses. First, the regional boundaries have not been standardized, and indeed the optimum number of regions for Ireland has not been established. This has the knock-on effect of inhibiting co-ordination between different

---

[6] Brunt, *The Republic of Ireland*, 71.   [7] Ibid. 70.

[8] Boylan and Drudy, *Towards a Regional Development Strategy for Ireland*, 5.

[9] Advisory Expert Committee, *Local Government Reorganisation and Reform* (Dublin: Stationery Office, 1991), 26.

agencies in the same general region, and indeed co-ordination can often be easier through central agencies back in Dublin, thus exacerbating part of the regional problem. Second, the powers granted to regional levels of administration vary considerably. Again, this inhibits effective co-ordination. A third weakness lies in the fact that no regional tier of government has been put alongside these sectoral agencies. Indeed, 'there was a horror of anything that savoured of regional government'.[10] This has meant that the case for regional economic policy has been unable to draw on a base of political support. The Regional Development Organizations that were created in the late 1960s and abolished in the late 1980s were non-statutory bodies which depended on consent to function from the local and central authorities.

This indicates that although there is a clear socio-economic rationale for some form of regional policy, there has never been a political or cultural need for regions. A survey of different attempts to measure ethnic diversity in western Europe concludes that the Republic of Ireland is 'more or less homogeneous'.[11] Identity and loyalty has been given either to the national or the local level rather than any intermediate tier. The local focus is the county, which attracts considerable traditional and sporting sentiment but at the same time has never been a source of political sentiment, and is coming to be recognized as less suitable from technical and administrative perspectives than regions. In these circumstances, no sense of regional identity has developed in Ireland, which clearly weakens the basis for regionalism: there must be standard regions if regions are to make any sense to people and if regional loyalties are to develop.[12]

The only instance of an alternative territorial focus providing an opening for a regional identity is in the Gaeltacht, the Irish-speaking region. The Gaeltacht provides an interesting summary of the way in which subnational identities and loyalties have failed to emerge. In the late 1960s, a Gaelic civil rights movement was founded, campaigning on broadcasting and local government issues. Agitation from this quarter led eventually to the establish-

---

[10] Barrington, 'Ireland: The Interplay of Territory and Function', 144.

[11] J. E. Lane and S. Ersson, *Politics and Society in Western Europe* (London: Sage, 1987), 67.

[12] Advisory Expert Committee, *Local Government Reorganisation and Reform*, 26.

ment of *Udarás na Gaeltachta* (the Gaeltacht authority) whose board of directors is partly elected and partly appointed. However, this elected regional body has not become a focus for regionalism. First of all, the Gaeltacht is a hugely dispersed and disparate entity. Three large pockets exist in Donegal, Connemara, and Cork/Kerry, which are isolated from each other and from the even smaller remnants in Meath and Waterford. Second, although the Gaeltacht might seem to give a separate cultural dimension to Ireland, it must be borne in mind that Irish is nominally the first language of the whole State. Although the Gaeltacht areas are unique in having Irish as the daily language, the separate cultural dimension is by no means as clear-cut as it might seem at first. Finally, even the elections to *Udarás na Gaeltachta* have succumbed to one of the overriding features of Irish political life: the intense localism, indeed parochialism, of Irish voters. This has caused a few problems for the national parties in these elections, but 'importantly, the effect of localism is something that operates not only against major party machines but also against a local pressure group which might seek to establish a "regional" identity covering the whole or even a single major Gaeltacht area'.[13]

Thus, there is no cultural background to regionalism. The cultural identity is either national or local, and local identities, though strong, are highly fragmented and largely apolitical. They do not pose a serious alternative to national parties and politics, and 'a political perspective which serves local and national issues means that a more co-ordinated and articulated political response to the problems of regional inequality is lacking'.[14] Brunt goes on to conclude that 'any form of regional devolution is not even worth considering', which is probably excessive. Local government at the county level is being recognized as less suitable from technical and administrative perspectives than government at regional level.[15] The political commitment to achieve some form of devolution of power to regions or even to local levels has been weak. Central administrative elements have been reluctant to cede any of their powers. Finally, the popular response has been limited at best. At the existing local level of government, elections have been post-

---

[13] M. Akutagawa, 'Elections to Udarás na Gaeltachta, 1979–1989', *Irish Political Studies*, 5 (1990), 66.

[14] Brunt, *The Republic of Ireland*, 97.

[15] Chubb, *The Government and Politics of Ireland*, 297.

poned, councils suspended or even abolished without effective public protest, which augurs ill for any future regional tier of government.[16]

The basis does exist for regional policy in Ireland, but not perhaps for regional politics. Although there are clear socio-economic differences between parts of the country, this is not backed up by any sense of regional loyalty or identity, and indeed there is still widespread disagreement as to which are the most suitable areas for any future regionalization. This has been combined with a considerable debate over how best to deal with the problems of spatial inequalities in Ireland—whether through regional policy or through overall national economic development. There is an additional dimension which deserves mention, revolving around the question of cross-border co-operation with Northern Ireland. In the past, such co-operation was limited to a handful of initiatives and to co-operation through all-Ireland bodies, such as the trade union movement. However, the EC's current move to complete the internal market has further challenged the continued existence of such borders.[17] Few would argue that the border between Northern Ireland and the Republic will disappear overnight, given the intransigent nature of the political problems involved. Both Unionist opposition to further co-operation with the south and the Republic's irredentist constitutional claim to Northern Ireland reduce the likelihood of co-operation. It is worth remembering that cross-border trade has been very limited in the past, accounting for no more than 4 to 5 per cent of exports for both north and south annually.

On the other hand, there have been a number of calls, on both sides of the border and from the EC, for greater economic co-operation between the two parts of Ireland. Some have even raised the possibility of an economic corridor between Belfast and Dublin. There are also a number of indications that co-operation between the two areas may increase in the future, for example, the proposed merger of the Republic's and Northern Ireland's tourist boards. Such unitary authorities might reduce competition and unnecessary duplication of tasks between the two parts of Ireland, competition which has in the past proved very counter-productive

---

[16] Chubb, *The Government and Politics of Ireland*, 289.
[17] T. Lyne, 'Ireland, Northern Ireland and 1992: The Barriers to Technocratic Anti-Partition', *Public Administration*, 68 (1990), 417–33.

for both, as the case of the Republic's Industrial Development Authority and the Northern Irish Industrial Development Board has demonstrated. Such agencies might prove more efficient and be able to attract more inward investment and tourism to both north and south if they could present a united stance outside Ireland. However, whether or not the two areas form one economic region is open to debate. In some matters there is a high degree of common interest, most notably agriculture, where the policies pursued by the UK Government are inimical to Northern Ireland's interests.[18] In others, such as those relating to Northern Ireland's declining traditional industries, the two have little in common. Furthermore, economic regions are not automatically political regions, a point most strongly borne out by the continuing political conflict in Ireland, leading one commentator to state that 'the Community dimension has failed to transcend sectarianism'.[19]

EC Regional Policy and Irish Regionalism

Ireland's membership of the EC has generally been understood in terms of the economic benefits to be derived from such an association, and other aspects of membership are afforded much less attention. Although generally supportive of the development of the Community, Ireland has been so in practical terms rather than out of any great idealistic commitment to the goal of integration. This attitude parallels the reluctance to devolve power domestically. Irish political and administrative élites have always been alert to any opportunity to expand their powers, be it via a centralized State or an intergovernmental Community.

The élite attitude is further reflected at the popular level, as has been demonstrated on two occasions at national referendums on membership in 1972 and on the SEA in 1987. This generally positive attitude is also evident in Eurobarometer surveys, although they also indicate that attitudes to the Community, though positive, are not strongly idealistic about integration. There appears to be a

[18] P. Hainsworth, 'Administering the European Community', in A. Aughey, P. Hainsworth, and M. J. Trimble, *Northern Ireland in the European Community: An Economic and Political Analysis* (Belfast: Policy Research Institute, 1989), 74.

[19] A. Guelke, *Northern Ireland: The International Perspective* (Dublin and New York: Gill and Macmillan and St Martin's, 1988), 164.

mercenary attachment to the EC in Ireland. This might explain one notable feature of Irish attitudes to the EC—their regional variation. Three distinct zones are evident. Support for the EC has consistently been strongest in the north-west periphery around Connacht-Ulster; in Munster and Leinster (excluding Dublin) there is an average level of support; and Dublin is the centre of the strongest opposition to membership. 'While this pattern is largely a function of the regional distribution of occupational groups, it is striking that support for the EEC tends to be strongest in the poorer areas.'[20] This might suggest that Irish regions were hoping that their position might be strengthened by Community membership—indeed, as Barrington comments, 'Irish regionalism looked to have some future [following accession] until the Irish government, true to form, got the whole state classed as a single region.'[21] Successive governments have been reluctant to adopt either subnational programmes or to consider decentralization, although Ireland's status as a single region in the EC does not preclude it from taking such actions.

The Irish Government has treated the European Regional Development Fund and the other structural funds as increasingly important sources of revenue. Ireland's receipts have grown dramatically from 5.21 million ECUs in 1975 to 132.39 million ECUs in 1988, although Ireland's percentage share of the fund has remained relatively static over the years. In Ireland the money was concentrated primarily on large infrastructure projects such as roads, sewerage works, and transport rather than on industry or services. Generally, the Government has favoured funding such projects which absorbed funds available under the ERDF and yet precluded intricate negotiations over a multitude of projects.

The major beneficiary of EC funds has been the eastern region of the country, dominated by Dublin, which has received over 269.35 million ECUs. In comparison the south-west, the second largest recipient, received 165.92 million ECUs and the north-east the least amount of money, at 20.82 million ECUs (1975–88). This distribution remains a source of some controversy in Ireland where those in the poorer regions of the west and north-east have con-

---

[20] Barrington, 'Ireland: The Interplay of Temtory and Function.'
[21] Ibid.

TABLE 10.2. *Regional breakdown of ERDF commitment to Ireland, 1975–1988*

(Million ECUs)	Total amounts	Amounts per capita (ECUs)
East	269.35	201
Donegal	23.98	185
South-west	165.92	309
Mid-west	124.88	396
South-east	71.69	186
West	61.08	208
North-east	20.82	105
North-west	34.29	412
Midlands	43.00	164

Source: Derived from CEC, European Regional Development Fund, 14th Annual Report (1988).

sidered this distribution of funds inequitable, especially as the wealthiest area, Dublin, has received the most funds. This perception is inaccurate, because ERDF aid gives a very different picture when broken down on a per capita basis, but it is persistent (see Table 10.2).

The EC has also financially supported a limited number of cross-border initiatives with Northern Ireland. It funded the upgrading of the Dublin–Belfast rail line by providing assistance totalling some £70 million. The EC also funded a gas interconnector between the North and the Republic through its Regen programme. In addition, a number of the EC's other programmes straddle the border. The Star and Valoren programmes encouraged co-operation in the fields of telecommunications and energy respectively. Perhaps the best-known programme has been Interreg, which was established in July 1990. This programme specifically supports cross-border initiatives in regions with special development needs, providing grants and loans for cross-border tourism, SMEs, infrastructure, pollution control, and rural development.[22] However, limited resources only allow it to support a small number of projects. The

[22] Notice to the member states, laying down guide-lines for operational programmes which member states are invited to establish in the framework of a Community initiative concerning border areas (interreg), *Official Journal*, C 215 vol. 33, 30 Aug. 1990.

Commission approved one joint Irish–UK initiative in July 1991 for general interregional co-operation between north and south,[23] with the first release of funds under the scheme being provided for the opening of a canal linking the waterway networks of the two areas.

The Community's regional policy has had more than a purely economic impact. It has clearly had a political effect on all levels of government, though the impact has varied between levels and departments, and over time. While membership of the European Community has had little direct effect on the machinery of government, it has had a number of important indirect effects on the Irish administrative system and in particular on the different government departments, their internal structures, and interdepartmental co-ordination. The Department of Foreign Affairs gained the most from EC membership, finding itself placed in the position of a powerful gatekeeper between the EC and the Government. Functionally, the Minister for Foreign Affairs exercises a co-ordinating role in this process rather than being intricately involved in the day-to-day management of EC affairs.[24] Most EC activities are channelled through the European Communities Division which was created at the time of membership.

Similarly, most other departments have created divisions or appointed staff with specific responsibility for EC matters. The Department of Finance has, however, retained its pivotal position. Its control of the budget and public expenditure shapes the role that Irish Ministers play in Community forums. In particular, the Department has had the difficult task of ensuring that Ireland's benefits from EC membership are not outweighed by the costs, notably in respect of regional policy by making sure that moneys committed to Ireland from the structural funds can be matched by national funds. Thus there have been some limited indirect changes in the machinery of government as a result of EC membership. Nevertheless, the Irish administrative system has absorbed EC matters into existing structures and daily routines, and EC matters have generally been dealt with within the executive branch of government.

Other national actors such as the Dáil and its Joint Committee of Secondary EC Legislation have had little influence over the process. EC membership also had little initial impact on either local

---

[23] See Commission Decision C (91) 1518/3, 25 July 1991.

[24] B. Burns and T. Salmon, 'Policy-Making Coordination in Ireland on European Community Issues', *Journal of Common Market studies*, 15/4 (1977).

government or other regional bodies in Ireland. In part this can be explained by the state of local government in Ireland and the lack of regional structures: 'local authorities . . . have reverted to what they were in the past—the providers of environmental services and the protectors of the environment'.[25] Paradoxically, local authorities might have looked to the European Community as a powerful ally but for the Government's successful campaign to have Ireland treated as one region in Europe. Local officials and councillors were actively discouraged from forming relationships with EC officials. Nowhere was this more evident than in a Department of the Environment memorandum issued in 1988 which required all County and City Managers to 'notify the Committee [on the European Community Internal Market and Structural Funds] of all contacts with the European Communities' made by local authority officers or members. In practice many of the county councils and regional bodies have established links with the Commission and especially with DG XVI.

The relationship between the Government, local and regional authorities, and the Commission has undergone a number of changes evident in the case of regional policy. There was an initial phase in which the relationship was principally governed by the strictures of the 1975 Council Regulation, which lasted up until the second reform of the ERDF in 1984.[26] This required only limited contact: national quotas were in operation, eligibility criteria were determined nationally and finances were constrained. The Irish Government supported the creation of a regional fund but principally for economic benefit rather than with any real commitment to regional policy. It was committed to a policy of national economic growth, and had embarked on a series of national economic recovery programmes, so regional policy was not a high priority. Administratively, the Department of Finance acted as a clearing-house for ERDF proposals, while a variety of other departments were responsible for the drawing-up of proposals and their implementation. A second phase stretched from the 1984 ERDF reform to the SEA. During this phase the Commission made a number of important operational changes that impacted on the relationship between the fund and the states: the quota system was replaced by a new system of indicative ranges and two new types of programme

[25] Chubb, *The Government and Politics of Ireland*, 289.
[26] EEC Council Regulation No. 724/75.

were introduced, which increased the overall control and discretion of the Commission. The Irish Government's response to these changes was both muted and slow. The Government for the most part ignored the changes in the regulation, as it had done in 1979, and continued to submit a steady flow of projects rather than programmes for assistance. For example, in 1985 it submitted 160 projects for assistance but no programme. The first and for a long time the only application for programme support was a Roads NPCI submitted in 1986.[27] Nevertheless, the Commission did little to encourage Ireland to change its approach, and indeed there was a general feeling in DG XVI that little could be done, as Irish attitudes and policies were entrenched.

A change in government policy did come about in October 1987 with an announcement of the Government's intention to adopt programmes. On the same day the Hume report on *The Regional Problems in Ireland* was debated in the European Parliament, suggesting a growing concern over Ireland's particular regional problems. These actions marked the third and most active phase of development, where the Irish Government has to some extent adapted its practices in responding to changes under way in the European Community. This was in part a reaction to the growing importance of economic and social cohesion in the EC. The Government announced in August 1988 that in drawing up a National Development Plan for EC assistance it would be developing operational programmes at the national and subnational levels. In the case of subnational programmes the country was to be divided into seven regions. The following month the Government stated that it would be creating a two-tier consultation system within the seven sub-regions.[28] This seemed to mark a particular turning-point, suggesting the growing influence of EC regional policy in Ireland. The consultation, however, was largely deemed to be token, and the consultative committees went into abeyance after the Government submitted its National Development Plan in March 1988. There is no indication that they can become a focus for regions in the future.

While the current phase of Ireland's relationship with the Commission has been characterized by a much closer working relation-

[27] B. Laffan, ' "While you're over there in Brussels, get us a grant": The Management of the Structural Funds in Ireland', *Irish Political Studies*, 4 (1989), 51.
[28] N. Collins, 'Regional Planning Structures under the National Development Plan for the Republic of Ireland, 1989–1993', *Irish Political Studies*, 4 (1989), 115–17.

ship between the two bodies, there is nevertheless a continuing tension between the two levels. The Government has resisted Commission attempts to develop a closer working relationship with the local and regional authorities. The Government has jealously guarded its policy prerogative in the face of pressure from the Commission and from local and regional interests.

Conclusions

There has always been an objective basis for regionalization in the Republic of Ireland in socio-economic terms, but this never developed into regional politics for two reasons. First of all, the socio-economic conditions were never reinforced by any cultural awareness. Since the hiving-off of Northern Ireland in 1922, Ireland has been a largely homogeneous ethnic and cultural entity, with popular loyalties funnelled either to the local or the national level. Secondly, the socio-economic differences were not always seen as being problems of internal spatial distribution, but rather as subsidiary consequences of the overall lack of development of the Irish economy. Cultural distinctiveness cannot be created overnight: however, the second factor is more amenable to change in the short term. Where previously regional development considerations tended to be submerged in national ones, there is now a growing feeling that the two are not synonymous. This need not even imply that each region is behaving more selfishly, because if each region were to pursue its own needs, it could well be that the collective benefits of all regions would amount to more than could be achieved through a single national approach.

Although the first Irish regional policy predates EC regional policy, the Community's regional policy has been a key factor in encouraging a more political perception of regionalism, particularly through the desire of the Commission and the European Parliament to have a greater degree of consultation and control devolved to subnational authorities. This has given regional groups in Ireland a rallying point, in particular since the inception of the National Development Plan, which was widely interpreted as no more than a sop to them. Regional demands are now receiving an increasingly sympathetic ear from opposition parties and consistent attention in the national media and the national political agenda.

At the very least, a regional debate has been created. Furthermore, the feeling that regional development must remain consequent upon national economic development has been challenged by other developments in the EC. The drive towards completing the common internal market and the further proposals for economic and political integration have highlighted the unequal distribution of the benefits from the EC in Ireland. There is a growing feeling that the Government's centralized approach to dealings with the Community is inhibiting more flexible and potentially more effective arrangements.

Community regional policy has thus served to foster growing support for some degree of regionalization in Ireland. In a passive sense, the source of finance available from Brussels offers regional authorities a financial base and so removes possible objections on the grounds of economic feasibility. Economically, the fact that Community regional funds constitute an important plank of Irish Government regional schemes has served to heighten the importance of the regional debate in Ireland. And politically, the desire on the part of the Commission to include regional groups in consultation, implementation, and monitoring of schemes has been a direct challenge to the usual centralization of Irish government. Irish regionalism remains weak, but the Community regional policy has at least ensured that regional issues are now a constant item on the Irish political agenda.

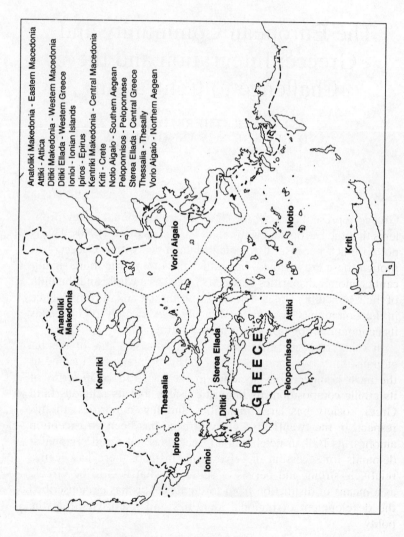

Anatoliki Makedonia - Eastern Macedonia
Attiki - Attica
Ditiki Makedonia - Western Macedonia
Ditiki Ellada - Western Greece
Ionioi - Ionian Islands
Ipiros - Epirus
Kentriki Makedonia - Central Macedonia
Kriti - Crete
Notio Aigaio - Southern Aegean
Peloponnisos - Peloponnese
Sterea Ellada - Central Greece
Thessalia - Thessaly
Vorio Aigaio - Northern Aegean

Map 10. Greece: regions.

11

The European Community and Greece: Integration and the Challenge to Centralism

KEVIN FEATHERSTONE
AND GEORGE N. YANNOPOULOS

Introduction

Greece represents one of the most difficult regional-policy problems that the European Community has to face in the 1990s. This is not so much because of regional inequalities within Greece—although these are serious—but rather because of the more significant economic disparities between Greece as a whole and the bulk of the EC member states. The aims of cohesion and of convergence in the Community pose major difficulties in relation to Greece, as its economic problems appear almost intractable.

In other respects, internally Greece possesses few of the regionalist tensions found elsewhere in the Community. It is one of the most homogeneous societies in the EC. Judged in terms of its ethnic composition, its linguistic usage, and its religious faith Greek society has large majorities and few minorities. In this respect, in the twentieth century Greece has been an exception amongst its Balkan neighbours. Greece has not faced regionalist demands for secession or separatism. Instead, there has been a relatively strong and pervasive sense of what it is to be Greek, as a means of distinction from foreigners. This has circumscribed the development of regional identities and interests within the polity.

Kevin Featherstone would like to express his gratitude to Susannah Verney and Constantine Ifadis (Research Unit on South East Europe, University of Bradford) for their comments on an earlier draft. Any errors are the sole responsibility of the authors.

In Greece, the sense of national identity has had an important inclusive character. The *ethnos* (nation) has assumed social primacy; indeed, it has superiority over notions of the individual rights of, and scope for dissent by, its citizens. As Pollis has argued, 'Greece is estranged from Europe because of the Greek conceptualization of the relationship between the individual and the state, because the state is considered the embodiment of the nation, and because the primary obligation of all Greeks is to protect and defend the transcendent *éthnos*.'[1] Indeed, Pollis has noted that in some respects this leads to a 'subordination of individual rights to one's obligation to the state.'[2] Certainly, the inclusivity of the prevailing sense of the 'ethnos' has limited the rights of Greece's small minorities; but, by being small they have not posed any significant challenge to the rest of society.

The instability in the Balkans prompted by the break-up of Yugoslavia poses external 'regionalist' problems for Greece and the EC to respond to. The demands for international recognition of its national independence made by the former Yugoslav republic of Macedonia, based in Skopje, in 1992–3 inflamed the sensitivities of almost all Greeks. Greek objections centred on the use of the term Macedonia, which Greece claims denotes an exclusive and integral part of its own history and culture, and the apparent irredentist claims made by political leaders in Skopje, seeking a Greater Macedonia. The Macedonian issue went to the very core of the Greek sense of *ethnos*, though it served to highlight the strength of its own national unity *vis-à-vis* outsiders. There remained no secessionist pressures of any significance within the Greek polity.

Another ethnic issue on Greece's borders seemed set to emerge in 1993: the dispute with Albania over Vorio Epirus, the southern provinces of Albania which have a predominantly ethnic Greek population.[3] The abuse of the human rights of the ethnic Greek population there has led to demands for a Vorio Epirus autonomous region to be created (similar to that demanded by Albanians in Kosovo, Serbia) or even for the *enosis* (union) of the provinces with Greece. In response, Albanian groups pressed for

---

[1] A. Pollis, Greek National Identity: Religious Minorities, Rights, and European Norms', *Journal of Modern Greek Studies*, 10/2 (Oct. 1992).

[2] Ibid.

[3] J. Pettifer, 'Greece: Into the Balkan Crisis', *The World Today*, 48/11 (Nov. 1992).

the return of the Cameria lands of southern Epirus, inside Greece, which have minorities descended from ethnic Albanians. In any event, worsening economic conditions inside Albania appeared to be leading to the disintegration of the border as an effective barrier, as many travelled to Ioannina, rather than Tirana, for scarce goods and services, and refugee ethnic Albanians crossed into Greece in increasing numbers.[4] The solution of this regionalist issue, like that of 'Macedonia', will require action by both the EC and the United Nations. Such issues will severely test the EC's foreign policy co-operation and the prospects for meaningful European Political Union envisaged by the Maastricht Treaty. The consequence of these ethnic problems is, of course, that Greece cannot expect harmonious relations with either its Tirana or Skopje neighbours in the medium term.

Domestically, the Greek State is highly centralist, possessing as yet only weak administrative structures for the articulation of regional interests. The consequence of EC policies and development aid, however, has been to boost the incipient internal pressure for greater administrative decentralization, to promote democracy and efficiency. The policy philosophy of subsidiarity and partnership underpinning much of the new EC funding has challenged traditional Greek centralism. Similarly, the deregulation and liberalization of the single market programme has encouraged opinion towards less statist public policies.

By virtue of its EC membership, Greece is thus importing new pressures for domestic political and economic reform. Modernization is equated with the attainment of EC norms and standards. Visions of a better future are now closely identified with action within the EC. Both élite and mass opinion, in the recent past, has been strongly pro-Community: some of the highest levels of support for integration have been found in Greece. Surveys conducted for the EC Commission have shown large majorities believing Community membership to be 'a good thing' and to have 'benefited' Greece (73 per cent in December 1991).[5] Those involved in Greek agriculture, and village communities, are well aware of the economic benefits they have obtained from the Community, as a result of its agricultural and regional development policies. Support

---

[4] Ibid.
[5] Commission of the European Communities, *Eurobarometer: Public Opinion in the European Community*; no. 36 (Brussels: EC Commission, Dec. 1991).

for Europe has been strong in recent years, constituting an important source for domestic unity. However, this majority support could be undermined by public dissatisfaction over issues such as Macedonia, and by the renewed opposition of the Communists (KKE) to the Community gaining more favour.

The present chapter discusses regional issues in Greece, in the context of its EC membership. Its central themes are: firstly, the extent to which EC membership is promoting a greater administrative decentralization from Athens—an external force overcoming entrenched national practices; and secondly, the more general effects of EC aid on regional development within Greece. The Greek State is vulnerable to EC pressures as a result, in part, of its increasing dependency on EC financial aid. Greece itself is an economically disadvantaged region of the Community, and it is recognized as such under the ERDF.

Regional Administration

Since its independence in 1832, the Greek State has been highly centralized, allowing little administrative decentralization. Indeed, given the reforms implemented elsewhere in Europe in the 1970s and 1980s, Greece may well be the most centralized state in the European Community. Its system of regional and local administration displays close parallels with the traditional French model, whilst some of its cultural traits—such as clientelism—are common to other southern European societies. Limited reform in the 1980s, and the pressures created by European Community membership, have challenged the traditional centralization, however, raising new questions for the future.

Historically, the power of the Greek State was derived not only from the weakness of regional and local government, but also from the relative underdevelopment of wider forms of pluralism. Limited industrialization, weak class structures, disorientation from the influx of refugees, and rapid urbanization undermined the emergence of pluralistic structures. Traditionally, charismatic leadership and clientelistic practices unified when ideologies and collective organization could not. Still today, the effective operation of democratic processes in civil society is limited by the weakness of social structures independent of the State and by the maintenance of traditional attitudes and practices. Political parties have seen the use of the State apparatus as a means of extending their own hegemony via intervention and incorporation, practices which received international attention with the scandals and controversies of 1988–9.[6] In sum, social structures and the prevailing political culture have supported centralism and clientelism: a dependency on the central State which has stifled other forms of autonomy and independence.

Traditionally, power and decision have extended out from the central State apparatus. The local administrative structure of Greece is based on the nomarchies, or prefectures (*nomarchia*). The *nomarchia* were developed as a branch of central government administration. Each one is headed by a *nomarchis* (or prefect) appointed by the Ministry of the Interior, who represents the central government in the area and who oversees the decentralized services of the central ministries there. Law 1235 of 1982 reinforced the ability of central government to appoint or dismiss a *nomarchis* at will. Until 1982 all decisions by local authorities within the area had to be approved by the *nomarchis*, and still the *nomarchis* must approve their legality: a power which can be used by central government to delay decisions if it finds it expedient to do so.[7]

The number of *nomarchia* has grown from ten to the current fifty-five. Technically, there are only fifty-two *nomoi*, or geographical departments, but that of Attica has been subdivided for administrative purposes.[8] The *nomarchia* are long-accepted administrative units, and they also serve as the basis for electoral constituencies at national elections. The size of the *nomoi* (the area of the *nomarchia*) varies considerably: from tiny islands like Lefkas or mountainous regions such as Evritania, to more populous units based on divisions of the urban centres of Athens, Piraeus, and Thessaloniki.

Councils for the *nomoi* (*nomarchiaka symvoulia*/prefecture councils) were established by Law 3200 in 1955. They were given an

---

[6] K. Featherstone, 'Political Parties and Democratic Consolidation in Greece', in G. Pridham (ed.), *Securing Democracy: Political Parties and Democratic Consolidation in Southern Europe* (London: Routledge, 1990).

[7] S. Verney and F. Papageorgiou, 'Prefecture Councils in Greece: Decentralization in the European Community Context', *Regional Politics and Policy*, 2/1, 2 (spring/summer 1992), 110.

[8] Ibid.

advisory role, to discuss the public-works programme for the area, to make proposals for area development, to consider the functioning of the public services and the issues of labour, health, and social welfare.[9] Given this talking-shop role, and the fact that they were to meet only twice a year, the *nomarchia* councils remained weak and ineffective.

A limited reform was instituted by the PASOK Government in 1982 (Law 1235). The councils' role remain essentially advisory, but with some upgrading.[10] The councils have to approve the fund budget of the *nomarchia*, previously the responsibility of the Ministries of Finance and of the Interior. They can propose particular projects for their public-works programmes, and they have decision-making powers on the drawing-up and amendment of these. They now meet once a month, and more regularly if demanded by two-thirds of their members. Their composition was also altered: they remain indirectly elected, but their membership was widened to reflect the various organized interests of the area. Local government representatives constitute half the members; the remaining members are chosen by the *nomarchia*-level governing committees of professional organizations; agricultural co-operatives; trade union organizations; and chambers of commerce. The *nomarchis* remains the president of the council, and he has power over its agenda. Other State functionaries in the area can attend the meetings, but unlike in the past they cannot vote.

Public attitudes suggest that *nomarchia* councillors are accorded less political significance than not only the prefect but also other actors in the area, such as party leaders, economic leaders, local personalities, and MPs.[11] Members of the public usually address councillors in their other capacities, such as mayor or union leader. The councillors see their role as akin to a pressure group defending local interests against Athens. In acting in this manner, however, they serve to raise the awareness of local interests.

Beneath the *nomarchia* level, there is a system of *demoi* (municipalities) and *koinotites* (communities), established in 1912. Communities are supposed to represent 1,000–10,000 people and municipalities populations over 10,000. However, in practice the sizes of both vary greatly: Greece, with a population of less than ten million, has some 5,999 local government units. The municipal and

[9] Verney and Papageorgiou 'Prefecture Councils in Greece'.
[10] Ibid.   [11] Ibid. 119.

community councils are directly elected, unlike those of the nomarchies.

The mayors of the municipal councils, and the communities, are directly elected, every four years. The politicization of these elections has varied, but it is usually high. In 1986, for example, New Democracy, then in opposition, put forward three of its leading figures to challenge the PASOK national Government. In the event, the strategy was successful: Evert won in Athens; Andrianopoulos in Piraeus; and Kouvelas in Thessaloniki. However, in 1990, when New Democracy held national government office, the party attempted to depoliticize the municipal elections: it successfully backed Antonis Tritsis against Melina Merkouri, one ex-PASOK member against a continuing PASOK member. The post of mayor in the three largest cities has thus been seen as an important political base.

For the new EC Committee of the Regions, established under the Maastricht Treaty, the Greek Government initially selected local mayors for eight of the nation's twelve places on the committee.[12] The remaining four were to be non-elected prefects, chosen by the Ministry of the Interior. This caused some controversy, though, as it seemed to flout at least the spirit of Article 198A of the Maastricht Treaty.[13] It is consistent with the tradition of political control from the centre, however.

The 1982 reforms of the *nomarchia* were intended to be the forerunner of further changes in local government. PASOK proclaimed its commitment to decentralization. Moreover, EC membership effectively required meaningful decentralization. The introduction of the Community's Integrated Mediterranean Programmes (IMPs), for which Greece had lobbied hard, assumed the operation of subnational planning authorities. For the purposes of the IMPs, Greece was divided into six areas: Aegean Islands; Crete; Northern Greece; Western Greece and the Peloponnese; Central and Eastern Greece; and Attica. The six regions had no other purpose than to facilitate the IMPs, with monitoring committees being established for them.

Later, the PASOK Government passed Law 1622 in 1986 which detailed a major extension of the power and role of the *nomarchia* councils.[14] It provided for 75 per cent of councillors to be directly

---

[12] *The Independent*, 20 Jan. 1993.   [13] *Eleftherotypia*, 30 Jan. 1993.
[14] Verney and Papageorgiou, 'Prefecture Councils in Greece'.

elected, with the remainder continuing to be interest-group representatives. The *nomarchia* councils were to be given significant new powers, including effective control over the public-works budget for their area. Though it was in power until June 1989, the PASOK Government did not implement this new law, maintaining instead its modest reforms of 1982. In March 1990, the 'ecumenical' Government of Greece's three major parties (PASOK, New Democracy, and the Communist-led alliance) legislated for elections to the bodies proposed by PASOK to be held the following October, with the new councils to start their work in January 1991. However, the new ND Government of April 1990 cancelled the elections. It has recently brought forward its own set of reforms: a draft law in February 1992 promised to delegate more spending powers to the *nomarchia* councils. Progress on this was slow, however.

The 1986 law also defined thirteen new administrative regions (*perifereies*). Thirteen regional councils (*perifereiaka symvoulia*) were established, grouping a number of *nomarchia* under the chairmanship of a Regional Secretary-General (*Perifereiarchis*). Both the councillors and the secretaries are appointed by the Government. The regional secretaries were first appointed in 1988, and the regional councils shortly afterwards. Following the June 1989 national elections, all regional secretaries, as party-political appointees, were replaced. The councils comprise representatives of both the central government and local authorities in the region. The regional councils have an ill-defined role concerned with planning, and in particular spending projects, affecting several *nomarchia*. Their role is essentially advisory, but the Athens Government can allow them a greater say. Political pressure led to further differentiation of development regions and regional-council areas.[15]

The creation of these thirteen regions was motivated by planning needs, including the stimulus of EC structural-aid programmes. They constitute a modest reform of the heavy-handed centralism of Greek administration, but they hardly represent a radical shift of power. As Papageorgiou and Verney have commented, 'The regions are meant to act as "watchdogs" over the regional budgets and to co-ordinate planning activities, but they do not as yet represent an administrative tier co-ordinating policies and ad-

---

[15] Verney and Papageorgion, 'Prefecture Councils in Greece.'

ministration between central government and the prefectures (nomarchia).'[16] Moreover, 'As long as the leadership careers of regional administrators depend on their role as obedient servants of the centre, they can never become effective exponents of regional and local interests.'[17] The regions are still struggling to establish their identity and their role.

Regional and local government in Greece has thus experienced only modest reform in recent years; the traditional centralization essentially remains in tact. However, the pressure for more meaningful reform has grown, in part aided by EC policies which presume a decentralized planning process. Any government currently in power would thus be urged to introduce reforms: both PASOK and ND have felt obliged to table such proposals. Lack of political will and/or bureaucratic inertia may yet stifle such reform: indeed, the climate of centralization has been well established over the course of modern Greek history. Some change is almost certain in the 1990s; the success of its implementation remains highly questionable, however, given the political manipulation, administrative inefficiency, and structural tensions endemic in the present system.

Regional Economic Inequalities

The most important regional-policy problem for the EC in relation to Greece is the glaring economic disparity between Greece as a whole and the average prosperity of the Community. Moreover, the relative inequality of Greece has worsened in recent years: by 1990 it was the poorest EC member state. Individual regions in Greece are amongst the poorest in the Community, and some have slipped further behind the rest of the EC. These regional disparities pose severe policy problems for both Athens and Brussels, with the onset of the single market and the prospect of EMU.

Economic disparities between Greece and the rest of the EC have widened considerably since 1981. GDP per capita as a proportion of the EC-12 average fell from 58.2 per cent in 1980 to 53 per cent in 1990. Whilst, admittedly, inter-country disparities in

---

[16] F. Papageorgiou and S. Verney, 'Regional Planning and the Integrated Mediterranean Programmes in Greece', *Regional Politics and Policy*, 2/1, 2 (spring/summer 1992), 141.

[17] Ibid. 159.

GDP per head widened within the EC as a whole in the first half of the 1980s, they fell below their 1980 level in the second half of the decade. Moreover, in 1990 Greece replaced Portugal as the EC nation with the lowest GDP per capita.

Throughout the 1980s the Greek economy suffered sluggish growth. Its growth was less than that for the EC as a whole: by 0.2 per cent per annum during 1982–5 and 1.3 per cent during 1986–90. Relative labour productivity deteriorated: GDP per person employed in Greece fell from 63.4 per cent of the EC average in 1980 to 56.7 per cent in 1990. In this respect also, Greece had fallen behind Portugal by 1990. For most of the 1980s, the Greek economy was characterized by a public sector with ever-increasing operating losses and financial markets run on administrative fiat. Adjustment to average EC economic levels was frustrated, as a large section of the domestic economy was shielded from competitive market pressures.[18] By the early 1990s, Greek government debt stood at 135–40 per cent of GDP, depending on how the figures are analysed, and inflation was the highest in the EC by far. Early in 1991 the Athens Government obtained a special EC loan of 2.2 billion ECUs to support a three-year stabilization programme, designed to allow the Greek drachma to enter the ERM by the end of 1993.[19] Economic prospects seemed dim, however.

If the disparities between Greece and the average EC levels are to be reduced—so that, for example, by the year 2000 Greek GDP per capita was to reach 75 per cent of the EC average (instead of the current 53 per cent)—then the Greek economy would have to grow every year during the current decade at a rate approximately 3.5 percentage points above the average rate of growth for the Community as a whole. To put this in perspective, it can be noted that during the period 1986–90 Greek GDP per head was growing at 1.5 per cent per annum compared to 2.8 per cent for the EC: in other words, by 4.8 percentage points less than the rate required for the 75 per cent convergence target. This indicates the magnitude of the Greek problem.

The regional disparities within Greece also pose severe problems. Of the ten poorest regions in the EC according to GDP per

---

[18] G. N. Yannopoulos, 'Integration and Convergence: Lessons from Greece's Experience in the European Economic Community', in G. N. Yannopoulos (ed.), *Greece and the EEC* (London: Macmillan, 1986).

[19] *Financial Times*, 30 Apr. 1991.

TABLE 11.1. *Regional income and productivity disparities within Greece and selected EC countries, 1985*

	Belgium	Greece	Spain	Italy
GDP per head at PPS and current prices	8.6	18.7	24.7	17.6
GDP per person employed and current prices	16.9	17.6	13.0	9.4

Source: Commission of the European Communities, *Third Periodic Report on the Social and Economic Situation and Development of the Regions of the Community* (Brussels: EC Commission, 1987).

capita measured by PPS (Purchasing Power Parities) average 1986–8, five are Greek development regions (the other five include three in Portugal, one in Spain, and the French overseas territories). Twelve of the thirteen new administrative regions in Greece are among the twenty poorest in the EC (the total number of EC regions being 171). The relatively more prosperous region of Greece (Sterea Ellada—Central Greece) ranks twenty-eighth in the list. In general, it is estimated that differences in regional productivity (and not just in agriculture) better explain these disparities in prosperity levels than do differences in industrial structures.

Despite the poor position of Greek regions when compared to the EC as a whole, disparities within Greece are not as great as in some other EC member states (see Table 11.1). The distribution of GDP per head appears more equitable in Greece than elsewhere in southern Europe or even within Belgium, a nation of comparable size. Caution must be exercised in making such interpretations, however, because of the differences in the number of regions in each member state and also the sensitivity in the values of the coefficient of variation to the number of regions used. It is possible that most of the extreme disparities in Greece are intra-regional (e.g. inside Attica) rather than interregional (e.g. between Attica and Thessalia). Labour productivity levels seem to diverge more strongly in Greece than in other EC states. This suggests pronounced regional differences in Greece in the proportion of the labour force in employment, or more particularly in participation rates. Overall, the range of economic disparity within

Greece (measured in GDP per head, 1981–8) has deteriorated marginally.[20]

The economic decline of Greece relative to the rest of the EC has not been equally spread across all regions within Greece. The change in income relativities was 6.5 per cent between 1980 and 1988 for Greece as a whole. The relative decline for five Greek regions (of eight regions for which data is available) was much greater: Epirus (−12.7 per cent); Crete (−10.2 per cent); the Peloponnese and Western Greece (−11.0 per cent); Central and Western Macedonia (−8.9 per cent); and Thessaly (−7.8 per cent).[21] On the whole, the relative position of the poorest Greek regions deteriorated more substantially than did that of the more prosperous Greek regions.

The EC and Regional Development in Greece

The role of the EC in promoting regional economic development in Greece has involved: (a) the allocation of a preferential share of aid under EC structural funds, boosting the strained resources of the Athens Government; and (b) the stimulus to domestic administrative reform to facilitate more effective regional planning, which has produced only modest changes as yet. Criticism of Greece has arisen in Brussels focused on the failiure of Athens governments to narrow the economic gap between Greece and average EC GDP, and also on evidence of the domestic mismanagement of the aid given by the Community. To some extent, such criticism presumes too much: it ignores the problems of the international economy in the 1980s and it neglects the evidence of financial corruption in other EC member states.[22]

---

[20] Commission of the European Communities, *The Regions of the Enlarged Community*: Third Periodic Report on the social and economic situation and development of the regions of the Community (Brussels: EC Commission, 1987). Commission of the European Communities, *The Regions in the 1990s* (Brussels: EC Commission, 1991).

[21] Communities, *The Regions of the Enlarged Community*; *The Regions in the 1990s*.

[22] K. Featherstone, 'Greece and the Single European Market: Integration and Liberalization', paper presented to the Modern Greek Studies Association symposium, Florida, 1991.

Without a doubt, EC aid has been very valuable to Greece.[23] Between 1985 and 1989, Greece received a total of 9.9 billion ECUs in payments from the EC budget, equivalent to US\$ 7.9 billion.[24] Over a slightly shorter time-span, Portugal received only 3.1 billion ECUs between 1986 and 1989 (or US\$ 2.5 billion). In other terms, ERDF aid alone to Greece was equal to 0.76 per cent of Greek GDP or 4.22 per cent of investment (Gross Fixed Capital Formation). Greece in the 1980s obtained a proportion of actual ERDF payments to initial commitments much higher than the EC average. In reality, the relative benefits of EC aid by member states vary from year to year, and are affected by the different programmes the EC has developed.

Greece has done well out of the EC budget but, contrary to some opinion, not exceptionally so. Per head of population, the total financial aid given to Greece (52.4 ECUs) in 1987, for example, was less than that transferred to Ireland (103.9 ECUs), Portugal (79.7 ECUs), Italy (77.6 ECUs), or even Denmark (76.5 ECUs).[25] Most of the aid given to Denmark and Italy was in the form of loans from the European Investment Bank, but even ignoring the loan element, both Ireland and Portugal did much better out of the EC, on a per capita basis, than did Greece.[26] Further calculations for the 1989 payments from the EC budget suggest that while the position of Portugal and Italy had deteriorated relative to that of Greece, Ireland continued to receive far more aid on a per capita basis than Greece.[27] More suprisingly, both Denmark and the Netherlands did about as well as Greece.

Infrastructure projects formed a larger part of ERDF payments (1981–8) to Greece (88 per cent) than for the rest of the EC (80 per cent). Approximately one-third of the spending on infrastructure projects was directed to the energy sector, a quarter to transport, one-fifth to telecommunications, and 14 per cent to water-engineering schemes. The expenditure on energy projects led to some regional imbalance in allocations: following the geographical

[23] P. Kazakos, *Hellada Anamesa se Prosarmogi kai Perithoriopoiisi: Dokimia Evropaikis kai Oikonomikis Politikis* (Athens: Diatton, 1991).

[24] Featherstone, 'Greece and the Single European Market'.

[25] Commission of the European Communities, *A Social Portrait of Europe* (Brussels: Eurostat, 1991).

[26] Featherstone, 'Greece and the Single European Market'.

[27] *Official Journal of the European Communities*, 12 Dec. 1990, 76.

distribution of energy resources meant concentrating spending in the relatively prosperous regions of the Peloponnese and Eastern Macedonia.

Following the terms of the so-called 'cohesion fund' agreed at the EC Summit in Edinburgh in December 1992, the Greek Government has announced how it will allocate its 6,670 billion drachmas (approximately £121 billion) between different policy sectors.[28] Approximately 55 per cent will be spent on what is termed 'human resources' and transport. Some 2,668 billion drachmas will be given to the thirteen regions. A special allocation of 5 per cent will be spent in the five border regions—Epirus, Western Macedonia, Eastern Macedonia and Thrace, Northern Aegean Islands, and Ionian Islands.

The scale of EC aid thus far has had little impact in reducing interregional disparities within Greece. In part this is because of the relatively modest sums involved in comparison to the size of the inequalities; the priority given to certain sectors conflicting with regional equalization objectives; and, perhaps, the emphasis placed in some instances on large-scale investment projects. A bias in favour of large projects could be the result of the centralization of both planning and implementation. As Tömmel has noted, it may also be a consequence of the 'additive' principle, requiring national aid to match that from the EC.[29] A breakdown of ERDF aid per capita (for 1981–8) on a regional basis is given in Table 11.2. The correlation between aid per capita and GDP per head in the regions was not significant, indicating limited redistributive effects (Spearman rank correlation coefficient: -0.428, not significant at 0.1 level).

The fiscal crisis of the Greek State in recent years also poses severe constraints on the effective use of ERDF aid. The Greek Government has been forced to cut its budgetary expenditure. This suggests that it will find it increasingly difficult to abide by the additionality principle of matching funds. The Greek contribution to the EC-sponsored regional development programmes, for example, approved in January 1990 for the period to the end of 1993, is such that if it comes entirely out of the Greek State budget,

[28] *Eleftherotypia*, 30 Jan. 1993.
[29] I. Tömmel, 'Regional Policy in the European Community: Its Impact on Regional Policies and Public Administration in the Mediterranean Member States', *Environment and Planning C: Government and Policy*, 5 (1987).

TABLE 11.2. *ERDF aid per capita, 1981–1988*

Region	ECU
Central Greece	264
Central and West Macedonia	444
Peloponnese and Western Greece	290
Thessaly	201
Eastern Macedonia	295
Crete	304
Epirus	411
Thrace	233
East Aegean Sea	284

Source: CEC, ERDF Fourteenth Annual Report (1988).

it will tie up all the funds of the public investment budgets up to that year. There would be no independent Greek regional-policy action. These difficulties come amidst the challenge of the single market and the opening-up of eastern Europe, both of which have major implications for Greek regions. Recognition of these problems led to the EC Commission allowing Greece to use part of the receipts from its 1990 EC loan as its own contribution to meet the additionality target.

Of special relevance to Greece has been the aid given under the EC's Integrated Mediterranean Programmes (IMPs–MOPs in Greek), established in June 1985. Half the aid available under the IMPs was earmarked for Greece (3.3 billion ECUs). The PASOK Government, led by Andreas Papandreou, had pressed for such aid as a 'condition' of Greece's continued EC membership and as help in the face of the entry of Spain and Portugal into the Community. PASOK claimed the IMPs as its victory.

The initiation and implementation of the IMPs in Greece offers illuminating insights into regional policy and administration in that system. The IMPs were based on two principles which challenged the nature of traditional Greek administration: subsidiarity and partnership. Together, they required decentralization and co-operation between central, local, and EC authorities.

The experience of the IMPs testifies to the strength of centralism in Greek administration. Papageorgiou and Verney undertook a detailed investigation, involving a range of interviews in April–

June 1989, of how the IMPs were developed and implemented in Greece. They concluded that,

all the limitations of the IMP process . . . resulted from the Greek administration's attempt to run regional programmes without devolving any substantial powers to the regional level. Although the IMPs were regional programmes in name, in practice a sizeable component was centrally planned and centrally implemented. The degree of regional control was frustratingly small.[30]

They report an administrative process very much in contradiction with the original IMP philosophy. Central government ministries operated as 'watertight compartments' unable to engage in integrated planning. The Ministry of the National Economy drew up the IMP bids, adopting a narrow view of essential EC rules, rather than studying the effects of projects on regional development. Prefectures (*nomarchia*) were not told and had no influence over the implementation of IMP measures in their areas. The share of the IMP budget implemented by central agencies reached 90 per cent in Crete, instead of the intended 75 per cent. The inflexible procedures and structures of the central bureaucracy and accounting system in Greece drastically undermined the effectiveness of the IMPs. In short, the IMP process was an exercise in central control and stifled local efforts.

Such centralization has severely constrained the development of networks linking subnational and EC-level actors. Athens acts as the gatekeeper. Verney and Papageorgiou noted that, 'the Greek government seems to want to retain exclusive political control of all relationships with the EC'.[31] Indeed, they found no single regional agency in Greece participating in a European consortium or network: few had any knowledge of what they might involve, though prefecture councillors expressed keen interest in them.[32]

EC aid to Greece, including the IMP measures, has shown the compatibility between EC and subnational interests. EC action prompted the elaboration of new regional planning processes—IMP monitoring committees and the thirteen regional councils—and in the future Community policies may well require more substantive decentralization. The IMPs also affected the attitudes

---

[30] Papageorgiou and Verney, 'Regional Planning and the Integrated Mediterranean Programmes in Greece', 159.
[31] Ibid. 150.   [32] Ibid. 132.

of the subnational actors involved. Verney and Papageorgiou in their study of prefecture councillors found strong support across all parties for the EC to be given larger and wider policy responsibilities and for the creation of new EC-level institutions.[33] Set against the long-established criticisms of the autocracy and inefficiency of central administration in Athens, as well as the image of the EC possessing a pot of gold, no doubt Brussels can seem a most attractive suitor to fledgeling leaders at the grass roots.

Conclusions

The foregoing analysis has emphasized the challenges posed to Greece by EC integration in the 1990s. First, as a result of EC aid policies, a new stimulus has been felt towards administrative decentralization from Athens. As yet, progress towards decentralization has been modest: the culture and practice of centralism is well entrenched in the Greek polity. Yet, the issue is now firmly on the political agenda of each of the major Greek parties. The second challenge to Greece has been to converge more closely, economically, with its wealthier EC partners. This is especially important in the context of the stage-by-stage progression planned for EMU. The economic data portrayed above present a dim outlook: Greece has failed to narrow the gap with its partners since it joined in 1981. Greece clearly needs far more help to achieve such high targets.

Such pressures place the Greek State very much on the defensive in the 1990s. In the past, political manipulation has bedevilled the State machinery; now the major parties talk of decentralization. Whether there is the political will to carry through meaningful reform, and whether any such reform might be distorted by party interests, remains a pertinent question. In any event, the State machinery is failing to keep up with new administrative pressures and it has neither the resources nor, perhaps, the managerial ability to catch up with its EC partners. Seemingly inadequate to its tasks, the State machinery is undermined not only by dated administrative practices, but also by a clientelistic culture, involving an ever-increasing number of staff who have their own entrenched

[33] Ibid. 128–30.

interests. This culture and these interests may yet stultify meaningful reform.

The onset of the Single European Market has already widened the pressures on the Greek State, beyond those associated with direct EC aid and the EMU convergence targets. The 1992 process has obliged the Greek State to open up the domestic market to EC firms and to reduce its own regulation and support of that market. In increasingly important respects, the single market requires the Greek State to act as a local agency carrying out regulatory and distributive acts agreed at the EC level. The State machine thus faces additional pressures for its rationalization.[34] The process of market liberalization initiated by the 1992 programme was taken up by the (conservative) New Democracy Government of Constantine Mitsotakis after April 1990, which sought to introduce deregulation and privatization into Greece. The single market is thus set to have a profound effect on both the Greek State and the private sector. Private business has been conditioned to operate in a highly statist environment: in the past there was no effective force opposing the expansion of the State's distributive role. The statist approach at home was encouraged in response to the external vulnerability of the economy: with the aim of substituting its greater strength for the weakness of others. Now, it is precisely an external pressure which is set to weaken the domestic role of the State and expose the Greek private sector to the force of strong external competition.

The intensification of the EC regional integration process is thus increasing the pressures in Greece for 'modernization', involving less State regulation and less centralization. At the same time, the Greek economy remains weak and vulnerable, within the EC and beyond. In foreign policy matters, Greece faces major problems on its doorstep. The common element here is the increasing dependency of Greece on the rest of the EC. It remains to be seen whether the EC can cope with such intense Greek problems, or whether life on the Community's periphery will become relatively more difficult. The 'regional' problem for Greece is to be accepted as a full and equal member of the Community.

[34] Featherstone, 'Greece and the Single European Market'.

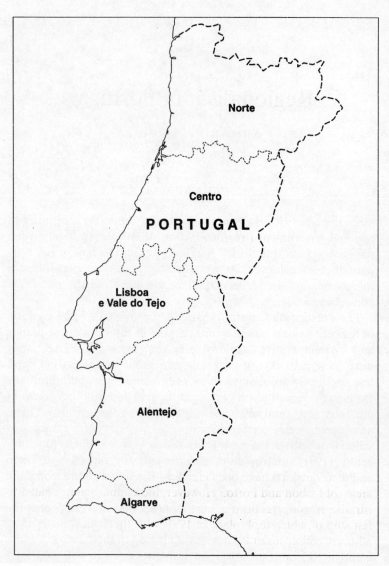

MAP 11. Portugal: regions.

12

Regionalism in Portugal

ARMANDO PEREIRA

Introduction

Since the late 1970s the process of creating autonomous entities of regional government ('regionalization') has been an issue on the political agenda, but so far regional institutionalization has only partially been achieved. Regional entities have been established in the Azores and in Madeira, but on the mainland the process is embryonic.

The Portuguese Constitution of 1976 provided for the creation of regions; namely 'autonomous regions' in the Portuguese islands and 'administrative regions' on the mainland. The latter were designed as self-government regional entities, but with less political autonomy than the islands. In addition, the Portuguese Constitution permitted the creation of 'other forms of autarchic territorial organization' in the 'large urban areas'.[1] The autonomous regions of the Azores and Madeira were established immediately after the new Constitution was approved. More recently (1991), metropolitan governments for Lisbon and Porto and their outskirts have been created—the so-called 'metropolitan areas' of Lisbon and Porto.[2] However, the establishment of administrative regions has been a more complex and slower process, the last step of which took place in 1991, with the achievement of an all-party consensus in Parliament. This lead to the Law on Administrative Regions,[3] a basic legal framework which will at a later stage allow for the implementation of regionalism throughout Portugal.

[1] Portuguese Constitution, Article 238 n. 3.
[2] Law no. 91, of 2nd August (Metropolitan Areas of Lisbon and Porto).
[3] Law no. 56/91, of 13 August (Basic Law on Administrative Regions).

The Regional Component in the Portuguese Political and Administrative System

The Portuguese political and administrative system has its roots in the administrative structure of the nineteenth century. Following the victory of liberalism, the administrative structure was reformed on the Napoleonic model characteristic of other southern Europe systems. Subsequently, partial administrative and territorial reforms were implemented reflecting either 'liberal' or 'absolutism' values, but the basic administrative structure remained substantially intact.[4] Some elements of the Portuguese political and administrative system differ significantly from other systems in central and northern Europe:

1. An electoral system based on proportional representation.
2. Diversity of parties.
3. Strong State centralism with Jacobinism a significant factor in the central political and administrative organization, and throughout the bureaucracy.
4. A legal and effective right of access to Government and Parliament given to the locally elected people, public officials, and higher civil servants.
5. A 'prefectural' administrative structure; the country is divided into eighteen administrative districts, which have some regional significance and are headed by a representative of the central government (civil governor) more or less responsible for some public services.
6. At a local level, the self-governing municipalities and parishes have a strong executive: a president rather like the French *maire*, who in the case of the municipalities, is called 'President of the Municipal Council'.

This political and administrative organization is essentially that adopted after the Liberal Revolution of 1820. The abolition of the monarchy and the inauguration of the republic in 1910 made little impact on the administrative and territorial system.[5] Between 1926

[4] A reference work of some interest, about Portugal and its political and administrative evolution, particularly on this historic period, is W. C. Oppelo, Jr., *Portugal's Political Development* (Boulder, Colo.: Westview Press, 1985).
[5] See D. L. Wheeler, *The First Portuguese Republic* (Madison, Wis.: University of Wisconsin, 1978).

and 1974 Portugal was governed by a political regime characterized by a powerful executive with a strong bureaucratic, corporatist, and autocratic emphasis. It depoliticized institutions, particularly the local units of administration, and reinforced Jacobinism in public administration.[6] After the revolution of 25 April 1974 was consolidated by the new Constitution in 1976, priority was given to the processes of democratization, decolonization, and decentralization, with the intent of developing the country along modern democratic and European lines.[7] The process of decolonization was implemented, a new political-electoral framework was organized, democratic local authorities were re-established and the autonomous regions of the Azores and Madeira were created. In the new Constitution, the administrative regions were anticipated and other forms of territorial organization for metropolitan areas were allowed. In this context the creation of administrative regions is the unfinished business of the democratization process.

This is not altogether surprising since Portugal has been a unitary state for the last 850 years; its borders were settled a long time ago. There are no major differences in ethnic, linguistic, or racial terms and, there have been virtually no regionalist pressures, except in the islands of the Azores and Madeira for obvious geographical reasons.[8] Thus, regionalism is not a strong tradition in the Portuguese political and administrative system; indeed at a territorial level, a basically municipalist tradition predominates. However, throughout the centuries of Portuguese history, different administrative formulations of a regional or provincial character have survived. In the fifteenth and sixteenth centuries, the country

---

[6] About this period of the Portuguese life and its political and administrative implications, see e.g. P. C. Schmitter, The ' "*Régime d'Exception*" that Became the Rule: Forty-Eight Years of Authoritarian Domination in Portugal', in L. S. Graham and H. M. Makler (eds.), *Contemporary Portugal: The Revolution and its Antecedents* (Austin, Tex.: University of Texas Press, 1979), 3–45; also in L. S. Graham, *Portugal: The Decline and the Collapse of an Authoritarian Order* (London: Sage Publications, 1975); and yet P. C. Schmitter, *Corporatism and Public Policy in Authoritarian Portugal* (Beverly Hills, Calif. and London: Sage, 1975).

[7] The literature in English concerning the above-mentioned historical period of Portuguese life is rich, as far as the analysis of political and administrative implications goes. See e.g.: T. C. Bruneau, *Politics and Nationhood: Post-Revolutionary Portugal* (New York: Praeger, 1984); and also R. J. Morrison, *Portugal: Revolutionary Change in an Open Economy* (Boston: Auburn House Publishing, 1981).

[8] T. Gallagher, 'Portugal's Atlantic Territories: The Separatist Challenge', *The World Today* (1979), 353–60.

was divided into provinces, for administrative purposes, and this regional structure survived more or less until the liberal reforms of the nineteenth century. Until 1959, these regional provinces survived episodically, embodying some morphological, economic, and cultural differences.

With the administrative reforms of the nineteenth century, the districts and municipalities were created; the former under the rule of a prefectural authority, the civil governor, and the latter led by elected local politicians. Together they deprived the provinces of most administrative meaning. In particular, the municipalities, relatively large in population and area, were powerful representative local government units and almost totally dominated their internal self-governing parishes.[9] The autonomous regions of the Azores and Madeira are the only institutionalized regional governments in Portugal and were given a series of devolved powers: to legislate on all matters of regional interest; to regulate regional legislation emanating from national government; to initiate legislation in the national legislature; to exercise their own executive authority; to spend autonomously all revenues collected by the regional government and allocated by the central government; and to supervise their local governments. The organic structure of the autonomous regions comprises an assembly and an executive. The regional assembly is a unicameral legislative body, elected for four years by direct universal suffrage in accordance with proportional representation. The regional executive is appointed by the Government, having given due consideration to the election results for the assembly.[10]

Finally, the administrative regions on the mainland constitute a 'prefigurative' intermediate level of government at a not-yet attained decentralization goal.[11]

---

[9] See developments in A. Pereira, 'The System of Local Government in Portugal', in R. Batley and Gerry Stoker (eds.), *Local Government in Europe* (London: Macmillan, 1991), 134–45; W. C. Oppelo, Jr., 'Local Government and Political Culture in a Portuguese Rural County', *Comparative Politics*, 13/3 (1981), 271–89.

[10] About the model of the Azores and Madeira autonomy, see the opinion of R. M. Stevens, 'Asymmetrical Federalism: The Federal Principle and the Survival of the Small Republic', *Plubius*, 7/4 (1977), 177–203; R. Paddison, *The Fragmented State* (Oxford: Basil Blackwell, 1983), 27–33.

[11] Developments on the subject of the efforts of democratization and decentralization made after the upheaval of the 25 April 1974, in W. C. Oppelo, Jr., 'The Second Portuguese Republic: Politico-Administrative Decentralisation since April

Advances and Regressions in the Regionalist Process

The lack of a tradition of regional self-government necessitated an extensive debate to define the goal of territorial administrative reform. The debate involved the political parties, the media, representatives of industry, the universities, public administrators, and local authorities. In the early 1980s, the Government promoted studies into regionalization, and broadcast information on the subject. The Portuguese candidacy to the EEC, the prospects of integration, and the importance of regional policies all gave urgency to the process of regional institutionalization.[12]

By the mid-1980s a dynamism for regional reform animated governments of all political colours. Precise legal definitions of the regionalization process and its timing were agreed, and decisions were taken to create administrative regions and to take those actions necessary to complete the process successfully.[13] However, the regional euphoria suffered some set-backs. In the first phase of the discussions on regionalization, local authorities saw the administrative regions as a threat to the newly established local democratic system. They were afraid that the new regions would oppress local governments and regulate them more closely than the central government. The situation in the autonomous regions of the Azores and Madeira was cited as a paradigm. There the municipalities were weaker, in part because they were under the tutelage of an autonomous region and because 'regional autonomy' rather than 'municipal autonomy' was thought of as the more effective democratic achievement in the islands. The consequences of creating new political and bureaucratic headquarters in the regional capitals were also pointed out. However, attitudes changed with time.[14] By the second half of the 1980s, local government had adopted a 'pro-regions' strategy. The ghosts and dangers of regionalization had faded away, and now it is being argued that the

25, 1974', *Iberian Studies*, 7/2, 43–4; and K. Maxwell (ed.), *Portugal in the 1980s: Dilemmas of Democratic Consolidation* (Westport, Conn: Greenwood Press, 1986).

[12] For an example of the rising interest about the regional development on the second half of the 1970s, see J. Gaspar, 'Regional Planning, Decentralization and Popular Participation in Post-1974 Portugal', *Iberian Studies*, 5/1 (1976), 31–4.

[13] Resolution no. 231/81 (DR no. 264 of 16 Nov. 1981) and Resolution no. 1/82 (DR. no. 2 of 4 Jan. 1982).

[14] See e.g. views expressed by the ANMP—*Associação Nacional dos Municipios Portugueses* (National Association of Portuguese Municipalities).

creation of administrative regions is an indispensable step towards the accomplishment of a fully decentralized administrative reform. Local authorities now claim that the municipalities, which are sometimes in disagreement with the central government and administration, will be more secure in administrative regions, and will see their own role strengthened. For these reasons they are now favourable to regionalization.

To some extent this change in the attitudes of local government is the product of the growing maturity of local democracy. But equally important has been the emergence of a socialist political leadership which has adopted more 'regionalist' positions than the central government for partisan reasons. Finally, some local political élites exhibit political ambitions which are not confined to the narrow municipal level but which cannot be attained at the national level. In this case, the regional dialectic has become a platform from which to promote their points of view.

One of the most significant participating actors in the regionalization debate is private industry. In Portugal the business community and its associations have grown in strength and prestige with the country's economic development. This is particularly so in banking and insurance sectors, but also in some industrial and rural enterprises. The full integration of Portugal in the EC and the process of privatization developed during the last few years have also contributed to the enhanced status of the business sector. There are two types of associations: those of local or regional scope and those which are national. The local or regional associations tend to support regionalization as a means of strengthening local and regional economics. National associations are clearly against regionalization, arguing that it will mean more bureaucracy.

Trade unions and political parties are also sceptical about regionalization. The former, with their central organization and unified national leadership, see regionalization as something which might eventually divide the labour movement and weaken the negotiating strength of the unions. For the political parties, there is a strong dependence on central political leadership.[15] In some cases, there is a subservience of local political leaders to central strategies and national politicians—a tribute of loyalty which is the cost for career advancement in national politics. But there are

[15] T. C. Bruneau and A. MacLeod, *Politics in Contemporary Portugal: Parties and the Consolidation of Democracy* (Boulder, Colo.: Lynne Rienner, 1986).

other cases where local politics are not submissive and remain at the local level, 'calling in the wilderness' for regional autonomy. Clearly the logic of political parties is centralist and is involved with national strategies, where the regional issue does not have much weight. The party in power is more conservative as far as regionalization is concerned, but the political opposition always tends to be regionalist, claiming the creation of administrative regions as the possible solution for the 'salvation of the motherland'. The vested interests of some natural politicians and administrators keen to preserve their privileges and powers is undoubtedly significant.[16] Other reasons may be added to this general picture of regionalization and the fears it causes. Not least is the power of the Communist Party. In the metropolitan area of Lisbon, eleven of the eighteen municipalities are pro-Communist; and in the so-called 'Region of the Alentejo', the Communists rule twenty-nine of the forty-six municipalities included in this territorial unit. If administrative regions were established, the Communists would win a big political share, and this has been a reason for some non-Communist political leaders showing excessive caution in their support for regionalism.[17] It is against this background of divided opinions that the development of regional institutions has taken place. It has not been an easy process. Undergoing discussion are two projects of territorial division, supported by the major political groups. One of the projects sees the Portuguese mainland territory divided into five administrative regions: North; Centre; Lisbon and Tagus Valley; Alentejo; and Algarve. Against this model, the other project supports the 'complementarity' component and prefers the creation of seven regions, dividing both the North and the Centre into coastal and interior regions. In the first

[16] About the intrinsic centralist character of the Portuguese administrative system and the difficulty of operating any transformations in it, as well as the administrative resistances opposed to changes, see the work published in 1988, by A. Pereira, *Disruptions and Continuities in Portuguese Politics: The Effectiveness of Decentralizing a Napoleonic-type State* (dissertation, 151 pp; University of London—London School of Economics and Political Science, 1988); and also J. Story, 'Portugal's Revolution of Carnations: Patterns of Change and Continuity', *International Affairs*, 52 (1976), 417–33; and W. C. Oppelo, Jr., 'The Continuing Impact of the Old Regime on the Portuguese Political Culture', in L. S. Graham and D. L. Wheeler (eds.), *In Search of Modern Portugal: The Revolution and its Consequences* (London: Wisconsin Press, 1983).

[17] In this example there is a repetition of the Italian case of some years ago, about the same fears of the regional 'Communist belt', relating to the regions of Tuscany, Umbria, and Emilia-Romagna.

of the two proposals there is concern to create 'big regions' which will be strong enough to compete in Europe. In the second proposal, for smaller regions, the emphasis is on the homogeneity of the respective areas in terms of culture and socio-economic development—emotional arguments with which the local population is more able to identify.

There are other proposals—for administrative regions which coincide with the districts proposed by the Communists, and for 'natural regions' so limited that they would be little more than small groupings of neighbouring municipalities—but these carry little weight.

Late Developments in the Regionalist Process: Regional Institutions and Regional Policy

The most significant development of regionalism to date was the creation in 1991 of the metropolitan areas of Lisbon and Porto. They are self-governing, elected indirectly by the representatives of the municipalities belonging to the metropolitan area, and have a deliberative assembly and an executive board. Strictly speaking the metropolitan areas are not regions. However, because of their supramunicipal scope, they are seen as a major step in the process of regionalization since they allow the development of relationships between the local, regional, and central levels of administration in the co-ordination of policies.[18]

As regards the regional sphere of competence, the Portuguese Constitution mentions three general functions;[19] administration of public services in the regional area; co-ordination and support of municipalities while respecting municipal autonomy; elaboration of regional plans and the participation in the national planning process. There are doubts as to the precise scope of the regions' competence but they will only be answered at a later phase of the regionalization process. Meanwhile, regional policies continue to

[18] See developments on the metropolitan areas of Lisbon and Porto, especially on their regional meaning and the realignment of political forces propitiated by such metropolitan structures, in A. Pereira, 'The New Metropolitan Governments in Portugal: Realignment of Local, Regional and Central Powers', in Ita O'Donovan and Risto Havisalo (eds.), *Finnish Administrative Studies—Special Number: 25 Years* (1992).

[19] Portuguese Constitution, Articles 255–62.

be managed by central government departments but the Commissions of Regional Co-ordination (CCRs—*Comissoes de Coordenação Regional*), essentially entities of regional co-ordination, have a significant role in the formulation of policies for regional development. Their final goal is the development of their respective regions. They have been playing an active role in the country, and are recognized at the international level, particularly by the EC. Created in the late 1960s and early 1970s, they were organized as study commissions to feed into the national development plan, but during the 1980s they have acquired greater technical capacity and significant political weight.

The CCRs are based on five regional areas: North, Centre, Lisbon and Tagus Valley, Alentejo, and Algarve, and are concerned with planning projects, support of municipalities, dialogue with universities and business associations. They have specific executive functions in urban and countryside planning and co-ordinate closely with local municipalities in the selection of local projects to be financed by Community funds, and in the management of EC regional funds for those projects. In the absence of self-governing regions the CCRs have assumed a major role in defining their regional identities. In strict constitutional terms they are extensions of the central government. Nevertheless they are firmly rooted in their respective regions. Their structure consists of the directors of State public services in the regions who constitute the Co-ordination Council and who seek to co-ordinate the administrative actions of the CCRs and discuss matters of mutual regional interest. In addition, representatives of the local authorities within the region, usually the presidents of municipal councils, are assembled in a regional council to debate the guidelines for regional development, in particular infrastructural development, whether supported by national or EC funds; to co-ordinate local investment within the region; to define local projects which will be financed by Community funds; and, often, to play the part of a regional forum in debating those national or Community policies which could effect the regional interest. Thus regional policies, while applied by central government departments, are considered and co-ordinated by the CCRs which have gone some way towards filling the gap produced by the delay in creating regional governments.

The very success of the CCRs has provoked political questions. For some people opposed to the regionalization process, they have gone beyond the formal limits of their legal competence and through their activities have sustained and promoted the regional spirit. For the pro-regionalists, the CCRs, while filling the gap, are delaying the implementation of regional governments and legitimizing a level of regional administration which is non-democratic and centralist. However, the political debate on regionalism has cooled in recent years, partly because of the successful passage through Parliament of the Law on Administrative Regions and partly because of the emergence of a pragmatic consensus: to avoid excessive and divisive discussions and to allow the idea of regionalism to mature at a pace which will avoid political upsets. In this context the political leaders are mindful of the experience of other European countries where regionalism has been a sensitive subject which has, in some cases, led to the defeat of the political leadership.

The Portuguese Government is more concerned with the delivery of public services at the territorial level and, aware of the difficulties consequent upon an overcentralized bureaucracy, has moved to deconcentrate the provision of public services through the creation of administrative units with increased human resources and administrative capacity at the designated territorial level. This 'process of deconcentration' is regarded by the national government as a rational way of improving public services by restructuring government departments at the subnational territorial level. For some departments deconcentration will involve the transfer of human and other resources from the centre to the territory (or the periphery). Clearly this development has implications for the process of regionalization. However, the question is whether deconcentration is a driving force for or a restraining power against regionalization. Some analysts argue that the process of administrative deconcentration of government departments will serve to rationalize and harmonize administrative functions at the regional level and that this will assist in the future construction of autonomous regions. However, there is a fear that as the reorganized and deconcentrated government departments improve the delivery of public services, so the expressed need for regional autonomy will weaken. Some suspect that government interest in strengthening State services in the periphery is no more than a manœuvre to postpone regionalization. Whatever view one takes in the controversy the two concepts, deconcentration and regionalization, are linked.[20] The deconcentration exercise requires clear and consistently defined territorial areas for the organization of public departments in order to make the delivery of public services coherent and effective. Furthermore, the pattern of administrative deconcentration must take account of the different levels of administrative authorities—local, regional, and central—in order to establish the preferred model of co-ordination.[21] How, for example, should policies be co-ordinated at the regional level so as to balance the requirements of central government departments with sectoral policies and the regions with territorial priorities? It is not difficult to understand how the multiple corrections and interfaces between 'deconcentration–regionalization' in Portugal have led to a complex debate on the creation of a regional system.

The European Community has played a part in the debate on the development of Portuguese regionalism. Community influence, reflected in its regional policies and structural and regional funds, has, in a general sense, been a driving force for regionalization and very few voices have been raised against the regionalist implications of European integration. However, in practice the operation of the structural funds has not contributed to the regionalization process because the whole country is included in objective 1 of the Structural Funds Regulation.[22] Different positions at the regional level are mainly the result of policies and strategies of a rational or partisan character. And given the small dimensions of the country, such regional diversities as exist have not led to marked differences on the big issues of European integration: the single market, Economic and Monetary Union, and eventual Political Union. On the question of regionalization, Euro-

---

[20] The connection between the two political–administrative phenomena (decentralization–deconcentration) is dealt with by some authors in an interesting way, as in B. C. Smith, *Decentralization: The Territorial Dimension of the State* (London: Allen & Unwin, 1985), 18, applying to the concept of decentralization a broader meaning in which are included elements of deconcentration. On the other hand, he refers to deconcentration as a sort of 'bureaucratic decentralization'.

[21] A frequent debate about the more convenient model for public services at a territorial level is often heard: is it based on the French model, of concomitant existence in the territory of central and regional services; or mainly based on the British model, with its dominion in the provision of public services by local governments and a sort of agencies: or yet, on the Norse model in which the public services are essentially provided for by local governments, sometimes according to their own competence, at other times by delegation representing the central State?

[22] Regulation (CEE) no. 2052/88, of 24 June 1988 (Structural Funds Regulation).

pean Community membership has been used to justify an emphasis on regionalism and the institutionalization of administrative regions by reference to the notion of a Europe of the Regions. But the European argument can, and has been, used in the opposite direction: that the priority for Portugal is in the concentration of efforts and resources to integrate the country into Europe and that a diversion towards regionalization would disperse resources and provoke divisive discussions.

13

Danish Policy-Making, Regionalism, and the European Community

ALASTAIR H. THOMAS

As the oldest kingdom in Europe, Denmark has a clear sense of national history and identity, which is reinforced by a common language and culture; also, 95 per cent of the population belong to the national evangelical Lutheran Church. Thus Danish society is cohesive and integrated. Although socio-economic factors are the most important influence on voting behaviour, social inequalities are not extreme. For most of the twentieth century, there has been a four-party system comprising Social Democrats, Radical Liberals, (agrarian) Liberals, and Conservatives, the first two of which predominated in government between 1929 and 1964. A fifth party, the Socialist People's Party, entered the system in 1958, and an 'earthquake' election in 1973 doubled the number of parties, to the cost of all the established parties. For most of the ensuing decade, the Social Democrats led a succession of minority governments.

From 1982, the Conservative Poul Schlüter has led successive minority coalitions in partnership with the Liberals. Additional partners have included the Centre Democrats, the Christian People's Party and, more recently, the Radical Liberals. Further parliamentary support for economic and social policy has come from the Social Democrats and the centre-right, but has generally been withheld by the Socialist People's Party on the left and the Progress Party on the right. During 1982–8, on certain issues of foreign and security policy and environmental policy there was a majority opposed to the Government, comprising the Socialist People's Party, the Social Democrats, and the Radical Liberals. The Government accepted, and had to act upon, adverse votes on these issues, arguing that, more importantly, it had parliamentary support for its economic policies.

Leaving aside the home-rule arrangements for the Faeroes and Greenland, Denmark is a unitary state, so expressions of regionalism amount to relatively minor variations of emphasis within a unified political and governmental system, in a small country with a population of 5.1 million, a high standard of living, and a highly developed system of communications.

Like the other Nordic countries, however, Denmark is among the most decentralized of the European unitary states. Comparing government centralization measured by central government's share of total tax receipts, Arend Lijphart found that federal systems became less centralized (from 69 per cent to 58 per cent) during the period 1955 to 1979,[1] and this trend probably continued in the 1980s. Following extensive local government reorganization and devolution of taxing and spending powers, in the 1970s Denmark, Finland, and Norway had centralization figures of 70 or 71 per cent, while the figure for Sweden was 62 per cent. In all these countries, local government is the most important agency implementing welfare programmes, being responsible for between 50 and 60 per cent of total public outlays and more than 50 per cent of GDP.

Reform of local government in 1974 reduced the number of municipalities by 80 per cent, abolished urban/rural distinctions, and reduced the twenty-five counties to fourteen. This reform was achieved without political discord, because structural reform and financial reshuffling, and extensive decentralization of tasks and functions had been deliberately tackled together. Subsequent reallocation of functions gave the enlarged counties responsibility for secondary schools and hospitals. The municipalities have responsibility for primary schools, social security and assistance, individual health services, local roads, and the environment. Financial reforms followed: from 1973 counties were empowered to tax personal incomes, and itemized grants and reimbursements were consolidated into a block grant, the value of which was indexed to the value of the transfers which it replaced. Social assistance was reimbursed at 50 per cent of the running costs, while pensions (including pensions for invalidity, early retirement, and the elderly) were fully reimbursed. In sum, the reforms aimed, with substantial success, at enhancing efficiency, increasing access to all types of

---

[1] Arend Lijphart, *Democracies* (New Haven, Conn.: Yale University Press, 1984).

local government services, which had often been lacking in the rural areas, and enhancing a sense of financial responsibility. Many of the smaller local government units disappeared and larger bureaucracies were created, but most daily services were delivered by the lower-tier units, which covered the whole national territory except a few small islands. In the 1980s, a tight legal and regulatory financial framework was selectively relaxed to allow local experiments in the delivery of new types and methods of service delivery.

Within Denmark proper there is some recognition of regions in electoral law, which ensures proportional representation within each of Jutland, the Islands, and the Capital. Variations in voting patterns among these regions are small, but they show the Social Democrats to be weaker in Jutland than elsewhere. The Socialist People's Party is especially strong in the Capital. The Conservatives' greatest strength is in the Islands. The Liberals, with their strong agrarian base, have established themselves in the Capital only recently, and have always been strongest in Jutland. The Progress Party is also strongest in Jutland and weakest in the Capital.

The overall result of the 1992 Maastricht referendum was, of course, NO but there was a small YES majority in Jutland. The NO vote was clearly strongest in the Capital. This is also where the strength of the Socialist People's Party is greatest, and it was especially active in the broadly based June Movement, which coordinated the opposition vote.

There are cases of public investment involving the Danish Government loan capital and international finance, notably the proposed Skan Link, a 17.6 km road/rail bridge and tunnel across the sound to Sweden. The largest party of domestic Danish regional policy, however, operates through the well-established system of local government finance. Substantial infrastructure

TABLE 13.1. *Regional variations in the referendum on the Maastricht Treaty, 2 June 1992 (% vote)*

	Denmark	Capital	Islands	Jutland
YES	49.3	38.3	49.6	51.6
No	50.7	61.7	50.4	48.4

Source: Statistisk Arbog, 1992.

projects funded by Government or through loans repaid by revenue are much more significant than EC-assisted programmes which, while of some help, are quite small-scale.

The Regions

Within the Danish realm, the Faeroe Íslands and Greenland both have home rule. Denmark retains control over foreign policy, defence, the Church, the judiciary and police, and the monetary system. The chief representative of the Danish State in the Faeroes is the *rigsombudsmand*. The 47,500 inhabitants speak a distinct Faeroese language, close in form to Icelandic and west Norwegian dialects, and with a flourishing literature. There is a locally elected assembly of thirty-two members, the *Løgting*, and a six-member *Landsstyri* (executive council) responsible for internal affairs. Two representatives from the Faeroes and two from Greenland sit in the Danish Parliament.

Greenland is the largest island in the world, with an estimated 55,500 inhabitants, mainly Eskimo (Inuit) or of mixed Eskimo and European origin. Although Danish is widely spoken, the indigenous language is Eskimo, and a growing sense of Inuit identity recalls their non-European origins and explains their rejection of the EC. About 83 per cent were born in Greenland and 21 per cent live in the capital, Nuuk. Greenland had colonial status until the 1953 Constitution accorded it the status of a Danish county, with its own ministry between 1955 and 1982. In 1979, Greenland attained home rule. Functions have been transferred gradually over the period 1980–9, with the intention that the administration should have similar responsibilities to those held by the Faeroes Government. The health service was the last major function to be transferred. Because of its high cost this transfer was postponed to 1992. This partly explains why the level of transfer to Greenland is higher than it is to the Faeroes.

In both regions, party systems have developed which differ from their counterparts in Denmark. In the Faeroes the Social Democratic Party was formed in 1928 and retains close links with its counterpart in Denmark. The Home Rule Party originated in 1906. Social-liberal in outlook, its links are to the Danish Radical Liberals and it advocates political independence for the Faeroes within the Danish kingdom. The Union Party also originated in 1906. Conservative in internal affairs, it favours maintaining close relations between the Faeroes and Denmark. The People's Party was formed in 1940 and advocated free enterprise and wider political and economic autonomy for the Faeroes, within the Danish kingdom. The Republican Party dates from 1948 and advocates secession from Denmark. The Christian People's Party, like similarly named Nordic parties, opposes moral permissiveness. It works closely with the Progressive and Fishing Industry Party, a social but non-socialist and anti-Communist centre party closely linked to the Fishermen's Association. None of the Faeroese parties advocates EC membership. Although greater independence from Denmark is one of the aims of most of the Faeroese parties, they are likely to remain linked to Denmark so long as the Danish economy remains such an important component of the Faeroese economy. In the 1991–2 recession, the Faeroese economy was very heavily hit and Denmark had to support the Faeroese national bank.

In Greenland, too, the relationship with Denmark forms an important dimension of the party system. The three largest parties were formed as recently as 1977–8. *Atassut* (the Feeling of Community Party) is a moderate, non-socialist party which wishes to see Greenland back in the EC. *Akuliit Partiia* (the Centre Party) is a liberal party with policies very similar to those of *Atassut*. *Siumut* (Forward) has links with the Danish Social Democrats and aims to improve the status of hunters, fishermen, and workers, to promote collective ownership and co-operation, and to develop greater reliance on Greenland's own resources. It led the campaign to take the country out of the EC. The *Inuit Ataqatigiit* (Eskimo Brotherhood) is a socialist party. It wishes to restrict Greenlandic citizenship to those of Eskimo parentage, opposes home rule, and advocates Greenland's eventual independence from Denmark. As in the Faeroes, the Danish State is represented in Greenland by the *rigsombudsmand*.

In the *Folketing* the four Faeroes and Greenland representatives largely avoid direct involvement in Danish domestic politics, but occasionally their numbers can be pivotal. In 1960–4, for example, a Greenlander was brought into the Government to give it a practical majority. However, the strong pattern of consensus in the *Folketing* encourages governments to seek broad support for major legislation from the main Danish parties, and this pattern means that for most of the time the Faeroes and Greenland representatives are mainly concerned with representing the interests of their home territories in budgetary and other negotiations.

With an economy heavily dependent on fisheries, the Faeroes never joined the EC. As part of the Danish realm, Greenland joined the EC in 1972, although the referendum vote in Greenland was 68.9 per cent NO and 28.5 per cent YES. In a further referendum in Greenland in 1982 the vote was 52 per cent NO and 46.1 per cent YES.[2] Following difficult negotiations, Greenland left the EC with effect from 1 February 1985 and was accorded the status of an overseas territory in association with the EC, with preferential access to EC markets. The failure of those making EC fisheries policy to recognize the overwhelming dependence on fish resources of Greenland and the Faeroes explains much of the opposition to the EC in these regions. Neither the Faeroes nor Greenland are eligible for EC regional funding but both continue to receive substantial block grants from the Danish State. In 1991, the grants totalled Kr. 3,125 million; but these are only a fraction of the credit transfers by Denmark to the EC of Kr. 9,118 million and significantly less than the foreign-aid budget of Kr. 7,320 million. [3]

EC-Assisted Programmes

Regional funding in Denmark is administered by *Industri og Handelsstyrelsen* (the Industry and Trade Directorate) located in Silkeborg in mid-Jutland, which maintains regular contacts with the regions, with Brussels, and upwards to the Ministries of Trade and of Foreign Affairs in Copenhagen. Counties or *kommunes* have direct contact with EC offices in Brussels, but the Directorate advises on and co-ordinates the preparation of applications for funding.

A range of programmes has been implemented to draw on the EC's structural funds, both before and after they were reformed. Examples will be discussed of EC-supported regional development programmes for which the Industry and Trade Directorate and the

---

[2] L. Lyck (ed.), *Denmark and EC Membership Evaluated* (London: Pinter, 1991).
[3] *Statistisk Arbog 1992* (Copenhagen: Danmarks Statistik).

various county councils (*amtsrad*) have overall administrative and co-ordinating responsibility. Each has a steering committee composed of representatives from each of the relevant authorities and the Commission. EC support is normally conditional upon at least 50 per cent national co-financing, which may be derived from the State, the county, the *kommune*, or the private sector.

Nord-Tek (the North Jutland Technology Programme) ran during 1986–91 and aimed to introduce and strengthen the use of new technology in small and medium-sized firms in order to improve the competitivity of industry and thus increase employment and incomes. In North Jutland the legislation for the Great Belt link also included a commitment to build a motorway between Åalborg and Århus and to extend the road network in North Jutland. Similar technology programmes were centred in Viborg and Århus, major urban centres in North Jutland. Stride programmes running during 1991–3 in Åalborg (North Jutland) and Nakskov (Storstrømsamt) supported productive investment, business education and advice, and the development of industry and tourism in the period of transition after the shipyard closed. Renaval programmes in Åalborg and Nakskov were for restructuring the ship-building areas of the two towns. Objective 2 funding during 1989–91 for both cities was obtained for restructuring areas in industrial decline. Over the period 1989–93, these programmes brought in sums totalling about kr. 145 million to Åalborg and about kr. 51 million to Nakskov.

Southern Jutland is the predominantly agricultural region bordering Germany. A substantial area was lost in 1864 following war with Prussia. In 1920 the border was settled by plebiscite. The issue was raised again in 1945–7 but the border remained undisturbed. There is a significant Danish-speaking minority south of the border with representation in the Schleswig-Holstein *Landtag*, and Flensburg supports a Danish-language newspaper. German speakers north of the border are fewer. A Slesvig party had a single representative in the Danish *Folketing* until 1939 and during 1953–64. During 1973–9 the Centre Democrats nominated a German-minority candidate who represented this constituency. The EC programme in southern Jutland (SEP) ran during 1987–92, with the aim of expanding knowledge of new technology and technological development by supporting projects and consultancy which would improve firms' ability to compete in quality, design, high technology, and production methods. From the fund kr. 4 million was reserved for consultancy, and the aim was to see higher turnover, exports, and employment. During 1990–3 the Interreg programme funded cross-border co-operative projects in southern Jutland and also in the counties of Storstrøm, Bornholm, and Fyn.

Storstrømsamt (including the two southern islands of Lolland and Falster) lies in the main route southwards from Copenhagen to Germany via the ferry from Rødbyhavn to Puttgarten, so much of the traffic is transitory. There is a distant plan to replace the ferry with a fixed road and rail link. The Start-Lolland EC programme ran during 1987–91 with the aim of securing a well-planned business-development initiative which would increase employment on the island by broadening the industrial and commercial structure, at the same time ensuring that firms developed a future earning capacity and growth. The shipyard in Nakskov, established in 1914 by S. Breseman (the first Social Democrat governing mayor outside Copenhagen) encountered difficulties in the 1980s and then closed. Stride funding was designed to support the area during the ensuing restructuring process through product-development by firms in the area, and Renaval and objective 2 funding was also obtained. Like the other technology programmes the one on Bornholm (Borntek), which ran during 1988–92, aimed to get small and medium-sized firms to develop their levels of technological competence.

14

Conclusion

BARRY JONES

The central focus of this work has been the evolving relationships between regions and various institutions of the European Community. There is no single relationship. Rather the chapters reveal a plurality of relationships which reflect not only the energy and aspirations of the regions but also the nature of the political systems of the respective member states. Furthermore, the concept of region held by the European Commission and which is the basis of 'regional' policies does not always coincide with regional self-perceptions and structures. Thus, although regionalism is a common theme running through the chapters of this book, it tends to represent a variety of different legal competences, political processes, and policy outputs.

One conclusion that can be drawn from even a cursory reading of the foregoing chapters is that the European nation-state is not what it used to be. In the introduction Keating noted some of the reasons for the creation of a European Community, which reflected concerns with military security and economic development; the implication was that neither of these goals was fully attainable within the boundaries of the nation-state, but that some integrative framework was necessary. Since the founding of the Community in the late 1950s other changes have taken place with implications for the traditional European nation-state, not least the development of a global economy mirrored in multinational corporations, rapid and (relatively) free transfers of capital between different financial centres, and the erosion both in theory and practice of autonomous national economics. In this context the political institutions of states have been subject to unique pressures and have been obliged to adapt. There has been what has been described as a process of structuration whereby State structures or institutions change according to a mix of factors including the political market, the hierarchical State, and, increasingly, external forces. As a result, the Welfare State associated with post-war social democracy and based on 'national' norms is being replaced by the Competition State which has to operate within an ever-more interdependent world.[1]

This trend is particularly apparent within the member states of the European Community. The continuing integrative process and the increasingly qualified concept of national sovereignty poses profound questions for national political institutions. National parliaments are circumscribed by European regulations and national politics have become so porous that within the European Community the distinction between 'national' and 'international' politics is becoming difficult to draw. It is against this background of historic political change of the traditional European nation-state that our examination of regional institutions and regional initiatives must be viewed.

Just as regionalism cannot be fully understood without reference to changes in the nation-state, so it is necessary to examine the attitude of the European Community to regions and regionalism. It is undeniably the case that the EC and particularly the Commission is concerned with the regions but this concern is less for the regions themselves than for regional disparities and the implications and possible dangers which they pose for the cohesion of the Community. Consequently, the focus of EC regional policies has been directed at the least developed regions, particularly those in Greece and Portugal. In this context regional policies have not been particularly successful. World economic trends have tended to overwhelm EC regional initiatives, and unemployment in the peripheral Mediterranean regions was disproportionately high in the early 1990s as it had been in the early 1980s. The Director-General for Regional Policy concedes that 'over the decade, the differences between the less developed regions themselves and between those regions as a group and the rest of the Community, have not changed appreciably.'[2] Given the objective of cohesion, the EC is understandably preoccupied with the less developed regions, where the social and economic problems are greater. But

[1] This view is very much based upon the stimulating analysis of the State presented by Philip C. Cerny in *The Changing Architecture of Polities: Structure, Agency and the Future of the State* (London, Sage: 1990).

[2] Commission of the European Communities, *The Regions in the 1990s; Fourth Periodic Report on the social and economic situations and development of the regions of the Community* (Brussels, 1991), 13.

whereas this is the central thrust of the EC regional policy, it is not the central focus of this book. There are two explanations for this difference. The definition of regions for the purposes of EC regional funding does not necessarily coincide with 'constitutionally' defined regions and, secondly, the more vulnerable the socio-economic base of a region the more limited its political options are likely to be. What the foregoing chapters reveal is that the more forceful innovative regions, such as Bavaria, Catalonia, and Lombardy are amongst the most wealthy European regions for which the importance of the European Community lies not in its regional, structural funds but in the opportunities for interregional co-operation which transcends national boundaries and which is legitimized and encouraged by the institutions and ethos of the Community.

This 'political' aspect of regionalism in the European Community has produced two distinct, although linked, consequences. First it has affected a change either in the political debate or in some cases the power relationships within member states; and, secondly, it has stimulated the growth of cross-national consultative regional networks the full implications of which are not yet clear but which carry the potential for significant change within the Community.

Within the political process of member states the regionalist factor has not worked consistently. In Germany, the only real federal state within the EC, the European connection and the implications for the German regions (*Länder*) have been ambiguous. As Gerstenlauer points out, German federalism is executive federalism and it is not so much the German regions which have stronger participation in EC affairs as the regional bureaucracies. According to this analysis, regional initiatives by both the German *Länder* and the EC have not reduced but reinforced the democratic deficit. In France the decentralist initiative of the early 1980s, which was a response to both domestic and EC considerations, has not realized the hopes of the regional reformers and some EC policies geared to further integration are actually strengthening local government. Although Balme makes the valid point that the relationship between the French state and the regions are subject to constant negotiation and renegotiation, the drift of events in favour of the regions appears to be in doubt. Within the UK, the only large member state without a defined regional structure, the EC's impact has been upon the political debate between the various regions and peripheries on the one hand and the central government on the other in which EC policies (not just regional) are presented as more sympathetic to regional interests than those emanating from London.

The most dramatic change in terms of regionalism is to be found in Italy. Desideri strongly makes the point that the 'regional revolution' epitomized by Bossi and the Northern League is the product of domestic factors some of which are rooted in the creation of the Italian State. However, he argues persuasively that the internationalization of the Italian economy and the process of European integration caused the collapse of the ingrained approach towards the north–south gap in Italian politics. Desideri doubts whether regionalism can solve the problem, given the weakness of regional sentiments in the south and the quasi-separatist character of northern regionalism. In this as in other political contexts Italy would appear to have developed its own unique political dynamic. The same can also be said of Spain, whose regional autonomous communities have a much stronger linguistic and ethnic character than most European regions. In this context the European Community has been critical in establishing a framework which has enabled Catalans and Basques to emphasize their European identity without threatening the coherence of the Spanish State. However, Morata points out that the ambiguities of the Constitution have fed traditional centre–periphery conflicts and that political actors, both national and regional, have been unable to co-operate to facilitate the framing and implementation of Community policies.

The smaller member states of the European Community have only limited regional frameworks. Luxembourg is little more than a small but wealthy city region. For both Greece and Portugal the regional problem is to become equal economic partners of the Community and while Portugal is making hesitant moves towards a regional structure Greece's geopolitical position renders such a policy-shift unacceptable in the context of contemporary Balkan politics. In the other small countries regionalism is tied in with the local government system. In the Netherlands the European connection has provided the provinces with arguments to strengthen their role within the Dutch State system while in Ireland, community regional policies have stimulated regional lobbies calling into question the traditional centralization of Irish government but, as Holmes and Rees emphasize, regionalism remains weak. In Denmark, aside from the quasi-autonomous islands of the Faeroes and Greenland there is no significant regional dimension to the political debate or policy implementation. Amongst the small member states only Belgium has a clearly discernible regional framework but this is the product of indigenous linguistic differences. Although the European Community deals directly with the regions and language communities, Hooghe can find no evidence of conscious EC efforts to play the regional card. However, the EC's ability and willingness to deal with *all* levels of Belgian society, national, regional, local, and private could very well point to a future pattern of increasingly decentralist, self-organizing, and porous societies with policy networks at a variety of levels. To date Belgium seems unique in this respect.

The second aspect of the European Community's impact on regionalism, that of the creation of consultative interregional networks, is less problematic. As Keating points out, there have been a wide range of informal and semi-formal associations such as the Assembly of European Regions and the Consultative Council of Regional and Local Authorities. Both these bodies and others, following a parallel course of constructing policy networks, have been weakened by ambiguity as to what their respective constituencies are: local government areas or regions. The problem has been compounded because designated regions possess such a wide range of legal competences ranging from the precise powers and functions of the German *Länder* to the vaguely defined English 'region'. However, in the midst of this complexity one thing is clear: the eagerness of regions of all kinds to lobby the Commission in Brussels. The growth of regional offices is one of the most positive illustrations of increased regional awareness and self-confidence. Although a clearly defined regional base and strong financial resources facilitate the lobbying process they are not a prerequisite. The evidence presented by the chapters suggests that the relative weakness and even the absence of regional institutions can stimulate a region (such as the north-east of England) to lobby that much harder for recognition of its regional interest.

The regions least satisfied with the informal or quasi-formal arrangements have been those regions with developed political institutions, a democratic base, and significant financial resources.

These include most of the German *Länder* but particularly Bavaria and Baden-Württemburg and some of the Spanish autonomous communities, most notably Catalonia. In this context the continuing debate on the 'democratic deficit' has been linked to the institutional development of regionalism within the European Community, specifically by exploiting the December 1992 declaration on subsidiarity and by pushing for a Committee of the Regions with clearly defined functions and powers within the formal structure of the EC.

Subsidiarity is an ambiguous concept and its presentation in the Maastricht Treaty as a substantive principle left it unclear whether it merely related to when the Community rather than the member states should take action or whether a comprehensive interpretation was appropriate—that decision-making should be taken at the lowest appropriate level. This second interpretation has implications for the internal political processes of member states and while it would pose relatively few problems for a federal state like Germany it would run counter to the politics of those member states, particularly Britain, unwilling to cede authority downwards. For Euro-sceptics the more comprehensive interpretation of the subsidiarity principle appeared to lead towards a federal Europe with defined juridical powers at all levels from the local community up to the Council of Ministers. With such a proliferation of levels of decision-making the dominant role of member states' national parliaments would be seriously undermined, leading to a Europe of the Regions.[3] Although the British Government has been the most articulate and intransigent in rejecting this view of subsidiarity, it is doubtful whether the government of any member state (save possibly that of Belgium) could seriously contemplate any such development.

Subsidiarity is, however, a dynamic concept which is likely to be subject to a process of clarification and redefinition as the policy-making process develops. Furthermore, the presence of federal or quasi-federal states within the Community is likely to promote the more comprehensive interpretation of the subsidiarity principle. The dominant position of a united Germany increasingly willing

[3] For a fuller discussion of this issue, see A. Scott, J. Peterson, and D. Millar, 'Subsidiarity: A Europe of the Regions v. the British Constitution?', *Journal of Common Market Studies*, 32/1 (1994).

to exercise its enhanced political clout would be crucial in this context.

If the jury is still out on the significance or otherwise of the subsidiarity principle for regionalism, the other pillar linking the democratic deficit with regionalism is now in place. The Committee of the Regions (COR), the newest of the European Community institutions, met for the first time on 9 March 1994. Although it is less than dedicated regionalists had hoped for, it will occupy a significant position within the EC policy-making process. It consists of 189 members who will be entitled to be consulted on a range of EC policies including public health, education, and culture, trans-European networks, as well as policies leading to economic and social cohesion. The COR will also be able to make pronouncements on policies or issues which possess a regional dimension. But its views and recommendations will carry no formal weight, nor will it be able to exercise any veto. For many critics the COR could degenerate into yet another European talking-shop. Furthermore, the initial composition of the Committee, determined by the respective governments of member states, reveals a significant dilution of the regional element. With the exception of Belgium all the 'national' representatives will include some from local communities. Only Germany, Spain, and Italy will send a majority of regional representatives to the Committee while those of Ireland, Luxembourg, Denmark, United Kingdom, and Greece will consist exclusively of representation from local government.

Overall a clear majority of the COR membership will be made up of representatives from local government and local communities. It already seems likely that tensions will develop along the local community/regional fault-lines. Despite these limitations the Committee none the less possesses a clear potential. Its prime concerns, public health, education, and culture, are the precise policy-areas which are the responsibility of the German *Länder* and the Spanish autonomous communities. One can confidently predict that they will be keen to preserve and enhance their role in these policy-areas. Furthermore, it is not inconceivable that leading regional politicians from Germany, Spain, Belgium, and elsewhere will decide that their respective regions could be more effectively promoted if they were to take up seats in the COR. With politicians of the calibre of Jordi Pujol from Catalonia the Committee of the

TABLE 14.1. *Representation on Committees of the Regions*

Country	Number of Representatives	
	The regions	Local communities
Belgium	12	0
Denmark	0	9
France	15	9
Germany	21	3
Greece	0	12
Ireland	0	9
Italy	17	7
Luxembourg	0	6
Netherlands	6	6
Portugal	3	9
Spain	17	4
United Kingdom	0	24

Regions could develop as an effective counterweight to the European Parliament. This is not to say that a 'Europe of the Regions' is an immediate prospect; but the COR could accelerate the process of structural pluralism within the EC, strengthen the decentralist forces both within the Community and member states, and play an increasingly important role in determining regional policies. In such circumstances the unitary member states might consider it appropriate to develop more regionalist structures on their own, if only to protect their national interests. All this is necessarily problematic and speculative. However, it is clear that there is now a regional dynamic within the structures of the European Community whose potential has yet to be realized.

Index